THE IDEA OF INDIA

ALSO BY SUNIL KHILNANI

Arguing Revolution: The Intellectual Left in Postwar France

Incarnations: A History of India in Fifty Lives

THE IDEA OF INDIA

Twentieth Anniversary Edition

SUNIL KHILNANI

Farrar, Straus and Giroux

New York

SANJAY SARABHAI

In Memory

Farrar, Straus and Giroux
175 Varick Street, New York 10014

Grateful acknowledgment is made for permission to reprint the following material:
Excerpt from "Partition" from *Collected Poems* by W. H. Auden. Copyright © 1976 by
W. H. Auden. Reprinted by permission of Random House.
Excerpt from "'Irani Restaurant Instructions" from *Collected Poems 1952–1988* by
Nissim Ezekiel. Copyright © 1989 by Nissim Ezekiel. Reprinted by permission of
Oxford University Press.

The Library of Congress has cataloged the hardcover edition as follows:
Khilnani, Sunil, 1960–
    The idea of India / Sunil Khilnani.
        p.   cm.
    Includes bibliographical references and index.
    ISBN: 978-0-374-17417-0
    1. India—Politics and government—1947–   I. Title.

DS480.84.K47   1998
954.04—dc21   97033205

Revised paperback edition ISBN: 978-0-374-53762-3

Our books may be purchased in bulk for promotional, educational, or business use.
Please contact your local bookseller or the Macmillan Corporate and Premium Sales
Department at 1-800-221-7945, extension 5442, or by e-mail at
MacmillanSpecialMarkets@macmillan.com.

www.fsgbooks.com
www.twitter.com/fsgbooks • www.facebook.com/fsgbooks

1   3   5   7   9   10   8   6   4   2

CONTENTS

PREFACE TO THE TWENTIETH
ANNIVERSARY EDITION

In 2017, as India prepared to celebrate its seventieth year of freedom from colonial rule—cultural pageants in foreign capitals to puff India's cachet abroad, military parades to impress Indians at home—I found myself gripped by two images, taken a few weeks apart. I still haven't been able to shake them from my head.

The first image—a grainy video still—was captured in one of India's most brutalised peripheries, the state of Jammu & Kashmir. The video had been taken by a fearful passerby and uploaded to numerous Kashmiri websites, which the Indian government immediately tried to shut down. The picture shows a young Muslim man in a traditional woollen *pheran* and blue jeans, immobilised and dazed. On previous days, Farooq Dar made a living embroidering shawls. Now he is bound to the bumper of an Indian military jeep, his beaten hands hanging limply at his sides. The Indian army has forced him to become a human shield as it advances through a crowd of other young Muslims, who are protesting against military repression.

The other image: a professional photograph seemingly designed to be iconic. It shows a bald, saffron-clad yogi, trim and almost boyish in looks, smiling and flashing a victory sign. He has just been installed by representatives of his Hindu nationalist party as the chief minister of Uttar Pradesh—with more than 200 million people, the country's most populous state. Yogi Adityanath, the leader of one of India's influential Hindu monasteries, had made his political career by advocating extremist causes and inciting hatred towards Muslims, who comprise nearly one-fifth of his state. This photograph of a beatified, menacing man would be tweeted and Instagrammed millions of times.

India likes to define itself as a democracy—the world's largest and most diverse, no less—and since Independence in 1947, democratic pluralism has been at the core of the country's self-image. That democratic pluralism is the primary idea of India I explore in the book. It has been a way of looking its former colonisers in the eye, distinguishing itself from its neighbours, standing up to the ideological bullying of the world's superpowers, and claiming a certain modern global status. But to me, these two images, set against each other, raise profound questions about India's identity—questions that parades and pageants are meant to deflect: What does it mean to be Indian today? Who amongst the citizenry counts, and who is expendable?

When the prospect arose, early in the twentieth century, that an independent India might become a democracy based on universal suffrage, the subcontinent's numerous minorities had reason to fear for their future. Muslims, Sikhs, and Dalits—known formerly as untouchables—took the lead in articulating the dangers, and in fighting for safeguards, territorial or constitutional. In the end, two-thirds of the subcontinent's Muslims chose the territorial option—leading to Partition in 1947.

In the years after, India reconstructed itself as a constitutional democracy committed to the protection of minority beliefs of every kind. Some of the architects of that order worried that it might provoke majoritarian counterreactions or erode under the pressure of social and religious prejudice. But as the country worked to build its economic and military standing, reduce poverty and redress staggering caste injustice, the fact that its government was freely elected by almost one-fifth of the world's population, and one as humanly varied as any, bestowed a vital, sustaining legitimacy.

Yet could that democracy vaunted by Indians also be a delusive falsehood, used to justify the routinised cruelties practised by their state—whether in heavily militarised Kashmir, the barely pacified North East, or far-flung, insurgent Adivasi tribal regions? And has it now become a self-righteous alibi for the exercise of state power, supposedly at the service of an assertive Hindu majority, convinced that its numbers lend its claims irresistible force?

As such questions mount today, I feel once more the urgency of twenty years ago, when *The Idea of India* was first published. This book came out in 1997, the fiftieth year of Indian Independence and another moment of celebration and of anxiety. Earlier in the decade, Hindu agitators had hacked to rubble a Mughal-era mosque, the Babri Masjid, in hopes of replacing it with a temple to the popular god Ram, who many believed had been born at the mosque site at Ayodhya. Subsequent riots across the country left hundreds dead and propelled further the rise of Hindu nationalism: led by a renascent political party, the Bharatiya Janata Party, or BJP, it threatened to overturn the pluralist character of India's democracy. Against the efforts of founders like Mahatma Gandhi and Jawaharlal Nehru to preserve space for a diversity of beliefs, a singular cultural template would, it seemed, be imposed.

The danger of majority capture of the state has loomed over many postcolonial polities. But it wasn't until the 1990s that this possibility gained likelihood in India. As the BJP grew in strength, one of my hopes in writing this book was to reconsider the animating principles of the people who created this remarkable political invention, modern India.

The debates that underpinned the making of modern India are amongst some of the most intricate in recent political history— arguments about identity and difference, representation and dignity, liberalism and communitarianism, justice and inequality, freedom and power. They emerged from a long, contentious national struggle, and they were voiced with compelling sharpness as well as grace—not just by Gandhi and Nehru, but by

B. R. Ambedkar, Vallabhbhai Patel and a host of others. The legacy of these shaping arguments is an immense political and intellectual resource, of value to us today.

As I wrote the manuscript, I was seeking to parry the self-satisfaction of many of my compatriots ('Yes, we may be a little vicious to one another, but we *are* a democracy . . .') as well as the reductive condescension of some Western commentators about the Indian experience ('Yes, you may call yourselves a democracy, *but* . . .'). I wanted to place India, for all its political particularities, in the universal context in which I believed it rightly stood: as one of the world's great experiments with democracy, alongside the United States and France—every bit as convulsive as those histories have proved to be, and potentially even more consequential for democracy's future, in Asia and across the globe. I thought that if we could see more clearly the complex history that had made modern India, and recognise the hard-won principles that emerged from intense intellectual arguments about nation and statehood, we might better understand the significance of India's foundational choices. I hoped, too, that we might realize we needed to sustain those choices far better than we were managing to do.

As I pursued my research in archives and libraries, I travelled across the country as well. In Ayodhya I spoke with smiling police guards at the site of the Babri Masjid—all Hindu, and pleased by what their co-religionists had done to the historic mosque they were supposed to protect. In Tumkur down south, I watched L. K. Advani, a campaigning BJP leader and one of the instigators of the mosque's demolition, extol his deeds in rousing language. I stopped in Chandigarh, and saw its monumental Corbusier buildings sandbagged against extremists who had been fighting for a Sikh homeland. Making my way through the spoiled beauty of Nagaland and parts of the North East, I met Angami, Ao and Konyak youths to whom Delhi seemed a distant imperial capital. Back then, I felt I was straddling fault lines that might widen to become nearly as perilous as those that, in 1947, had split the country apart.

In one of the chapters of this book, titled 'Who is an Indian?', I wrote: 'For a few parenthetic decades, Nehru's improvised conception of a tolerable, common Indianness seemed to suggest a basis for India's sense of itself. It was an explicitly political conception and to sustain itself it had to constantly persuade.' But that conception, I argued, was giving way. I saw my book both as an historical analysis of the processes leading to that collapse and as my own effort at political persuasion, aimed at renewing public investment in the Indian wager on building a pluralist democracy.

As I rushed to finish the book, I wasn't certain what it added up to. I would have chuckled if told that, over the next two decades, the phrase 'the idea of India' would trip off the tongues of prime ministers and leaders and enter the mainstream of public debate.

At first, the phrase served as a shorthand for the unusually plural view of national identity that I identified with India's founding. Later, it become a sneer of choice—used by right-wing nationalists to denigrate those who believed in an India more complex than a Hindu state. And yet, interestingly, they sought also to appropriate the phrase for themselves: in a speech in parliament, for instance, Prime Minister Narendra Modi, the first leader of a BJP majority government, incanted it nineteen times in service of his own Hindu nationalist vision. I'd like to think that these tussles over four words do more than just demarcate the divide between pluralist and majoritarian conceptions of India. Perhaps they could help the arguments to engage with one another, and even move them ahead.

To me, in 1997 as now, the idea of a plural India, open to diverse and competing beliefs, is not an achieved ideal. It is a work in progress: a field of tension, or arena of debate, where differing conceptions of India can encounter one another, seeking to persuade—and willing to listen. Yet that conception, of a nation advancing through self-criticism to a more complex understanding of itself, is regularly threatened by more exclusivist views of nation and of community. So the book, in tandem with its historical diagnosis of how that had come about, contained an argument for what we lose when we fail to keep the debates alive.

After 1947, the idea of India served as an instrumental fable to rally support in the newly independent but still fractured country. Yet it was also much more than that. It provided the principles upon which the founders built a political order. As articulated through independent India's Constitution, it defined in unprecedented ways the relationship between state and nation.

Unshy of ambition, the Constitution aimed to create space for religious and cultural differences, to address age-old social inequalities, to foster individual liberties and to disperse power across the branches of government so that legitimacy could not inhere in any single arm or office. It placed sovereignty—long usurped by the British—in the hands of Indians, though not in the hands of any particular Indians. The Indian founders refused the usual anchors of national identity, such as religion, race and language, which classical European nationalism advertised (foreign comforts that were gratefully embraced by the subcontinent's religious nationalists, whether Muslim or Hindu). The founders thus implicitly acknowledged that to keep this political contraption working would require, in addition to legal design, contingent skills—judgement, abilities to improvise and compromise, and plenty of luck.

For all its vision, the Constitution was prey to subversions—through consequences unintended, of course, and through cynical manipulation by subsequent generations more weakly committed to foundational principles. B. R. Ambedkar, one of the constitutional drafters, noted, just before the Constitution was adopted, one of its inevitable limitations. All it could hope to do was establish the basic structure of the state—the distinct legislative,

can pluralism be a sustained identity?

xii

executive and judicial arms. How in practise this apparatus came to be worked would inevitably depend on 'the people and the political parties they [Indians] will set up as their instruments to carry out their wishes and their politics'.

As Ambedkar predicted, after 1947 the Indian fiction would come under constant strains—many of which are examined in this book. When the withdrawal of colonial power removed an opponent Indians could unite against, the democratic process incited new conflicts. More groups began to speak for their own interests, including non-elites who had felt sidelined in many of the debates of the Independence movement. The intense political mobilizations produced by democracy engendered mobilizations of India's history, too. New heroes were consecrated, others retired to storage godowns. (I traced some of that furious historical re-pedestalling, and its political consequences, in my recent book, *Incarnations*.) *← Monuments*

The opening chapter of *The Idea of India* is devoted to the Constitution's biggest act of faith, or—depending upon your point of view—its most reckless risk: the adoption of universal adult suffrage as the basis of political authority in India. Assessed purely by the fervour with which they have adopted the practise of voting, Indians have rewarded the founders' faith. Surveys reveal that today more Indians than ever believe their votes actually count, and in elections in 2014, a record 66 per cent of India's 814 million eligible voters turned out to cast their ballots.

But what kind of democracy was this? To some left-wing critics, India's constitutional order—rooted as it was in a society where religion and caste retained their grip—would always necessarily favour the religious majority. (Through this prism, Yogi Adityanath was a monk simply awaiting electoral coronation.) Inevitably, the argument went, the strong suppressive powers inherited from the colonial past would be used whenever and wherever the majority felt numerically challenged or politically threatened. From this point of view, that regions like Kashmir and the North East have been kept essentially subject possessions is equally no cause for surprise.

To critics of the right, on the other hand, India's constitutional democracy encouraged a bias towards India's minorities, Muslims and lower castes in particular, at the expense of Hindus. It was a Constitution riddled with minority exceptionalism, imposed upon a disprivileged majority, and its provisions of secularism and toleration had become little more than opportunities for self-interested manipulation by a Congress-dominated political establishment. When I wrote this book, that establishment's failures were clear, and right-wing suspicions of the Constitution were threatening to prevail. Twenty years later, its advocates are in power, its goals more closely in sight.

National State

In 1997, I wrote that the ambition of Hindu nationalism 'was to complete the project of achieving an Indian nation state by piloting it towards what it saw as its logical terminus: a culturally and ethnically cleaned up homogenous community, with a singular Indian citizenship, defended by a state that had God and nuclear weapons on its side. It was the BJP which kept alive most devotedly the ambition of modernization based on Western experiences of nationalism.' All the BJP lacked when I was writing back then was a pilot for its modernizing, Westernizing project.

When that beacon emerged, it was in a form I had not thought likely: a dominating leader, Narendra Modi. Since its inception as a modern political movement in the 1920s, Hindu nationalism had avoided strong individual leaders, in favour of tightly run organizations, disciplined cadres and, to an extent, collective leadership. In that respect, Modi's ascension, through a display of political entrepreneurship so far unmatched in India's democratic experience, was as unnerving to some in his own movement as it has been for India's political system.

Modi appealed to voters to trust his economic vision and

developmental prowess: he was a moderniser who got things done. But his political intentions were not so simple. He also envisioned the creation of a strong state commanded by Hindu interests, with economics as a means to that end. As the chief minister of his state, Gujarat, he had overseen an acceleration in its growth and development, as well as the worst violence directed against Muslims since the Partition riots of 1947.

That combination—growth and the ever-present threat of religious vengeance—became a trademark as he went on to build a national image by propagating a new version of Hindutva. Originally, Hindutva had been an early-twentieth-century mash of ingredients from Hindu scriptures, Mazzinian nationalism, anti-individualist communitarianism and nineteenth-century European race theories—an ideology designed to show that India rightfully belonged to Hindus. But Modi seasoned the religious ideology with one of economic efficacy. He claimed to have cracked the secret of economic development: centralised management and tight, chaebol-like ties with the corporate world. And he served it up just as many predominantly Muslim countries were being torn apart, undermined first by Western military interventions and then consumed by internal violence—violence that sometimes brought terror elsewhere, including to India. What better moment for political entrepreneurs in societies where Muslims formed minorities to play on stereotype and fear?

In India today, as the BJP's hard ideology consolidates its hold over political power, as its religious affiliates expand their grip across civil society and as opposition parties languish, it might seem that the country is merely conforming to a global pattern. Across many parts of the world, entrenched elites have lost power to movements led by authoritarian figures, most of whom advocate more singular views of national community and are intolerant of dissent. In this harsher world, it seems inevitable to some that the idea of India will be permanently displaced by a narrower, more aggressive nationalism. It is not inevitable, in my view, but considering the likelihood is becoming more difficult to resist.

As Modi and his allies seek to eliminate all political opposition and produce a 'Congress-free India', criticism and dissent are branded as anti-national—an excrescence on the politics of democracy rather than its natural, enabling condition. Spaces of free thought—universities, the media, civil society organizations—are subject to pressures from state power, sometimes insidious and other times direct and brutal. Modi and the Hindu right are by no means unique or exceptional in the assault on these spaces: across the states of the union, regional leaders of all political hues have time and again cultivated authoritarian personality cults and tried to centralise control. Installed at the centre, though, this will to power has effects more wide-ranging and damaging— conniving with, if not actually inciting, attacks on citizens who stray from ruling diktats, and crippling intellectual independence. To conceive of the country in such ways is ultimately to weaken the very sinews that have given modern India its strength: the capacities of creative political argument, critical social imagination and an independent-mindedness that questioned and even redefined—as Gandhi did—the nature of power itself.

If there is one theme that drives this book, it is the utter centrality of politics to modern India's experience—the fundamental fact that, as I put it, India does not merely 'have' politics; India is constituted by politics. In the years since the book came out, that view, never particularly fashionable, has become less so. Economics, many have argued, will provide the solutions to India's dilemmas—stepping in where politics has so conspicuously failed.

Certainly India's economic surge over the past two decades has been spectacular, more rapid than anything I had expected. For twenty-five years now, beginning in the early 1990s, GDP has grown around 7 per cent a year, driving an eightfold expansion of the Indian economy and taking average incomes more than five times higher. With that growth came rising self-confidence amongst Indian elites that the country's moment had come. Simultaneously, the Indian state's tax revenues spurred an expansion of military expenditure—enough to move India into the top five military spenders in the world. (The United States is the only other democracy amongst the five.) Under Manmohan Singh's Congress-led coalition government, ambitious policy began directing some of the growth revenues into education and social provision. Poverty, as measured by official statistics, plummeted, and India experienced relative communal peace. *inequality*

Yet also during those years, corruption spread, political inertia and complacence set in and that age-old affliction of India's Congress party, governmental *droit de seigneur*, took hold. Just as stubborn to change were many human development indicators as Indians' respective life chances, already in different universes, moved further apart. Mumbai now has twice as many billionaires as Los Angeles and San Francisco combined, while half of India's population has had no more than a primary school education.

I had expected, writing in 1997, that regional disparities, already deep-set, would persist for decades, testing in various ways the union and the idea of a shared national identity. As I wrote in my chapter on India's cities, the choices of global and Indian capital, drawn to invest in already successful places, helped compound the disparity—a pattern intensifying now.

The result is deepening economic divergence both between states and *within* them—the latter a hint that the problem lies not just with the varying qualities of governance across states but with India's pattern of economic development itself. The Modi economic doctrine of 'competitive federalism'—the optimistic belief that market discipline will push regional state governments to converge on investor-friendly policies, so reducing regional unevenness—evades the political strains that India's growth trajectory will place on the union. Already, economic divergence at the regional level is stirring demands for the creation of new states, and for India's more populous, poorer existing states to receive greater national representation.

The very fact that growth is being experienced so differently by citizens across the country makes it unlikely that pan-Indian social classes, whether poor or prosperous, might emerge and sustain themselves long enough to mitigate divisions or moderate conflicts. Faced with actual tensions, parties like the BJP assert that the solidarities of culture will best allow Indians to transcend divisions—but that too is an attempt to deny India's inescapably political condition.

As I wrote in 1997, there are no guarantees—economic, ideological or cultural—that can hold a nation together: 'It just depends on human skills. That is why politics, as an arena where different projects are proposed and decided for and against, has never been more important for Indians.' What continues to keep India a functioning union, and has made it one of the world's largest markets and a potential engine of the global economy, is not innate virtue or cultural uniqueness—an Indic tolerance, let us say. It's the fortunate result of keeping a political invention working—the imperfect architecture of state, nation and constitutional democracy set in place by India's founders.

It was already clear to me in 1997 that rising prosperity would not necessarily produce a more open-minded middle class, potential stalwarts of liberal democratic politics. Surveying the expanding market and rising consumerism during these years, I wrote that it 'did not fuel an individualistic hedonism nor breed liberal individuals. Rather, it was experienced as an opportunity to sample the pleasures of modernity within collective units like the family' or, I might have added, religious community. 'For many in India, modernity has been adopted through the conservative filters of religious piety, moralism and domestic virtue'. What better example than Modi's home state, Gujarat: a textbook case of political stability and economic vigour? With per capita income more than three times that of India's poorest state and an aspirational middle class networked to a global diaspora, it was also the epicentre of a novel bloody religiosity. For days, in the spring of 2002, Hindu gangs led by the rich and educated—amongst them doctors and lawyers—drove through the city, using mobile phones and government-supplied computer printouts of electoral rolls to identify Muslims' homes and direct attacks on them. That murderous efficiency provided the basis for Modi's rise to national power.

If a civic-minded middle class is no guarantor of India's political cohesion, what is? When it comes to holding India together as a territorial state, one should not underestimate the sometimes brutal or high-handed roles of India's bureaucracy and its military. These legacies of the Raj have been periodically deployed by Indian authorities with a callousness and savagery at least equal to their colonial predecessors. Though tying young men to the front of army jeeps, using citizens as human shields, may be something of a new tactic (the officer who commanded the action was suitably honoured and awarded for his innovation), it comes from a deep bag of techniques gathered by the Indian state in its efforts to maintain territorial unity. Yet military and bureaucracy alone have never been enough to hold India together, nor will they be. Equally important has been, and must continue to be, India's constitutional democracy.

At its inception, the founding architects of the Indian state wagered on a design that might resist succumbing to any singular impulse or ideology, to a strong man or woman at the centre. That design has not always held up against immediate pressures. It will, in coming years, face its strongest challenges yet. An impulse is alive in India, and a strong man is there to rouse it through democratic means: the idea of a national mission, an urge to remoralise politics and social life and to make the state its vehicle. It's a recurring wish, across time and place, a wish to put government securely in the hands of those privy to the voice of God—or of History, or of the People. "I am merely the medium," Narendra Modi said before his 2017 Independence Day speech. "It is the people whose voice is resonating." The historical record of such political ventriloquy has been disastrous. If it comes to pass in India, that will be a failure not so much of the idea of India itself as of its present-day advocates: a failure on their—on our—part to persuade. It will be a failure of democratic argument.

Farooq Dar, the man the Indian military lashed to their jeep, had voted in elections to his state assembly held a few weeks before the army seized him—making him one of only a few Kashmiris to cast a vote. Returning home after his release, he made a promise to himself: 'I will never ever step out of the house on election day.' Perhaps a trivial, if regrettable, decision when set against the heavy logbook of India's grander dilemmas—until it gets multiplied again and again and again.

BIBLIOGRAPHICAL SUPPLEMENT TO THE
TWENTIETH ANNIVERSARY EDITION

Since 1997, India's expanding presence in the world, driven by accelerating economic growth and more pronounced geopolitical ambitions, has made it an object of greater global attention, and has generated more intense debate and inquiry within India itself. There has been a surge of writing about contemporary and modern India, some of it notable for its quality. I've picked out some of the work published in recent years that is of direct relevance to the themes developed in my book.

Among the general histories of the subcontinent, one of the most accessible is Barbara and Thomas Metcalf's *A Concise History of India* (Cambridge, 2002), which emphasises the historicity of many of the basic organizing categories applied to Indian history (such as caste and religious communities); also useful are Peter Robb, *A History of India* (London, 2002), and David Ludden, *India and South Asia: A Short History* (New York, 2002). Dietmar Rothermund's *India: The Rise of an Asian Giant* (New Haven and London, 2008) is an informative survey of India since 1947 with a focus on the economy. By far the best history of post-1947 India is Ramachandra Guha's *India After Gandhi: The History of the World's Largest Democracy* (London, 2007), rich in detail and confident in its judgements. My own *Incarnations: A History of India in Fifty Lives* (New York, 2016) offers a connected account of the broad sweep of Indian history, through the lives of figures whose ideas and legacies still illuminate and animate conflicts and struggles in India today.

Our understanding of India's politics, both regional and national, has benefitted from several significant collaborative works.

Important, encyclopaedic compendia are: Niraja Gopal Jayal and Pratap Bhanu Mehta (eds.), *The Oxford Companion to Politics in India* (New Delhi, 2010); and Atul Kohli and Prerna Singh (eds.), *The Routledge Handbook of Indian Politics* (London, 2012).

Shifts in the structure of India's electoral politics, especially the regionalization of the post–Congress Party system (a system explained in the first chapter of this book) and the consequent development of a 'two-party coalition system' at the national level, are authoritatively captured in Suhas Palshikar, K. C. Suri and Yogendra Yadav (eds.), *Party Competition in Indian States: Electoral Politics in Post-Congress Polity* (Oxford, 2014). The 2014 national election was the first since 1984 to produce a parliamentary majority, and for early insights into whether it marked a significant reversal of the regionalizing trend in Indian electoral politics, see the special issue of the journal *Contemporary South Asia* (2015, vol. 23, no. 2), edited by Louise Tillin, in particular the articles by Tillin and Christophe Jaffrelot; see also Suhas Palshikar, 'India's Second Dominant Party System', *Economic and Political Weekly*, 18 March 2017, vol. 52, no. 11; and Suhas Palshikar, Sanjay Kumar and Sanjay Lodha (eds.), *Electoral Politics in India: The Resurgence of the Bharatiya Janata Party* (New York, 2017). A relatively new publication that has established itself as the house journal for Indian electoral and political analysis is *Studies in Indian Politics* (launched in 2013).

On the entry of lower castes into electoral politics, and on the changing social composition of India's political elites, see Christophe Jaffrelot, *India's Silent Revolution: The Rise of the Lower Castes in North India* (New York, 2003), and his 'The Plebeianization of the Indian Political Class' in *Religion, Caste and Politics in India* (New Delhi, 2010). Also, from a different methodological perspective, see Kanchan Chandra, *Why Ethnic Parties Succeed* (Cambridge, 2007), which points to some of the incentives driving caste politics.

The role of violence, patronage and corruption in India's

democratic politics has attracted much recent attention. On violence and elections, compare the contrasting arguments of Steven Wilkinson, *Votes and Violence: Electoral Competition and Ethnic Riots in India* (Cambridge, 2004), and Ashutosh Varshney, *Ethnic Conflict and Civic Life: Hindus and Muslims in India* (New Haven, 2002); and the views of a doyen of the field, Paul Brass, *The* ✴ *Production of Hindu-Muslim Violence in Contemporary India* (Seattle, 2003). Though its focus is Sri Lanka, a fundamental work on the topic is Jonathan Spencer's *Anthropology, Politics and the* ✴ *State: Democracy and Violence in South Asia* (Cambridge, 2007). A compelling argument for the non-pathological uses of the classical concept of patronage to understand the politics of the region is Anastasia Piliavsky (ed.), *Patronage as Politics in South Asia* (Cambridge, 2014). See also Milan Vaishnav, *When Crime Pays: Money and Muscle in Indian Politics* (New Haven, 2017).

Caste continues to be a focus of attention, both as a unit of choice and self-identity in democratic politics and as a gauge of social change or stagnation. For different perspectives on the category, compare: Anupama Rao, *The Caste Question: Dalits and the Politics of Modern India* (Berkeley, 2009); Ghanshyam Shah et al., *Untouchability in Rural India* (New Delhi, 2006); and Ashwini Deshpande, *The Grammar of Caste: Economic Discrimination in Contemporary India* (New Delhi, 2011). For a sober and illuminating historical account, see Susan Bayly, *Caste, Society and Politics in India from the* ✴ *Eighteenth Century to the Modern Age* (Cambridge, 1999).

Legal history and studies have been a rich field in recent years. Sujit Chaudhry, Madhav Khosla and Pratap Bhanu Mehta (eds.), *The Oxford Handbook of the Indian Constitution* (New Delhi, 2016), is an essential guide to the scope and dilemmas of India's constitutional jurisprudence. For an excellent account of the vicissitudes of free-speech provisions, see Gautam Bhatia, *Offend, Shock or Disturb: Free Speech Under the Indian Constitution* (New Delhi, 2016).

Two important volumes that review the condition of India's

institutions are Devesh Kapur and Pratap Bhanu Mehta (eds.), *Public Institutions in India* (New Delhi, 2007), and its sequel, *Rethinking Public Institutions in India* (New Delhi, 2017).

We still await a cool, analytical account of the emergence of Narendra Modi; in the interim, Kingshuk Nag, *The NaMo Story: A Political Life* (New Delhi, 2013), has some useful information. On the anti-Muslim violence in 2002 in Gujarat, see for first-hand accounts Siddharth Varadarajan (ed.), *Gujarat: The Making of a Tragedy* (New Delhi, 2002); and, for a determined investigation into the subsequent cover-up of the role of political leaders and government officials in the killings, see Rana Ayyub, *Gujarat Files: Anatomy of a Cover Up* (New Delhi, 2016).

We are finally beginning to get some rich historical studies of the mechanics of India's democratic institutions: see Ornit Shani's study of India's first national election in 1952, *How India Became Democratic* (Cambridge, 2018), and, across a number of essays, the work of David Gilmartin.

For important interpretations of India's democratic politics, see the collection of Sudipta Kaviraj's essays, *The Enchantment of Democracy and India* (New Delhi, 2011); and Pratap Bhanu Mehta, *The Burden of Democracy* (New Delhi, 2003). John Dunn, *Breaking Democracy's Spell* (New Haven, 2014), weaves India's democratic experience into the wider history of the term, and our multiple over-investments in it.

On India's economic horizons, three important general surveys are: Arvind Panagariya, *India: The Emerging Giant* (New York, 2010), whole-hearted in its advocacy of market-oriented liberalization; Jean Drèze and Amartya Sen, *India: Development and Participation* (New Delhi, 2002), alert to the distortions and limits of India's chosen growth pattern (some of these arguments and data are updated in Drèze and Sen's *An Uncertain Glory: India and Its Contradictions* [Princeton, 2013]); and, for an impressively balanced perspective on the challenges India faces, Vijay Joshi, *India's Long Road: The Search for Prosperity* (New Delhi, 2016).

With the end of economic planning and the withdrawal of the central state from economic regulation, some now describe India's economic model as 'competitive federalism'. This directs attention to the twenty-nine states of the union and their widely differing economic performances. Aseema Sinha, *The Regional Roots of Developmental Politics in India* (Bloomington [IN], 2005), studies some of these divergent trajectories across three states and over several decades. On welfare outcomes across India's states, compare Rajeshwari Deshpande, Louise Tillin, and K. K. Kailash (eds.), *Politics of Welfare: Comparisons Across Indian States* (New Delhi, 2015), and Prerna Singh, *How Solidarity Works for Welfare: Subnationalism and Social Development in India* (Cambridge, 2015), which argues for a correlation between regional or subnational solidarities and better welfare outcomes, thus questioning the social utility of an overbearing national ideology. For useful studies of particular states, see N. K. Singh and Nicholas Stern (eds.), *The New Bihar: Rekindling Governance and Development* (New Delhi, 2013); and two studies that complicate the view of Gujarat as a model for other Indian states: Nikita Sud, *Liberalization, Hindu Nationalism and the State: A Biography of Gujarat* (New Delhi, 2012), and Indira Hirway, Amita Shah and Ghanshyam Shah (eds.), *Growth or Development: Which Way Is Gujarat Going?* (New Delhi, 2014). For some preliminary evidence suggestive of economic divergence across districts within states (and not just between states), see Praveen Chakravarty and Vivek Dehejia's IDFC Institute Briefing Paper, 'India's Income Divergence: Governance or Development Model?' (Mumbai, 2017).

Across rural and agrarian India, longstanding conflicts over land and basic rights have gained new intensity. For two accounts of the violent insurgencies under way in parts of the country (many inspired by Maoism and Naxalism), see Sudeep Chakravarti, *Red Sun: Travels in Naxalite Country* (New Delhi, 2008), and Nandini Sundar, *The Burning Forest: India's War in Bastar* (New Delhi, 2016). On the role of state legislation and market pressures upon land issues in urban as well as rural India, a useful guide is Sanjoy Chakravorty, *The Price of Land: Acquisition, Conflict, Consequence* (New Delhi, 2013). In the now-sparse field of village studies, two noteworthy publications are: Himanshu, Praveen Jha and Gerry Rodgers (eds.), *The Changing Village in India: Insights from Longitudinal Research* (New Delhi, 2016); and a provocative essay by Dipankar Gupta, 'Whither the Indian Village: Culture and Agriculture in "Rural" India', *Economic and Political Weekly*, 19 February 2005. On India's large 'informal economy', Barbara Harriss-White, *India Working: Essays on Society and Economy* (2003), is very illuminating, as is the work of Jan Breman.

The consequences of India's increasing exposure to the global economy remain hard to fathom for non-technical readers. For an account of how India managed the 2008 economic crisis, see the account by the man who was governor of the Reserve Bank of India at the time: Y. V. Reddy, *India and the Global Financial Crisis: Managing Money and Finance* (New Delhi, 2009). See also the book by one of his successors, Raghuram Rajan, *Fault Lines* (Princeton, 2010), especially 'Afterword: What Lies Ahead for India'.

The China-India comparison has become standard fare. The best study by far is Pranab Bardhan, *Awakening Giants, Feet of Clay: Assessing the Economic Rise of China and India* (Princeton, 2010).

Cities and urbanization have seen a boom in scholarship. The work of the architect and urban historian Rahul Mehrotra is one of the surest guides for understanding the built environment: see his *Architecture in India* (Berlin, 2011), *The State of Architecture* (Mumbai, 2016), and the catalogue of the landmark exhibition he organised with Kaiwan Mehta and Ranjit Hoskote. For an exploration of the cultural imagination of India's greatest modern city, Mumbai, see Gyan Prakash, *Mumbai Fables* (Princeton, 2010). For an investigation of that same city's contemporary underbelly, Katherine Boo's prize-winning *Behind the Beautiful Forevers: Life, Death and Hope in a Mumbai Undercity* (New York, 2012) sets a new standard.

The shifting character of nationalism and its various labile elements—religion, language, culture—have drawn much study. Essential to understanding the place of language in the life of the subcontinent over a long historical span is the magisterial collection edited by Sheldon Pollock, *Literary Cultures in History: Reconstructions from South Asia* (Berkeley, 2003); see also his *The Language of the Gods in the World of Men: Sanskrit, Culture, and Power in Premodern India* (Berkeley, 2006). Two other important studies on the politics of language are: Sumathi Ramaswamy, *Passions of the Tongue: Language Devotion in Tamil India 1891–1970* (New Delhi, 1997); and Alok Rai, *Hindi Nationalism* (New Delhi, 2000).

The continuing revision of Indian secularism and the many uses of religion in the country's public life have produced much debate and some illumination. The single most important collection, from a flood of titles, remains Rajeev Bhargava (ed.), *Secularism and Its Critics* (1998). A useful collection of articles on Hindu nationalism is Christophe Jaffrelot (ed.), *The Sangh Parivar: A Reader* (New Delhi, 2005).

A number of recent studies have emphasised the long, inconclusive and humanly painful process of subcontinental boundary-making and its fraught relationship to national identity: Joya Chatterji, *The Spoils of Partition: Bengal and India, 1947–1967* (Cambridge, 2007); Vazira Fazila-Yacoobali Zamindar, *The Long Partition and the Making of Modern South Asia: Refugees,*

Boundaries, Histories (New York, 2007); and Bérénice Guyot-Réchard, *Shadow States: India, China and the Himalayas, 1910–1962* (Cambridge, 2017).

On the intricate politics behind the creation of new states—an increasingly pressing issue—see Louise Tillin, *Remapping India: New States and Their Political Origins* (London, 2013).

For a wider argument about the particularity of the Indian case as a federal model based on 'holding together' rather than 'coming together', see Alfred Stepan, Juan Linz and Yogendra Yadav: *Crafting State-Nations: India and Other Multinational Democracies* (Baltimore, 2010).

In recent years, *The Caravan*, a monthly magazine, has established itself as an outstanding platform for narrative and investigative journalism, and is essential reading for anyone interested in contemporary India. Among numerous websites, *Scroll* and *The Wire* maintain robust critical positions (the former is strong on politics and culture, the latter on foreign policy and security issues), while Indiaspend.com provides a range of statistics and data to fact-check India's rapid-fire public discourse.

PREFACE

This is a book about India's public life in the twentieth century. Its focus is the turbulent, intricate and decisive passage of history since India's independence in 1947, but since its interests are in historical continuities as well as symbolic and real ruptures, it roves freely back into the period before independence. With a population approaching one billion, India is after China the most populous country in the world and its physical proportions too are vast: only six countries are larger. Faced with India's scale, diversity and sheer complexity, this book is necessarily fiercely selective. Its treatment of events and personalities is dictated by larger thematic and interpretative concerns. Twentieth-century India has produced a host of formidable public figures, many of whom have played a decisive role in the subcontinent's history. Some of these people move through the pages of this book, but they are evoked rather than explored. The compressions of the essay form require that they function essentially as icons, and – like other essays – this one has its central icon: Jawaharlal Nehru. The historical Nehru is alluded to here, but not presented in any detail. That is the task of a biography that I am currently researching. But I hope here to make clear why Nehru is so fundamental a figure in modern India's history, and why he demands to be understood anew in this period of flux in India's life.

In writing this book, I have relied in different ways on the assistance of many others. My debts to the specialist literature on India are noted in the bibliographical essay. For institutional support, I would like to record my thanks to Birkbeck College for a small College Research Grant during 1995–96, which relieved me from one of my teaching responsibilities. I thank Andrew Franklin and Peter Carson at Penguin Books for their initial enthusiasm when I suggested the idea of this essay; I am particularly grateful to Peter Carson for adopting it, and for all his help from beginning to end. Elisabeth Sifton at Farrar, Straus and Giroux provided very acute and improving suggestions, and the text has benefited greatly from these. In Gill Coleridge I could not have hoped for a better agent, and it has been a pleasure to be able to rely on her guidance and support. Most of all, I have drawn on the patience and indulgence of friends and family. Takashi Kato first gave me an opportunity to try out some of the arguments on various occasions at Seikei University, Tokyo, and I am grateful to him for his interest and kindness. For their generous encouragement, suggestions, and in some cases comments on draft sections of the book, I am indebted to Biancamaria Fontana, Ramachandra Guha, Keith Hart, Ron Inden, Rob Jenkins, Vijay Joshi, Pravina King, Arvind Krishna Mehrotra, Ben Pimlott, Suguna Ramanathan, Asha Sarabhai, Martand Singh, Giles Tillotson and Stephen Wilson. The bulk of the text was read at short notice by Gyanendra Pandey and Yogendra Yadav, and I am very grateful to both of them; to Yogendra Yadav I owe special thanks for his extremely thoughtful and careful comments. Various constraints have meant that I have not always been able to incorporate or respond to the suggestions and reactions so generously given. I am deeply grateful once again to John Dunn, Geoffrey Hawthorn and Roy Foster, for their criticism and advice, their intellectual example and their unfailing support – especially at precarious moments. My own ideas about India have developed over the past few years in dialogue with Sudipta Kaviraj: his extraordinary intellectual generosity, his friendship, and his stern encouragement have been vital. My debt to Rebecca Wilson is of a different order from any of the above: I thank her most of all.

SUNIL KHILNANI
26 January 1997

AUTHOR'S NOTE

Brief biographical notes on some of the characters who appear in the pages of this book, as well as glosses on terms that may be unfamiliar, will be found in the index entries. References for direct quotations are given at the end of the book.

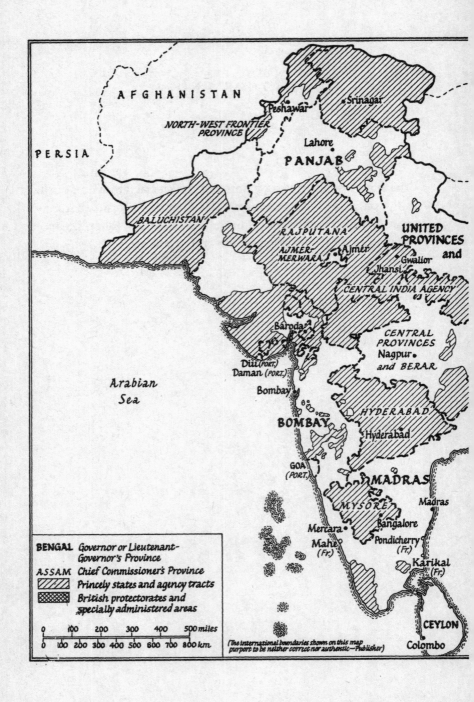

AFGHANISTAN

PERSIA

NORTH-WEST FRONTIER
PROVINCE

Peshawar

Srinagar

Lahore

PANJAB

BALUCHISTAN

RAJPUTANA

AJMER-
MERWARA

Ajmér

UNITED
PROVINCES

and

Gwalior

Jhansi

CENTRAL INDIA AGENCY

Baroda

CENTRAL
PROVINCES

Nagpur

and BERAR

Diu (PORT.)
Daman (PORT.)

Arabian
Sea

Bombay

BOMBAY

HYDERABAD

Hyderabad

GOA
(PORT.)

MADRAS

MYSORE

Mercara

Mahé
(Fr.)

Bangalore

Pondicherry
(Fr.)

Madras

Karikal
(Fr.)

CEYLON

Colombo

BENGAL   Governor or Lieutenant-
         Governor's Province
ASSAM   Chief Commissioner's Province
▨   Princely states and agency tracts
▩   British protectorates and
         specially administered areas

0   100   200   300   400   500 miles
0 100 200 300 400 500 600 700 800 km

(The international boundaries shown on this map
purport to be neither correct nor authentic—Publisher)

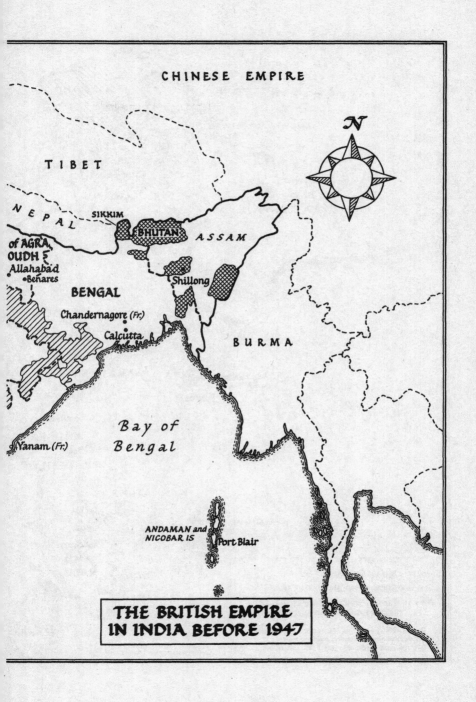

THE BRITISH EMPIRE
IN INDIA BEFORE 1947

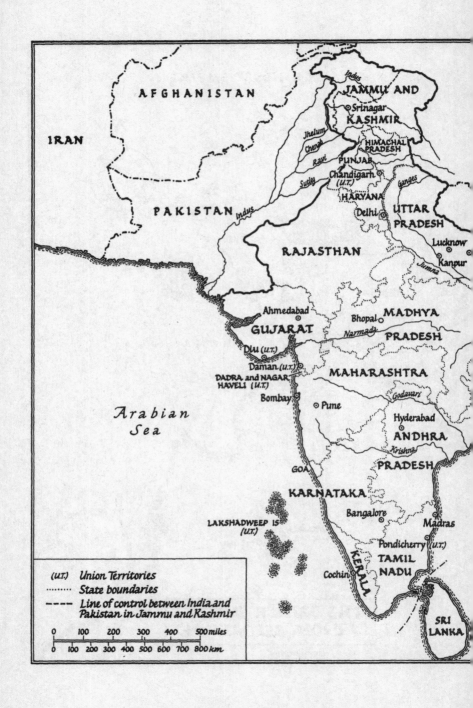

AFGHANISTAN

IRAN

PAKISTAN

Indus

Jhelum

Chenab

Ravi

Sutlej

Indus

JAMMU AND
KASHMIR

Srinagar

HIMACHAL
PRADESH

PUNJAB

Chandigarh
(U.T.)

HARYANA

Delhi

Ganges

UTTAR
PRADESH

Lucknow

Kanpur

Jumna

RAJASTHAN

Ahmedabad

GUJARAT

Bhopal

MADHYA

Narmada

PRADESH

Diu *(U.T.)*

Daman *(U.T.)*

DADRA and NAGAR
HAVELI *(U.T.)*

Bombay

MAHARASHTRA

Godavari

*Arabian
Sea*

Pune

Hyderabad

ANDHRA

Krishna

GOA

PRADESH

KARNATAKA

LAKSHADWEEP IS
(U.T.)

Bangalore

Madras

Pondicherry *(U.T.)*

KERALA

TAMIL
NADU

Cochin

SRI
LANKA

(U.T.)   Union Territories
.... State boundaries
- - - - Line of control between India and
        Pakistan in Jammu and Kashmir

0   100   200   300   400   500 miles

0   100 200 300 400 500 600 700 800 km

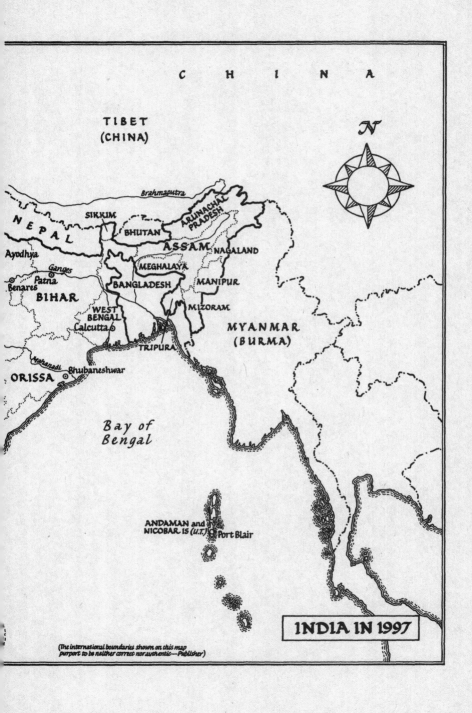

INDIA IN 1997

(The international boundaries shown on this map
purport to be neither correct nor authentic—Publisher)

India was in my blood ... And yet I approached her almost as an alien critic, full of dislike for the present as well as for many of the relics of the past that I saw. To some extent I came to her via the West and looked at her as a friendly westerner might have done. I was eager and anxious to change her outlook and appearance and give her the garb of modernity. And yet doubts rose within me.

JAWAHARLAL NEHRU, 1946

While everywhere multitudes cried for bread, the leaders of the nation made a great feast and praised the gods of gold, and of silver, of brass, and of iron. In the same hour came forth five fingers of a hand and wrote on the wall, and the leaders of the nation saw a part of the hand that wrote. Then their countenances were changed and their thoughts troubled them. The leaders of the nation cried aloud to bring in the astrologers and the soothsayers. Then came in all the wise men; but they could not read the writing, nor make known to the leaders of the nation the interpretation thereof. And no one with light and understanding and excellent wisdom could be found to read the writing, and make known the interpretation and dissolve the doubts.

VED MEHTA, 1970

INTRODUCTION

Ideas of India

Since its inauguration amidst the intense drama, excitement and horror of 1947, the public life of independent India has presented a scene of vivid collective spectacles and formidable individual characters, of unexpected achievements and unforgivable failures. The detail and sometimes the texture of this passage of history has been evoked in a rich tradition of reportage and travel writing, of fiction and cinema, as well as a huge and uncontrollable specialist literature. But what is it all about? What story is being told? What is the history of India since 1947 the history *of*?

Imperial and post-imperial accounts, as well as nationalist ones, all had their implicit answers to this, and they have suffused the sensibilities of popular and specialist writing about India. The post-imperial story cultivated a plot line of decline and fall. It told of a slow but irresistible erosion of the sand-castles of the British Raj, washed by the rising tides of India's ineffaceable past: a revival of the passions of community, religion and caste, stalking the scene in old and pristine form, the ageless subjects of India's history, ancient and modern. This story continues to sustain an often very sophisticated post-Raj literary style, an historicist nostalgia – a sense that without the carapace of imperial authority, things fall apart. It has produced the kitsch Gibbonism of a Nirad Chaudhuri and the more studiedly dark meditations of the younger, fastidious, V. S. Naipaul, drawn like a melancholy moth to his grandfather's land, always nervously reminding himself that 'it is necessary to fight against the chilling sense of a new Indian dissolution'. The temper of this nostalgic vision of India is reflected casually and unthinkingly in journalistic evocations of 'eternal India', of 'political dynasties' and 'feudal corruption'. For long, a standard Indian response to this dull narrative bass has been a percussive nationalism. For nationalists, 1947 marked a keypoint on a still building crescendo, a thrilling movement to a brighter future, where a settled and defined modern Indian nation, mature in its 'emotional integration', would come to preside over its own destiny.

But over the past generation the presumption that a single shared sense of India – a unifying idea and concept – can at once define the facts that need recounting and provide the collective subject for the Indian story has lost all credibility. This has been due partly to the direct practical challenges made to the Indian nation state by those who find reasons to dispute its authority to rule over them. And partly it has arisen through the efforts of a new generation of historians who, in an array of specialist and often innovative studies, have introduced a host of novel subjects and concerns, immeasurably widening the scope of any future History of Modern India. Research on 'non-national' identities has proliferated, and some historians have begun subtly to examine the processes through which national identities have been moulded out of the pressures and opportunities of power, often by active gerrymandering of the boundaries of individual and collective selves. If there is a single thrust to this intellectual assault on imperial and nationalist presuppositions, it has been to highlight the sheer artifice of all forms of political community on the subcontinent, whether religious or national. In itself, it is hardly a new point (it would not have surprised Hobbes). One benefit is that we can now see how those situated at different locations in Indian society have produced their own distinctive conceptions of the nation. But the costs have been heavy. Political history has been neglected – the doings of the state, of its elites, and of the many significant individuals in

India's twentieth-century history. Whatever political history has been written has remained imprisoned by the imperial mode of administrative history or, in its post-1947 analogue, diplomatic history, or it has been repetitious nationalist hagiography. The attempt to see the larger picture through new eyes has rarely been risked.

The choice seems stark. On the one hand, the old opposition between the monochromy of the post-imperial imagination and that of nationalist histories of a unified people; and on the other hand, set against both, the pointillism of the new Indian historians, ever more ingeniously trawling and re-reading the archives for examples of 'resistance' (textual or practical) to the ideas of nation and state. Yet there must still be room to navigate between these: to find new routes, that do not altogether abandon the terrain of political history, but recount it in different terms. This book is an initial venture into the task of retelling the political history of independent India. If its argument manages to encourage or irritate others into thinking about the larger picture, it will have served one of its main purposes.

In the first instance, the history of independent India can be seen, most narrowly but also most sharply, as the history of a state, one of the first, largest and poorest of the many created by the ebb of European empire after the end of the Second World War. The arrival of the modern state on the Indian landscape over the past century and a half, and its growth and consolidation as a stable entity after 1947, are decisive historical facts. They mark a shift from a society where authority was secured by diverse local methods to one where it is located in a single, sovereign agency. Seen in this perspective, the performance of the Indian state invites evaluation by external and comparative standards: for example, its ability to maintain the territorial boundaries it inherited from the British Raj, to preserve its domestic authority and the physical security of its citizens, to act as an agent of economic development, and to provide its citizens with social opportunities. Unlike the states of modern Europe, which acquired these responsibilities in gradual sequence, new states like India have had to adopt them, and be seen to pursue them, rapidly and simultaneously. The ability of a modern state to meet these heavily instrumental criteria is undoubtedly crucial to the life chances of its citizens. But these responsibilities have raised expectations often very distant from the state's practical capacities.

Rather more expansively, the period of Indian history since 1947 might be seen as the adventure of a political idea: democracy. From this perspective, the history of independent India appears as the third moment in the great democratic experiment launched at the end of the eighteenth century by the American and French revolutions. Each is an historic instance of the project to resuscitate and embody the ancient ideal of democracy under vastly different conditions, where community is no longer held together by a moral ideal or conception of virtue but must rely on more fitful, volatile solidarities and divisions including those produced by the exigencies of industrial production and commercial exchange. Each of these experiments released immense energies; each raised towering expectations; and each has suffered tragic disappointments. The Indian experiment is still in its early stages, and its outcome may well turn out to be the most significant of them all, partly because of its sheer human scale, and partly because of its location, a substantial bridgehead of effervescent liberty on the Asian continent. Asia is today the most economically dynamic region in the world, but it is also one where vast numbers of people remain politically subjugated. Its leaders have confidently asserted that the idea and practice of democracy is somehow radically inappropriate and intrusive to the more sober cultural manners of their people. The example of India is perhaps the most pointed challenge to these arguments.

The history of a state and the history of an idea: each provides ready if contrasting perspectives on contemporary India. But

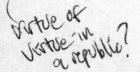

4

the most imaginatively ambitious if also analytically elusive perspective on India since 1947 shows a rapid acceleration and intensification in the long-running encounter between a civilization intricately designed with the specific purpose of perpetuating itself as a society, a community with a shared moral order, one of the world's most sophisticated assemblages of 'great' and 'little' traditions, and, set against it, the imperatives of modern commercial society. This is presumed somehow to link a political order that enshrines individual rights and representation to an economic system of private property rights and market exchange – but it stands under permanent threat of being unable to reproduce itself, and is fundamentally unstable. Seen from this angle, the many civilizational strands on the Indian subcontinent have uncomfortably but inescapably been confronting modernity: a seductively wrapped and internally inconsistent mixture of instrumental rationality, utilitarianism, and respect for individual autonomy and choice. From this perspective one can focus on the question of whether a culture and its members can sustain their distinctive character once they entrust their destiny (as they must) to a modern state.

In fact these three perspectives are not mutually exclusive. For all its magnificent antiquity and historical depth, contemporary India is unequivocally a creation of the modern world. The fundamental agencies and ideas of modernity – European colonial expansion, the state, nationalism, democracy, economic development – all have shaped it. The possibility that India could be united into a single political community was the wager of India's modern, educated, urban elite, whose intellectual horizons were extended by these modern ideas and whose sphere of action was expanded by these modern agencies. It was a wager on an idea: the idea of India. This nationalist elite itself had no single, clear definition of this idea, and one of the remarkable facts about the nationalist movement that brought India to independence was its capacity to entertain diverse, often contending

visions of India. 'One way of defining diversity for India,' the
poet and critic A. K. Ramanujan once wrote, 'is to say what the
Irishman is said to have said about trousers. When asked whether
trousers were singular or plural, he said, "Singular at the top
and plural at the bottom".' But Indian nationalism before Independence was plural even at the top, a *dhoti* with endless folds.
Its diversity was emblematically incarnated in the gallery of
characters who constituted the nationalist pantheon, a pantheon
whose unageing, cherub-like faces are still on display, painted
with garish affection on calendars and posters or moulded into
just recognizable statues and figures, in tea-shops and at cross-
roads across the country.

It contains people from markedly different backgrounds, yet
whose trajectories were often parallel. Most passed through some
form of Western education (often a training in law), and some
led strikingly cosmopolitan lives. At the head of this pantheon
is of course Mohandas Karamchand Gandhi, the Mahatma. Born
in 1869 in the Gujarati port city of Porbandar to a line of Dewans,
he experimented as an adolescent with ways of becoming more
manly and strong, like the colonial masters, travelled to London
to study law (disembarking at a grey Southampton dressed, to
his chagrin, in white flannels), and discovered vegetarianism in
Holborn, before moving to South Africa to practise as a barrister.
Politicized by the brutalities of the regime, he returned to India
to become, from the 1920s, the dominating leader of the Indian
National Congress and the most remarkable public figure of the
twentieth century. It also contains less distinctly remembered
men, like Vallabhbhai Patel, born also in Gujarat six years after
Gandhi, to a family of substantial landowners, who too passed
through London's Inns of Court and who worked himself up
through municipal and provincial politics to become for a brief
moment – between Gandhi's death in 1948 and his own in 1950
– one of the most powerful men in Indian politics. It has room
for men such as Subhas Chandra Bose, born in 1897 in Orissa,

6

the son of a Bengali lawyer, who qualified for the Indian Civil Service, became a radical Congressman and spokesman for Bengal, lived in Europe during the mid-1930s, and grew fascinated by the examples of Mussolini, Hitler and Ataturk. He persuaded the Nazis and the Japanese to support the creation of his own army to fight the Raj, only to die in a plane crash days after the end of the Second World War. And it also encompasses figures like Bhim Rao Ambedkar, born to parents of the 'untouchable' Mahar caste in Maharashtra six years before Bose, who lifted himself out of the near universal illiteracy of his caste to gain doctorates from Columbia and London universities, pass the bar at Gray's Inn, and become the leader of India's most oppressed groups. A thinker of lucid and focused anger, and one of the main drafters of India's Constitution, he was until his death in 1956 a perpetual thorn to the upper-caste pieties of the nationalist elite. But surpassing all in his influence on independent India's political possibilities was Jawaharlal Nehru. Born in 1889 to an astoundingly successful and ambitious provincial Brahmin lawyer, he was dispatched to be educated at Harrow, Cambridge and London's Inner Temple. On his return he drifted into nationalist politics through the influence of theosophy and Annie Besant, established a powerful and intriguing relationship with Gandhi, and, as India's first prime minister after 1947, decisively shaped his country's politics.

These figures, like other nationalists, and in conformity with the universal demands of modernity, had to invent and fashion their public selves. They created and expressed these selves sometimes through that literary genre which Indians embraced in the nineteenth and twentieth centuries, the didactic autobiography: a genre that in Indian – as in Irish – hands conveniently fused picaresque personal adventures with the odyssey of the nation. But often more important than their intellectual pronouncements were their practical actions – the dress, gestures, tone and style they self-consciously adopted to express their

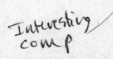
Interesting comp

distinct ideas of India. They had to make themselves Indian according to their own ideas of what exactly that meant. The presence of a foreign Raj had ensured that an Indian identity could not be assumed as a natural condition. Some, of course, chose to devise an ostentatiously 'traditional' self; others declared for a more stridently Western or modern one. But all had to make themselves out of the intimidations and possibilities posed by the West's modernity. Out of this experience, they had to forge their own distinctively Indian modernity. In the years after independence, the nationalist elite came to be dominated by a vision most closely associated with one man, Nehru. He was ostensibly the most anglicized of them all, and indeed it is impossible to bury the trail of his passage through British cultural institutions: public school, Cambridge, His Majesty's prisons. But in fact he had a profound sense of India's past, and of its own integrity, and this was matched by a personal life that was unmistakably Indian in its habits.

Nehru wished to modernize India, to insert it into what he understood as the movement of universal history. Yet the India created by this ambition has come increasingly to stand in an ironic, deviant relationship to the trajectories of Western modernity that inspired it. The processes of modernity within India have unravelled, and it has not kept to the script. In Nehru's rich metaphor, the 'garb of modernity' has not proved uniform, and Indians have found many and ingenious ways of wearing it. For Nehru and many nationalists, the West's present delineated the image of India's future. Yet the odd twist is that India's present may actually contain more than a premonitory hint of the West's own political future. The themes and conflicts that animate India's politics today have a surprisingly wide resonance – the assertion of community and group rights and the use of democracy to affirm collective identities; the difficulties of maintaining large-scale, multi-cultural political unions; the compulsion to make democracy work despite economic adversity, to sustain democracy without prosperity. The older democracies might recognize that each of these stands uncomfortably close to their own doorsteps.

In the four chapters of this book, I explore some of these twists, contradictions and themes. The thread that runs throughout is a concern with politics, understood as a necessarily undeterminable field of human agency, a space of constantly competitive, strategic and practical action, undertaken in conditions of imperfect and partial information. As both Gandhi and Nehru in their different ways had earlier seen, politics is at the heart of India's passage to and experience of modernity. In a fundamental sense, India does not merely 'have' politics but is actually constituted by politics. Once a society structured by stable hierarchies, where politics had a marginal – if spectacular – function, India is today the most intensely political society in the world. In a historical rebuff to Lord Curzon's solicitous advice – the salvation of India, he once declared, was not to be sought in the field of politics – Indians have poured their faith into politics, pinning their hopes to once-great movements like the Congress Party or to its current challengers like Hindu nationalism or the surging movements of India's lower-caste and Dalit parties. Politics at once divides the country and constitutes it as a single, shared, crowded space, proliferating voices and claims and forcing negotiation and accommodation. It is through politics that Indians are entering the contemporary world.

This is so above all because of the presence of democracy. The historic persistence of India's democratic routines, interrupted only by Mrs Indira Gandhi's Emergency – a twenty-two-month eclipse during the mid-1970s – is the single most remarkable fact about post-1947 India, distinguishing it from almost all the new nation states that emerged out of the disintegration of European empires. In India, democracy was constructed against the grain, both of a society founded upon the inequality of the caste order, and of an imperial and authoritarian state. If the initial conditions were unlikely, democracy has had to exist in circumstances that conventional political theories identify as being equally unpropitious: amidst a poor, illiterate and staggeringly diverse citizenry. Not only has it survived, it has succeeded in energizing Indian society in unprecedented ways. Introduced initially by a mincingly legalistic nationalist elite as a form of government, democracy has been extended and deepened to become a principle of society, transforming the possibilities available to Indians. They have embraced it, learning about it not from textbooks but by extemporary practice. Yet the very success of India's democracy also threatens its continued institutional survival. The idea of political equality has engendered the menace of a tyranny of the religious majority, a threat traumatically manifested in 1992 by the destruction of the Babri Masjid at Ayodhya, wrecked by militant Hindu activists.

In its politics, India has managed to achieve relative – if precariously balanced – success. It has allowed most of its citizens to live together with a larger measure of freedom than ever before and with more freedom than the citizens of other comparable new nation states (think of China). But by the standards of modern liberty, it has not allowed them to live well (China is again an instructive comparison). The aspiration to economic modernity has yielded a much more uneven picture: for most Indians, it has been a failure. Deprivation and maldistribution are the norm, for reasons that are numerous, often technical, and necessarily complex and disputed. But essentially it has been a self-produced political failure. It was political commitment to ideas, as well as politic concessions and compromises about these commitments, that created the curiously mixed and uneven character of India's economy: the close conjunction of fabulous luxury and abject destitution, of a lumbering state economy and nimble entrepreneurial capitalism, of the highest technology and grotesque physical labour. Competing ambitions collided to create this lopsided pattern of economic modernity followed after 1947: the interests of big industrialists, the hopes of Gandhian miniaturists, the ambitions of Nehru's intellectuals, and the power of those who controlled the land and its produce. No single vision triumphed.

What did carry the day was something no one had wanted but all had conspired to make, which gives India's economic life a painfully undecided character: poised for dramatic change yet never quite accomplishing it. While its politics have opened up its society to history in quite dramatic ways, in its economics India managed until the late 1980s to preserve what was, for a democratic country, a quite extraordinary insulation from the shaping forces of the global economy. Since the early 1990s, it has dramatically revised its economic identity, and has begun to open itself to greater international exposure and competition. This liberalization has raised high expectations, and has encouraged hopes of an Indian economic 'miracle' to rival those of East Asia. Economic possibilities have indeed rapidly changed for many Indians, yet the majority still find themselves waiting, some expectantly, most with no hope at all. Meanwhile, the state itself has also come to threaten its own citizens, often as a direct consequence of its commitment to the project of development, which has regularly placed enormous burdens on those people least able to defend themselves.

Modern India's political and economic experiences have coincided most dramatically in its cities – symbols of the uneven, hectic and contradictory character of the nation's modern life. From the ancient sacred space of Benares to the decaying colonial pomp of Calcutta, from the high rationalism of Chandigarh to the software utopia of Bangalore, from Bombay's uneasy blend of parochial politics and cosmopolitanism to the thrusting new cities of the north, driven by surpluses from a selectively prosperous countryside, India's cities express the country's unruly historical rhythms, and vividly reveal the harshly unequal opportunities of its denizens. They have become distended both by pressures from the countryside and by the insistent cultural and economic pulls of the world beyond. They have emerged out of an intricate, discontinuous history: remade by the will of the Raj, with its shifting, precise and – for most Indians – bewildering sense of what a city was; rearranged again by a nationalist conception of what the modern Indian city should be; and now once again subject to rearrangement by new post-nationalist ambitions. In India's cities, democratic equalization confronts the actual disparities of economic and social opportunity. The evident urban disjunctions have enlivened distinct political sentiments, and released unanticipated, sometimes dark potentialities, but they have also generated inventiveness and experimentation. Only a fragment of India's population has direct access to the cities, but images of them have spread throughout the society and have fired the imagination of all Indians.

The extension of democratic politics and electoral competition, the imbalance in available economic opportunities, and the real and imagined experience of the city have individually and together reconstituted both the nature and the range of the selves, the 'identities', that Indians can call their own. The nationalist confidence of 1947 that the definition of 'Indianness' and of those who possessed it would be permanently settled with the inauguration of an Indian state, was overly optimistic. The acquisition of a state, and regular, steadily intensified competition to enter and control it, has incited India's social identities to new potentialities for political organization and action. The emergence of a political Hinduism, of regional voices, and of the claims of caste identities – some of these last created by constitutional law, others worn as a defiant badge of historical oppression – has given the question of 'who is an Indian?' a sometimes lethal vitality.

Nehru's idea of India sought to coordinate within the form of a modern state a variety of values: democracy, religious tolerance, economic development and cultural pluralism. The unexpected historical trajectories of these various components since 1947 have changed the conditions of political competition in India, as well as the identity of the competitors, and as a result, it has become much more difficult to sustain a vision of a single political community.

And yet the idea of India retains a remarkable tenacity. Like their nationalist predecessors, Indians of vastly different backgrounds and ambitions today all wish to claim it for themselves. Modern Indian politics continues to plunder the nationalist pantheon for its iconography, while, at the same time, in its practical struggles it moves further and further away from the nationalist world and its distinctive temperament. The old arguments and battles are replayed today with the current generation's new meanings and desires: Ambedkar is once again ranged against Gandhi, Patel is brought into battle against Nehru. Even as they divide, these struggles themselves testify to the presence of a common history, a shared Indian past. The struggle for that past is of course a struggle to determine the future ideas of India. It is a struggle whose protagonists are at once products of ancient habits and of modern ambitions, who have found in democracy a form of action that promises them control over their own destinies. These struggles constitute the identity of India's history since 1947. And, in its ability constantly to encompass diverse ideas of what India is, this history is itself expressive of the Indian idea.

ONE

Democracy

In politics we will be recognizing the principle of one man one vote and one vote one value. In our social and economic life, we shall, by reason of our social and economic structure, continue to deny the principle of one man one value. How long shall we continue to live this life of contradictions?

B. R. AMBEDKAR, 1949

1

On 15 August 1996 the Indian tricolour was hoisted from the ramparts of Delhi's Red Fort in an annual ritual of state invented forty-nine years earlier by India's first prime minister, Jawaharlal Nehru. The man who in 1996 presided over this ceremonial observance of the day India gained independence from British rule came from a world galactically removed from Nehru's. H. D. Deve Gowda had taken office a few months earlier, the first Indian prime minister to speak neither Hindi nor English. A self-proclaimed 'humble farmer's son' from the southern state of Karnataka, he had vowed to master Hindi in time for the traditional Independence-day address to the nation. He stepped to the rostrum and valiantly delivered his speech in halting, and sometimes comic Hindi. ('Given the fact,' explained one supportive newspaper, 'that Mr Deve Gowda's familiarity with Hindi is only a few months old his speech obviously lacked the rhetorical flourishes.') It was a talismanic moment in India's public life. The mighty Congress, the invincible juggernaut of

India's twentieth-century history, the party so intimately associated with Nehru and his family, which had set the terms of an Indian identity, had crashed to electoral defeat in May. No ready substitute had emerged. The strongest challenger, the Bharatiya Janata Party (BJP), representing a resurgent Hindu nationalism, had made unprecedented advances in the elections, and for a brief fortnight it had actually held office – so interrupting India's record of government by non-religious parties. But, short of a majority, the BJP too had fallen, and power had passed to the men from the regions, a hastily arranged medley of more than a dozen parties led by the farmer from Karnataka, Deve Gowda.

After almost fifty years of self-rule, the old certitudes of Indian politics had crumbled. Yet one powerful continuity stretched across this half-century of spectacular and often turbulent events: the presence of a democratic state. As a single territory commanded by a state, India has long posed something of a puzzle: even the British who had possessed it as an empire marvelled at its oddity. Macaulay, with characteristic but for once justifiable exaggeration, famously described it as 'the strangest of all political anomalies'. As an independent democratic state since 1947, India remains defiantly anomalous.

Few states created after the end of European empire have been able to maintain democratic routines; and India's own past, as well as the contingencies of its unity, prepared it very poorly for democracy. Huge, impoverished, crowded with cultural and religious distinctions, with a hierarchical social order almost deliberately designed to resist the idea of political equality, India had little prospective reason to expect it could operate as a democracy. Yet fifty years later India continues to have parliaments and courts of law, political parties and a free press, and elections for which hundreds of millions of voters turn out, as a result of which governments fall and are formed. Democracy is a type of government, a political regime of laws and institutions.

Not quite true - lots of practice

But its imaginative potency rests in its promise to bring alien and powerful machines like the state under the control of human will, to enable a community of political equals before the constitutional law to make their own history. Like those other great democratic experiments inaugurated in eighteenth-century America and France, India became a democracy without really knowing how, why, or what it meant to be one. Yet the democratic idea has penetrated the Indian political imagination and has begun to corrode the authority of the social order and of a paternalist state. Democracy as a manner of seeing and acting upon the world is changing the relation of Indians to themselves.

How did the idea arrive in India? And what has it done to India, and India to it?

2

Contrary to India's nationalist myths, enamoured of immemorial 'village republics', pre-colonial history little prepared it for modern democracy. Nor was democracy a gift of the departing British. Democracy was established after a profound historical rupture – the experience, at once humiliating and enabling, of colonialism, which made it impossible for Indians to regard their own past as a sufficient resource for facing the future and condemned them, in struggling against the subtle knots of the foreigner's Raj, to struggle also against themselves. But it also incited them to imagine new possibilities: of being a nation, of possessing their own state, and of doing so on their own terms in a world of other states. By gradually raising the edifice of a state whose sovereign powers stretched across the vast Indian landscape, the British made politics the unavoidable terrain on which Indians would have to learn to act.

In pre-colonial India, power was not embodied in the concept of a state, whether republican or absolutist. Across the subcontinent, varied economies and cultures were matched by an assortment of political arrangements. They were nothing like the static 'oriental despotism' conjured up by colonial and Marxist historians: deliberative and consultative forms of politics did exist, but there was no protracted historical struggle to install institutions of representative government, nor (despite a hardly passive rural or urban poor) did large-scale popular movements act to curb the powers of rulers. Most importantly, before the gradual British acquisition of most of India's territory no single imperium had ever ruled the whole, immense subcontinental triangle. India's social order successfully curbed and blunted the ambitions of political power, and made it extraordinarily resistant to political moulding.

The basis of this resistance lay in the village, and its distinct form of community: the *jati*. These groups, numbering in the thousands, were governed by strict rules of endogamy and by taboos about purity, and arranged a social hierarchy: *varna*. The precise ideological sources of this system are obscure, but elements may be traced to one of the very late hymns of the *Rig Veda*, which describes the dismemberment of the cosmic giant *Purusha*, the primeval male whose sacrifice created the world: 'When they divided the Man, into how many parts did they apportion him? What do they call his mouth, his two arms and thighs and feet? / His mouth became the Brahmin; his arms were made into the Warrior [*kshatriya*], his thighs the People [*vaishiya*], and from his feet the servants [*shudra*] were born.' The resulting intricate filigree of social interconnections and division – a hierarchical order of peerless sophistication – defies any simple account. Perplexed Westerners came to describe it by the term 'caste', but a wide distance separates the deceptively well-defined doctrinal claims of the caste order and the actual operations of what is an essentially local, small-scale system. Two of its characteristics, however, are particularly direct. The system of *jati* and *varna* deflected responsibility for social outcomes away from human individuals or agencies and diffused it in a metaphysical universe, so making it impossible to assign blame for social wrongs and oppressions to particular individuals or groups. *Jatis* themselves were far from immutable in their social rank, and regularly rose and fell within the *varna* order; but the structure itself showed remarkable resilience. Further, the system did not concentrate status, wealth and power exclusively in one social group but distributed them to different parts of the social order, with the result that no one social group could impose its will on the whole society.

Yet India was not simply an archipelago of villages imprisoned by the local ties of caste. The prevalence of common aesthetic and architectural styles, as well as myths and ritual motifs, attests to the presence of a larger, more cohesive power. This derived neither from a unique political authority, such as an absolutist state, nor from a monolithic, codified religion controlled by a Church, but rather from the ideological mechanisms of pre-colonial India. These rested on a monopoly of literacy vested in one social group, the Brahmins. The Brahminic order in India was certainly an oppressive system of economic production, and it enforced degrading rules about purity and pollution. But its capacity to endure and retain its grip over a wide geographical area flowed from its severely selective distribution of literacy. The Brahminic pattern survived not through allying with temporary bearers of political power, nor by imposing a single belief system on the society. Rather, it cultivated a high tolerance for diverse beliefs and religious observances, withdrew from political power – the realm of *Artha*, or mere worldly interest – and directed its energies towards the regulation of social relationships; it made itself indispensable to the conduct of essential rituals, and it provided law for every aspect of social life. Its interpretative powers were recognized as the ultimate sanction and authority for caste rules. By renouncing political power, the Brahminic order created a self-coercing, self-disciplining society founded on a vision of a moral order. This society was easy to rule but difficult to change: a new ruler had merely to capture the symbolic seat of power and go on ruling as those before him had done. India could be defeated easily, but the society itself remained unconquered and unchanged.

Politics was thus consigned to the realm of spectacle and ceremony. No concept of a state, an impersonal public authority with a continuous identity, emerged: kings represented only themselves, never enduring states. It was this arrangement of power that explains the most peculiar characteristic of India's pre-colonial history: the perpetual instability of political rule, the constant rise and fall of dynasties and empires, combined with the society's unusual fixity and cultural consistency. Its identity lay not in transient political authority but in the social order. The ambitions of political rulers could therefore never become absolute, as they readily became in Europe: the rulers could not transform or mobilize society for particular ends. The state as a sovereign agency with powers to change society, to alter its economic relations, to control its beliefs or rewrite its laws, did not exist. The political authority that the many territorial kingdoms of the Indian subcontinent possessed was more a matter of paramountcy than sovereignty: kingship was exercised through overlapping circuits of rights and obligations that linked together diverse local societies but also sheltered them from the intrusions of any one ruler. Rulers restricted themselves to extracting wealth in the form of rent; they had no means to rearrange the property order or effect large shifts in the balance of wealth from one group to another, and thus secure permanent allies.

Unlike the history of Europe, that of pre-colonial India shows no upward curve in the responsibilities and capacities of the state. The very externality of politics, its distance from what was taken to be the moral core of the society, was the key to the society's stability. But this also made politics an exposed flank, *social order* / *politics*

an arena of contact with the outside world. Along with routines of trade and commercial exchange, politics became the vestibule where the alien was received, entertained, and usually contained. Here Indians were willing to learn techniques of statecraft from others without feeling that this endangered the inner core of their own identities. This shaping of social space made it easy for the concepts of Western politics to force an initial bridgehead in India and then, with their historically unprecedented powers, to overwhelm the society itself.

No issue divides India's historians more sharply than the impact of colonialism. Did British rule ruthlessly fracture the patterns of Indian society, or was it compelled to adapt to native styles, and merely preside in glorified manner over the more subterranean movements of India's history? Whatever view one takes of its economic and social consequences, the political effect of the British intrusion was unambiguous and resounding. The foreign rulers brought with them to India a concept of the state – with its distinct, if often locally influenced, administrative and military technologies, its claim to rule over a precise territory, its determination to initiate social reforms, and its reorganization of the texture of community – that drastically changed ideas about power in India. The British gradually but decisively defined power in political terms and located it in a sovereign, central state. The colonial template of rule altered over time, diverted by changing British ideologies about the state's legitimate purposes and the character of Indian society. Shifting historiographical fashions in interpreting Britain's own medieval history, for instance, directly affected the Raj's political practices: the view of India as a 'feudal' society with a natural ordering of lords, chiefs and yeomen, which called for little interference by the British, by the end of the nineteenth century gave way to one of a society composed of permanently feuding 'communities' that had each to be represented and paternally protected by the British Raj. Initially, British rule was often little more than a

interesting

series of severely local expedients of a commercial agency, the East India Company, but by the end of the nineteenth century it began to acquire a more tangible presence. This imperial state was charged with relatively restricted duties: to siphon off commercial and economic benefits more efficiently and, above all, to prevent any repetition of the Uprising of 1857, when a rebellion begun by Indian troops in north India spread to become the most serious domestic military challenge the British Raj was ever to face.

The state which the British built in India came to stand in a peculiar cultural relationship with Indian society: the British considered their most urgent task the Hobbesian one of keeping order over a bounded territory, but the Raj could not rely on preserving the peace simply through coercion or even by the deft manipulation of interests. It had to govern opinion. This it did by ostentatious spectacle, imperial Durbars and ceremonial progresses. These despotic tea parties won over a small circle of British loyalists, but there was no reshaping of common beliefs in the society at large. The barrier was essentially linguistic, and it endured after 1947. The language of administration used by the Raj – for example, for revenue collection and property law – had to be understood if it was to be effective, and so an elaborate and sonorous mongrel jargon of everyday usage was created, a Hobson–Jobson vernacular vocabulary. But the language of politics and legislation did not stray from the Queen's English. The British rulers swathed themselves in mystique by proclaiming in an alien and powerful language, but few among the ruled could actually comprehend what was said.

The British began therefore to cultivate a local elite who could understand them and their concepts of rule, who were willing to be inducted into politics, into a 'public arena' where they would freely give allegiance and loyalty to the British crown, 'a class of persons', as Macaulay had put it in the blunt instructions of his 1835 Education Minute which led to the foundation of the

Indian university system, 'Indian in colour and blood but English in tastes, in opinions, in morals and in intellect'. The imposition of English as the language of politics transfigured Indian public life in at least two ways: it obviously divided the British rulers from their Indian subjects; and it also divided Indians themselves, between those who could speak English, who knew their Dicey from their Dickens, and those who did not. These often immaculately anglicized elites were also, it is essential to remember, fully bicultural, entirely comfortable with their own Marathi, Bengali or Hindustani *milieux*: it was, after all, exactly this amphibious quality which made them useful porters to the British Raj. The slow extraction of power from the society and its concentration in the state was in India's case crucially a matter of language. The social power that Sanskrit – and then Persian – had once held was replaced by a new, still more mysterious, more potent language of state: English.

The cultural reach of British rule was steady as far as it went, but it was never very deep. The enduring effect of the Raj lay not in its ability to implant affection among native hearts for the empress across the seas, nor even – contrary to fond post-imperial imaginings – to seal a deep bond of Anglo-Indian cultural intimacy, but in its structuring of political possibilities. The extractive, suppressive, strange-tongued Raj was no mere clone of the British state, an expatriate station in an exotic location. When Henry Sumner Maine spoke of how India's British rulers were required to keep their watches set simultaneously on two longitudes, he captured the foundational duality of the Raj: it faced in two directions, towards two audiences or 'publics', British and Indian. From its very inception, impelled by both secular and Christian solicitude for benighted idolaters, it spoke the language of reform. After the mid nineteenth century, resolutely this-worldly political doctrines of utilitarianism dominated, but by the time their remedies began to surface in the ordinances of British administrators in Calcutta and Bombay, their original radical impulse had wilted into what has been called 'Government House utilitarianism', a decisively authoritarian and paternalist vehicle for the ideas of intellectual bullies like James Fitzjames Stephen. The corrective accent inspired zealous administrators to enlarge the field of the Raj's activities: it began to pry into Indians' social customs and habits, legislated the abolition of *sati* (an interference in social customs by political authority without historical precedent in India), and established the principle – if a rather deformed conduct – of representative politics.

The language of representative politics thus entered India through a utilitarian filter, at a time when British liberalism was at its most rampantly collectivist and paternalist. The possible forms of liberalism in India were still further reduced. The idea of natural rights, essential to modern liberalisms, was only faintly articulated and failed to find a niche in nationalist thought. The interests of Indians, the British had decided, could not be individual. It followed that when elections to provincial legislatures were first introduced – as a result of constitutional reforms devised in 1909 by the Secretary for India, John Morley, and the Viceroy, Lord Minto – the units of representation were not defined (as they were in Britain) as territorial constituencies containing individuals with rights and changeable interests. The legislatures of British India's administrative provinces, arbitrarily demarcated territories, represented societies of communities, not individuals. The extent of that representation did widen over time, being increased by the 1919 Montagu–Chelmsford reforms which granted to Indians for the first time the principle of responsible government, and most of all by the Government of India Act of 1935, which established the Raj as a federal structure and brought more Indians into its administration; but even then, less than one-third of the Raj's subjects had the vote (the subjects of princely India – a quarter of the subcontinent's population – remained altogether excluded).

The groups who were accorded political representation were

identified as religious 'communities' with immutable interests and collective rights: these Hindu and Muslim, Christian and Parsi communities were tagged as the eternal elements of Indian society. Defined as majorities and minorities, they were shepherded into communal electorates whose interests the British had to protect from one another. Representatives of these communities, along with the princes, were inducted into an ambiguously political world where they had to mouth the language of legality and representation, but these municipal and provincial chambers had no powers to legislate; they were enjoined simply to nod their approval of colonial laws. This was an anaemic conception of public politics. Instead of the threatening spaces of India's streets, squares and bazaars, it offered the soporific chambers of Indo-saracenic municipal halls. Men like Lord Curzon, who worked his viceroyalty so hard to institute this twilight world of spectacular impotence, tried to restrict the scope of Indian politics by ruling through the Indian princes, who were required to be at once conservative and liberal, to blend eastern splendour and western constitutional propriety, to sport turbans and read Bagehot.

Yet even this stilted acquaintance with the inconsistent bundle of ideas and protocols of the British imperium began to excite and then to irritate the Indian elites. It led to their first organized response to the Raj: the formation in 1885 of the Indian National Congress. Initially Congress merely requested that the privileges of British subjects be extended to obedient Indians, but by the 1920s it started to lay claim, in the name of the nation, to possession of the state and its territory. The history of Congress is that of a protean party with an exceptional capacity constantly to reinvent itself. What unites the party of Allan Octavian Hume, the theosophist and ornithologist who helped in 1885 to launch the Congress Party as a stiff debating club that met annually during the Christmas vacation with that of Annie Besant and Motilal Nehru, or these incarnations with Mahatma Gandhi's squabbling but determined mass organization, or any of these with Jawaharlal Nehru's expansive yet prim ruling party, let alone with the bedraggled rump of jobbers it became by the mid-1990s, is far from plain to the naked eye. Nehru once described Congress as 'the mirror of the nation', and it is indeed best seen as a screen on which the nation has projected its shifting politics rather than as itself a coherent agent with a unified will.

From its very earliest days it claimed to speak for the nation and did so by stressing India's right to collective liberty. Even during Congress's most strongly liberal phase, the period of 'mendicant constitutionalism' which ran from 1885 until the end of the First World War, its demands were not for the equal rights of all individuals but that culturally Indians should be at liberty not to have to suffer the petty – and therefore all the more infuriating – slights of colonialism and that economically they should be free to enrich themselves. Liberty was understood not as an individual right but as a nation's collective right to self-determination. It is hardly surprising that the individualist accent was muted: Indian society did have a place for the individual, but in the form of the renouncer, a category relegated to the margins of the society. Individuality as a way of social being was a precarious undertaking. All this left Indian liberalism crippled from its origins: stamped by utilitarianism, and squeezed into a culture that had little room for the individual.

Gandhi entirely remade this fastidious rule-book liberalism of the first generation of Congressmen. He turned Congress into a mass movement, though paradoxically preserved its conservative, distinctly non-revolutionary character. Congress was never the voice of a single class, but its conservative temperament was encouraged by the manner in which it had to enter representative politics. The British Raj, in its efforts to widen its representative base and devolve more responsibilities to the method of indirect rule, had in 1937 held elections to the enlarged provincial legislatures announced by the Government of India Act in 1935. Congress, initially hesitant, decided to compete and to win it was forced into alliances with powerful landed interests, upper-caste landlords, and rich peasants in the countryside. During these years of slow entry into the portals of the Raj, democracy did not capture its concentrated attention. Nor (contrary to subsequent nationalist self-congratulation) did the internal rules of the party organization explain the choice of constitutional democracy after 1947. For the duration of Gandhi's dominance, from 1920 until the early 1940s, policy within Congress was determined by the Working Committee, known as the High Command: this small group included powerful leaders from the provinces. Typically, except for a brief period in the early 1920s Gandhi preferred not to be a formal member of the Working Committee, yet he used it repeatedly to push through decisions that contradicted the wishes of party members. Most conspicuous was his removal of Subhas Chandra Bose from the elected office of party president in 1939. Gandhi did establish a culture of dialogue and publicity with Congress, but his fierce disciplinary regimes – fasts, silences, penances – gave him a grip on the party that relied at once on coercion and seduction. These were the immensely effective techniques of an eccentric parent, but they were not designed to nourish commitment to democratic institutions. By the 1930s and 1940s, Congress nationalism was divided between opinions that had little interest in liberal democracy. Gandhi's powerful vision of direct self-rule, with the majority in possession of political power unmediated by a state, rejected talk of rights and constitutions, while a dissident strain, articulated by Bose and Nehru and more obviously influenced by Western ideas, held that liberal democracy had been historically superseded by socialism.

So, before independence Congress could not pretend to any developed meditation on democracy, though it did embody a formidable will to political power. Its history demonstrates the impressive capacity of Indians to respond to the opportunities offered by a state, their readiness to mobilize for power. But what was to be done with that power? As the prospect of independence approached and as the prize of power loomed, the fissures within Congress became prominent. Its diversity of voices – Gandhian, socialist, conservative, capitalist, Hindu – meant that Congress, like so many other visionary nationalisms, had no coherent programme of independent government. And democracy itself was certainly not the object of close study. India's history in the first half of the twentieth century teems with new ideas, arguments, languages, hopes, but amidst these intellectual festivities the idea of democracy stood in a lonely corner. Then, after 1947, it swept all before it. But there was no surrounding world of arguments, theories, commitments or speculations about the consequences of implanting it on Indian soil. Apart from the standard colonial thrust against it and the nationalist parry that Indians could be parliamentarians too, little prepared the people who would soon entrust their destiny to democracy's exigencies.

3

The end of British rule and the withdrawal of governing units whose authorization to rule rested on imperial force and majesty raised awkward questions about the authority of any successor state to possess and rule this territory. The British, sceptical that any unity could outlast their reign, inclined to a 'Balkanization' of British India – which would have left it sundered between the suzerainty of the princes and the rule of religious leaders. To Congress this was an inconceivable idea, a travesty of independence: as self-declared representative of the nation, it laid claim to the state and the entire territory of British India. But since the late 1930s, representatives of the Raj's Muslims had disputed this claim with growing energy. A partition between a Hindu India and a Muslim Pakistan was intended finally to resolve all contests over who had authority to rule the territory of British India by dividing and bequeathing the land to two successor states. But this partition did not resolve these contests. Rather, it became a recurring motif in the subsequent history of the subcontinent and never died away: simultaneously a fearful spectre in the cultural memory and a perpetual challenge to the territorial authority of the successor states. The evidence of its refusal to pass quietly into history litters the subcontinent's landscape. The secession of Bangladesh from Pakistan in 1971, the long and bloody engagement of India in battles to forestall secession of some territories and – on occasion – to acquire others, and the insistence of Hindu nationalists in India to decide who belongs exactly where on the subcontinent, are all revisitations of this original faultline.

Thus when Congress inherited the undamaged coercive and bureaucratic powers of the British Raj in India, and the major part of its territory, the circumstances were ones of uncertainty and crisis. The nationalist elite in command of the state had to act in a society alive with aspirations, divided between differing conceptions of who the nation was and what the state should do. Congress was in dispute with itself: Partition had emboldened its Hindu voices, meanwhile those on the socialist Left had exited, and Gandhi in characteristically gnomic fashion called for Congress's dissolution now that the appointed day had come and gone. It was far from inevitable that the Indian state would emerge from this flux as a parliamentary democracy based on universal suffrage, without religious affiliation and committed to social reform. Strong pressures were weighing the other way: towards a more traditionalist kind of state, tied to religion and defending the existing order.

The contingencies that put Nehru in control of his party and then over the state of independent India in August 1947 were decisive. But his was always a tenuous dominance, and throughout his career as prime minister Nehru was an isolated figure, having to act against the inclinations of both his party and the state bureaucracy. In the history of the Indian state, this inaugural span, from 1947 until Nehru's death in 1964, is of unsurpassed importance, during which the state stabilized, became a developmental agency that aspired to penetrate all areas of the society's life, and showed that it could be subject to democratic procedures. But the settled coherence of the Nehru era is in fact a retrospective mirage. He did have intellectual principles and a philosophy of history, both of which shaped his actions, and there were certainly others who shared his views, but he had no clear doctrinal plan of action, nor was there anything like a consensus, within either his party or the society at large, to impart cohesion. Nehru's view of historical possibility was determined by his understanding of the West's historical trajectory, in which he saw universal significance. He was convinced that to maintain their newly won independence, Indians would have to entrust their future to a national state, whose central responsibility would be to direct economic development; but it also had to build a constitutional, non-religious regime, extend social opportunities, and maintain sovereignty in the international arena. This expansive and imprecise vision became tangible after 1947. Nehru's argument was not ideological or theoretical: it emerged through constant practical adjustments in the face of political contingencies.

The early years of his premiership were strewn with such contingencies, none more serious than Partition. Few had foreseen its likelihood, and fewer still had expected it to come so precipitately or in the form it did. Indeed, even while it was actually underway no one quite knew what it involved, and many – including Nehru himself – thought it was a temporary adjustment that in time would be reversed. But it came as a fury. Partition, when it began in August 1947, was the starkest case of being in the wrong place at the wrong time, as trains steaming across the plains with their dead, and refugee columns stretching for dozens of miles, testified. When the communal killing erupted in Lahore and Amritsar, Nehru faced the crisis as head of a cabinet and a party that were far from united behind him. The creation of a Muslim-majority Pakistan led many within Congress to demand that the Indian state should explicitly declare itself defender of the interests of the nation's Hindu majority. Powerful Congressmen like Vallabhbhai Patel from Gujarat and Bihar's Rajendra Prasad called for the dismissal of Muslim state officials, and suggested that there was little point in the army trying to protect Muslim citizens. For Nehru, the Partition was a crushing personal blow – 'Life here continues to be nightmarish,' he wrote in October 1947. 'Everything seems to have gone awry' – but his personal response was exemplary: he took to the streets of Delhi, rushing to Connaught Circus and to the old city in order to try to stop the killing and looting, and to assure Muslim families that they could rely on the protection of the state; and he repeatedly spoke against the Hindu communalists, refusing to cede control of the state to them. Ironically, although Nehru was now head of a state, which Gandhi detested, the two men grew closer together in the face of the communal violence – Nehru visited Gandhi daily during the autumn of 1947. Gandhi's assassination at the hands of a Hindu extremist in January 1948 removed Nehru's most important personal and political ally within Congress, but it also justified a ban that outlawed the most extreme Hindu communal groups. Partition was above all, however, a test of the Indian state's sovereignty, its capacity to protect its citizens, keep order, and justify its territorial ownership.

Thus was the Indian state embattled in contests over rights to territory from its inception. In two regions the contests were never resolved and continue to this day: in the northeastern homelands of the Naga tribes, a region severed by the hasty scrawl of an imperial pen between India and Burma; and in

Kashmir, whose Hindu king decided in 1948 to accede, with his predominantly Muslim subjects, to the Indian Union under notoriously disputed circumstances. The details of this constitutive moment of the Indian Union, which established it as a secular republic that included a Muslim-majority regional state, remain obscure: typical of the general purloining of the relevant papers was the story reported in 1995 that the actual document of accession had 'disappeared' from the archives in Srinagar. These running sores of independent India's politics were in later decades joined by other secessionist claims, most notably from groups in Punjab and Assam. The state, for its part, made efforts to acquire or control territory: sometimes by successful conquest, as in the case of Portuguese Goa in 1961; sometimes by constitutional sleight of hand, as in the case of Sikkim in 1975; and sometimes through disastrous military intervention, as in its interference in a dispute between Tamil separatists and Sri Lanka in the late 1980s. On this vexed subject of India's boundaries and its authority to rule over territory, Nehru was evasive: he recognized the sense in which a democratic nation state was a 'daily plebiscite' – which led him to promise a referendum for the Kashmiri people – but equally he found himself subject to the dictates of *raison d'etat*.

In the cases of Kashmir and Nagaland, India enforced its claim to sovereign control of its territory by military means. Immediately after Partition, the first of several wars with Pakistan over disputed territory in Kashmir erupted. Soon after, as the hundreds of princely states were assimilated into the new Union, military force was deployed internally – against the private army of the sumptuously eccentric Nizam of Hyderabad, for example, who entertained the notion of setting up his own independent fiefdom, and to suppress a communist-led peasant insurgency in the adjacent region of Telengana. In each case, the military response ensured that precisely those traits of the Raj which Indian nationalists had struggled against were now reinforced:

the powers to coerce and keep public order. Military force was essential in establishing and securing the Indian state, but the generals never ruled. The military was successfully subordinated to civilian control, unlike the situation in many other South and Southeast Asian states.

The authority of the new state to command its territory and govern its people could no longer rest on the praetorian habits of the Raj, nor could the meaning of security be restricted to colonial definitions of order. As nationalists insisted, it had now to encompass the welfare as well as the freedom of citizens. How to embody these aspirations was the subject of protracted, often bitter debate in India's Constituent Assembly, an island of calm deliberation amidst the historical currents that swirled through the country. It met for the three years between 1946 and 1949 to debate and in some part settle the character of the new state, and it produced the nation's Constitution, promulgated on 26 January 1950, which announced that India would henceforth be a 'sovereign, democratic republic'. The evocative Gandhian vision of an independent India that would dispense with a state altogether and return to traditional habits of rule soon faded from view. The Constitution was squarely in the best Western tradition: as one mortified nationalist in the Assembly lamented, 'We wanted music of Veena and Sitar, but here we have the music of an English band.'

The real confrontation, both in the Assembly and within Congress, was between Patel and Nehru. Diametrically opposed in character, the two waged an emblematic struggle between rival conceptions of a modern India. One wanted the state simply to express and tend the existing pattern of India's society, with all its hierarchy, particularity and religious tastes; the other hoped to use the state actively to reconstitute India's society, to reform it and to bring it in line with what it took to be the movement of universal history. Ultimately, Nehru's democratic, reformist argument edged out Patel's more conservative, authoritarian one. But it was a precarious and partial victory: it persuaded few outside intellectual and English-speaking circles, and it could never rely on the support of any powerful group.

It did result in a democratic regime. Constitutional democracy based on universal suffrage did not emerge from popular pressures for it within Indian society, it was not wrested by the people from the state; it was given to them by the political choice of an intellectual elite. The Constituent Assembly was a remarkably unrepresentative body: around 300 men (more were added after the princely states entered the Union), elected on the restricted franchise of the provincial legislatures, and overwhelmingly dominated by the upper-caste and Brahminic elites within Congress. There was no organized representation of India's Muslims, no presence of Hindu communal groups (although Congress itself harboured many Hindu conservatives) and, after 1948, no socialist voice. To Gandhi, for instance, it was quite clearly not a sovereign body. Within the Assembly itself, the drafting of the Constitution rested in the hands of only about two dozen lawyers.

Most people in India had no idea of what exactly they had been given. Like the British empire it supplanted, India's constitutional democracy was established in a fit of absentmindedness. It was neither unintended nor lacking in deliberation. But it was unwitting in the sense that the elite who introduced it was itself surprisingly insouciant about the potential implications of its actions. The ample volumes of the Constituent Assembly debates contain superbly turned pieces of forensic reasoning, speeches about the relationship between the executive and the judiciary and about the optimum length of a presidential term. Yet they carry little trace of the classic fears that haunted both advocates and critics of democracy in nineteenth-century Europe: what would happen if the vote was given to the poor, the uneducated, the dispossessed? B. R. Ambedkar, the formidable leader of India's 'untouchables' – upon whom the caste system branded its most brutal stigmata of oppression – put the point searingly in a majestic closing discourse to the Assembly debates:

On the 26th of January 1950, we are going to enter a life of contradictions. In politics we will have equality and in social and economic life we will have inequality. In politics we will be recognizing the principle of one man one vote and one vote one value. In our social and economic life, we shall, by reason of our social and economic structure, continue to deny the principle of one man one value. How long shall we continue to live this life of contradictions? How long shall we continue to deny equality in our social and economic life? If we continue to deny it for long, we do so only by putting our political democracy in peril.

This fundamental contradiction, along with others, was inscribed in India's interminably long Constitution. The Constitution did not express the opinions or preferences of Indians, nor did it confine itself to a bare statement of procedural rules. It was a baroque legal promissory note, its almost 400 articles embodying what initially looked like a derisorily ambitious political design. Yet, despite some serious mishandling, it has had a commanding influence over India's subsequent history, representing an ideal of legality and procedural conduct – albeit regularly ignored with sublime talent by Indians at all levels – that has loomed in public life as a permanently embarrassing monument. The Supreme Court, its defender and interpreter, became a central institution of the nation's public life, resorted to by rich and poor, literate and illiterate.

Most decisively, the Constitution endowed the Union with a steady political identity. But it also implanted two fundamental lines of tension in India's politics. The first was between the powers of the central state – or the Centre, as it came to be called – and those of the provinces, or regional states that constituted the federal Union. Pre-independence nationalists had promised considerable autonomy to the provinces, but the actual circumstances in which the state was compelled to secure itself after 1947

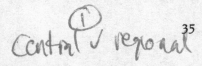

central / regional

35

encouraged the Constituent Assembly to retain the extensive central powers inherited from the Raj. Military powers and emergency provisions for constitutional dictatorship were concentrated at the Centre; so too were the fiscal powers to print money or borrow commercially (this last was a significant contrast to other large federal nations, like the United States or Brazil, which granted their constituent states greater fiscal freedoms). There were also concessions: in acknowledgement of Congress's dependence on the landed upper castes of rural India, the Constitution limited the Centre's ability to alter the rural property order (the promise to do this had been a loud part of the rhetoric of some within the pre-independence Congress). It left the matter of social and economic reform, whose significance Ambedkar had underlined and Nehru understood, to the regional legislatures, where the landed elites could bring local pressure against redistributive moves.

The second enduring tension concerned citizenship. The grant of universal rights to all was offset by a recognition of historical injustice suffered by particular communities. A principle of positive discrimination, or affirmative action, in compensation for past injuries inflicted upon the very poorest and lowest in the social order – especially those excluded from the system of castes, the 'untouchables' – was introduced in the form of a policy of 'reservation' of government jobs and educational places for members of these groups. The Constitution thus established a language of community rights in a society where the liberal language of individual rights and equality was little used. Rights were anchored in collectivities, now recognized as particular interests within the nation. The effect was to weaken the pressure to accord universal rights and to encourage demands for special dispensations for selected groups. Determining which groups and which interests – who exactly was eligible for the benefits of 'reservation' – was a job left to the regional legislatures, which gave local politicians a limitless resource for political manipulation.

interesting consequences of affirmative action

Reservations had been intended to be a temporary expedient to a less unjust society, but, ironically, the desire to dissolve what was seen as the eternal and internally undifferentiated categories of caste in fact gave them new vigour as political self-identifications. In later decades, as democratic struggle intensified, the ritual status and degradations of caste made for a proliferation of categories of economic opportunity and exclusion, subject to constant political negotiation and redefinition. At election time, politicians now promised – in the name of equality – to extend the proportion of reserved places, and to make them available to newly defined 'backward class' categories; caste groups, meanwhile, in a curious inversion of the ideal of social mobility, competed to be defined as 'backward' in order to corner the benefits of reservation. The policy of reservations was to become a sharp weapon in the hands of opponents and rivals of Congress, and by the 1980s these oppositional politicians committed themselves to proposals (contained in a report prepared by the Mandal Commission, set up in 1978 by a non-Congress governing coalition based around the Janata party, in order to recommend ways of improving opportunities for the 'backward classes') to extend the reservations to just under half of all government jobs, so inciting a fierce contest around caste entitlements. The Constitution, and the politics it sanctioned, thus reinforced community identities rather than sustaining a sense of common citizenship based on individual rights.

The Constitution established a democratic regime, but how the state would actually act was still undecided. No sooner had the Republic been declared in January 1950, than Nehru's wish to use the state to pursue policies of toleration and planned economic development came under fierce attack. In 1950 a new flow of migrants from East Pakistan into India revived the demands of the Hindu communalists to make the state an agent of Hindu interests, and within Congress Patel manoeuvred energetically to curb further Nehru's efforts to take control of the government. But at the end of 1950 Patel suddenly died, and with this chance event the command of the party passed into Nehru's hands. Nehru's often underrated skills as a party manager now showed clearly, as he quickly secured his organizational grip over Congress. He had few ideological partners, and could not rely on the party to understand or share his commitments, but his organizational powers, and Congress's electoral invulnerability – it easily won elections in 1952, 1957 and 1962 – gave him a stable political platform, though there was little broad enthusiasm for his reformist inclinations. The elite that collected around him was, effectively, an enclave within Congress, and Nehru relied, increasingly and despite himself, on the civil service rather than his party to be the main instigator of reforms. The diffuse aspirations of the pre-independence period were thus formalized and handed over to the bureaucracy's 'rule-bound incompetence'.

Very rapidly, the state accumulated for itself many quite disparate responsibilities, from patrolling borders that stretched across glaciers to abolishing untouchability, from constraining religious passions to building nuclear reactors. Convinced of its own ability to remould Indian society, it became a full-time trustee for its people: a guardian that – ominously – had also to guard itself in a world where most people were not well-versed in the rules and purposes of constitutional democracy. The observance of constitutional proprieties and democratic procedures was partly based upon a genuine idealism. Politics was still being played by men who were not professionals but had come to politics through the nationalist movement. But a sharper incentive derived from the Congress Party's scale: in order to maintain confidence and trust among its contending ideological preferences and interests, particularly between the modernizing, more radical elite and the conservative landed elite, neither of which was sufficiently powerful to dominate the other, it made sense to observe rules and to take turns in the exercise of power. Yet most citizens remained outside this conversation altogether, and were increasingly puzzled by its terms. Nehru himself was aware of this, and insisted constantly on the need to explain the operations of the state, and of democratic politics, to them; but he was caught by his own conceptual language, restricted by the boundaries of intelligibility set by the English language of power. Little was done to widen the circles of deliberation, to establish a public vocabulary through which Indians could talk to one another as Indians.

For Nehru, the authority of the new state rested not solely on domestic procedures of constitutional democracy but also on establishing its sovereignty in the international arena. Here, he had a virtually free hand, only lightly checked by domestic forces. In his determination to secure India's sovereignty, he developed the idea of non-alignment. The principles he enunciated at the Bandung Conference of Non-Aligned Nations in 1955 seem a faded and distant ideal now, but in the mid-1950s they were a radical departure from the obstinate polarities of the Cold War. There were a few stumbles in this doctrine of active neutrality – most notably India's momentary hesitation about condemning the Soviet invasion of Hungary in 1956 – but in the main Nehru achieved outstanding successes, establishing India as a forceful and independent voice in international politics. This was a staggering performance for a poor country that had only recently emerged from colonial rule. At the core of Nehru's idea of non-alignment was his conviction that Asia was finally taking charge of its own history as it emerged from the shadow of European domination. China and India were destined to be the prime movers in this new phase of world history – it was with China that he first outlined the *Panch shila*, the five principles that he hoped would make Asia an area of peace.

It is doubly ironic, therefore, that it was in foreign policy, and in particular in relations with China, that Nehru had his greatest failure: the disastrous war of 1962. His perception of China, rooted in his 1930s understanding of Asian civilizations, had led him to believe that conflict between China and India was an historical impossibility and blinded him to the rising evidence of China's aggressive intentions. This naivety became apparent when China invaded Tibet in 1950 and he raised no objection. As the Chinese were poised to move, he wrote to his ambassador in Peking, 'I attach great importance to India and China being friends. I think the future of Asia and to some extent the world depends on this', and he continued in this vein for the next dozen years, neglecting the advice of military officers to make adequate preparations in border areas. The result was a crushing humiliation for the Indian army in 1962, which left Nehru with nothing but pathetic fury ('I will fight them with a stick', he blustered to his cabinet colleagues). It was a brutal end to his effort to restructure international relations, and it forced India into greater external dependencies, for it had to turn initially to the United States and other Western powers; the road led ultimately to the treaty his daughter Indira Gandhi signed with the USSR in 1971, which finally buried the idea of non-alignment. The claims of the defence establishment received much greater attention after the war with China: the army, which grew huge and very well equipped, became a major drain on the Indian state's limited resources.

This debacle at the very end of Nehru's career inevitably overshadowed the more durable significance of his inaugural period in the history of independent India. There was a fundamental paradox. The Nehru era was permeated by the rhetoric of democracy and social reform, and indeed Indian democracy was exemplary as a system of government then; parliamentary and party procedures were priggishly followed, there were few scandals, enough Indians voted to give the system legitimacy without overtaxing its capacities (turnouts in the first three general elections averaged just under 50 per cent), Congress effectively filtered demands, and managed to contain religious and caste interests at local levels. Nehru rejected Jacobin notions of popular sovereignty, based on the expressed will of the current generation, in favour of the idea of an abstract, historically durable 'people' or 'nation': a conception of indirect sovereignty that was not shared by future generations of leaders and parliamentarians, who preferred to invoke the immediate, volatile authority of electoral majorities.

Yet the true historical success of Nehru's rule lay not in a dissemination of democratic idealism but in its establishment of the state at the core of India's society. The state was enlarged, its ambitions inflated, and it was transformed from a distant, alien object into one that aspired to infiltrate the everyday lives of Indians, proclaiming itself responsible for everything they could desire: jobs, ration cards, educational places, security, cultural recognition. The state thus etched itself into the imagination of Indians in a way that no previous political agency had ever done. This was the enduring legacy of the Nehru period. Democratic habits rapidly became hollow routines, and a bare decade after his death in 1964, his daughter had initiated the country into a very different politics. Perhaps it is unreasonable to have expected this brief and overactive period in Indian history to have installed invulnerable institutional structures. At the time, Nehru's achievement looked more solid than it was, a trick of his own formidable intellectual capacity to give shape to his projects, to tell persuasive stories about the significance of his actions. There was undoubtedly an element of self-persuasion to this: clear, for instance, in his resolution to treat the leaders of the tiny non-Congress parties in parliament as if they were genuine opposition leaders, in order to instil the habits of parliamentary democracy in India. The Nehru period made plain the centrality of leadership in the Indian state. But precisely because of this his death set India into a long succession crisis. As later decades revealed, leadership was crucial, given the misshapen muscularity of the state, which made it strong in certain respects but feeble in others.

4

In the two decades after Nehru's death the long-term historical centralization of power that had begun during the Raj and recently accelerated, continued; but for the first time new interests and groups in society began to gain access to this power. For most of that time, India was ruled by Nehru's only child, Indira Gandhi. It was accident that made her prime minister. The first succession, crucial for any democratic state, occurred under difficult circumstances. Nehru had not intended a dynastic succession, and though Indira Gandhi had certainly entered politics under her father's eye – she had served an annual term as Congress president in the 1950s, and he undoubtedly envisaged a public career for her – there is little reason to infer that she had been groomed to rule. It was the unexpected death in January 1966 of the man who had succeeded Nehru, Lal Bahadur Shastri – after less than two years in office – that propelled her to power, a chance event that transformed India's history.

When she was chosen leader of Congress, Mrs Gandhi lacked any power base in the party or in the country. Diffident and far from being driven by a burning ambition to command politically, she was also without any ideological passion. As a student in England she had moved in radical circles and in the late 1930s was probably further to the left than her father (writing from Oxford in 1938, she took it upon herself to advise Nehru against accepting an invitation to a house party given by Lord Lothian, warning that 'it would create a terrifically bad impression on all people in this country who are even slightly "left" '); but by the mid-1960s the doctrinaire fires had cooled. Exactly these apparent infirmities – plus the obvious advantage of being her father's daughter – made Indira Gandhi attractive to the powerful provincial leaders of Congress, the men who formed what was known as the 'Syndicate'. During the last months of Nehru's life, control of the party had passed to them, and it was this ageing quintet that had met on a moonlit night in Bhubaneshwar when Nehru was dying, and chosen Shastri as the new leader; and it was they again who in January 1966 agreed to make Mrs Gandhi their chief, secure in the belief that they could control her. It was a fateful misjudgement of their own abilities, and of her character. The story of Mrs Gandhi's metamorphosis during the last two decades of her life into a woman with a striking clarity of political purpose and an audacious, uncanny sense of pre-emptive timing, is a compelling one. It is more than merely biographically significant, for in her own determination to survive, she altered the character of the state and of democratic politics. She had first to act within and against her party, but its centrality in the political arena ensured that her actions transformed as well the internal operations of the state and its relation to the society.

Congress as she now led it was, in the late 1960s, at its most vulnerable since independence. The Indian economy was precarious, and Congress won the elections of 1967 – effectively the first it had to contest as a political party rather than as heir of the nationalist movement – but with much less confidence than in the past. It lost control of eight of the regional legislatures, including those of the most populous states of north India. A frazzled Mrs Gandhi saw in this drab performance an opportunity to assert control, and she proceeded to do so by radically revising the party's routines. Since the 1930s, a combination of strong central command and relatively independent provincial leadership was the axis of the Congress machine. This restricted the hand of the central leadership in New Delhi, as Nehru had known all too well, but it ensured that things were done with some efficacy, and it confined subjects of potential conflict to local and lower levels in the political order. It relied on provincial leaders building and tending their own branches of clients, who controlled the 'vote banks' (which delivered the votes of communities as a bloc) and had to be compensated through benefits negotiated from the central leadership.

Mrs Gandhi shattered this pattern. To get around the regional power brokerages, and to establish herself against the conservative Syndicate, she did the unthinkable: in 1969 she split the Congress Party, the great symbol and working engine of nationalism, going over the heads of its regional 'bosses', disrupting the filaments of patronage and dissolving the vote banks they commanded. By shifting her rhetoric to the left, she hoped to regroup society and appeal directly to India's millions of poor people. To mobilize what she correctly perceived as a powerful electoral resource, she devised a gestural radicalism: the banks were nationalized, constitutionally guaranteed privileges to the princes were abolished, and a devastatingly unexceptionable slogan was invented: *Garibi Hatao* ('Abolish Poverty'). The strategy – parallel to that adopted by her sparring partner across the border, Prime Minister Zulfikar Ali Bhutto of Pakistan – was deployed in electoral conditions custom-made for her purposes: she created a 'national' electorate by calling a general election in 1971, one year before it was due. This surprised her opponents, broke the synchronization between elections to the national parliament and to regional legislatures, and diverted the attentions of the electorate away from regional concerns and directly towards New Delhi.

The strategy was an intoxicating success, and gave her a landslide majority in 1971, bigger than any her father had ever enjoyed. Further triumph followed. Her decisive conduct in the victorious war against Pakistan that same year – which led to the secession of Bangladesh – helped her to sweep the elections to the regional legislatures in 1972. The Syndicate had been routed, and the fortunes of the Congress Party were on a crest.

But she had fractured Congress as an organization and opened a deep crevasse in Indian politics. The party itself swiftly degenerated into an unaudited company for winning elections. In the past, its factional conflicts had borne some relation to real ideological differences; now they became crudely instrumental, and the party simply acted as a mechanism for collecting funds, distributing 'tickets' or nominations for seats, and conducting campaigns. This myopic focus on elections was symptomatic of a deeper change. The subtle routines of politics between elections – when support must be nurtured, promises delivered on, things actually done – were neglected. Elections became spasmodic, theatrical events, when Indians gathered in hope and anticipation.

As the identity of Congress faded, Indira Gandhi's own profile began to fill its space. She offered herself as an individual object of adulation, identification and trust; it followed that she would also from now on become the object of all frustration and disaffection. A new pattern emerged: the massive support shown at elections rapidly evaporated, electoral majorities did not translate into durable opinion which governments could rely upon during a full term of office. Within a few years of her electoral successes, Mrs Gandhi had to face all those disappointed by her promises of a new dawn. But dissent was now no longer filtered through the Congress Party. It coalesced unexpectedly, around disgruntled men of the old Congress, previously marginal political groups, and even, in a final swansong, Gandhian socialism, in the form of Jayaprakash Narayan, who became the symbolic leader of countrywide protests and strikes that began to challenge Mrs Gandhi on the streets. Politics, both government and opposition, was no longer contained by the institutional form of the political party. In response to the spreading dissent, she clamped down. Invoking dictatorial powers inherited from the British Raj and carefully preserved in the Indian Constitution, she prevailed upon the president to proclaim an Emergency in

June 1975, which suspended democratic rights and judicial procedures.

The Emergency accelerated the concentration of power within the interiors of a few bungalows and offices in New Delhi. The cabinet and parliament were now excluded from decision-making, which was transferred to the prime minister's office. The PMO, as it became known in Indian political acronymese, was henceforth the sanctum sanctorum of the Indian state. The civil service and the judiciary were exhorted to display 'commitment' to the government's policies and importunities. But if all this appeared to brace India for a programme of vigorous authoritarian reconstruction, in fact hardly anything was actually done. There were some prodigious but restricted cruelties: slum dwellers had to make way for bulldozers, as vain sycophants like the Lieutenant Governor of Delhi, Jagmohan, were given powers to 'Make Delhi Beautiful'; men and women were handed transistor radios in return for terminating their reproductive futures; trees were planted and left to wither. Since the Emergency bore so clearly the hand of its immediate maker, a popular psychology of the leader was evoked to explain it: lonely, insecure, and believing herself to be persecuted, Mrs Gandhi cast a veil over liberty's figure, it was said.

Indira Gandhi declared herself committed to the project her father had begun, but her tolerance for the unpredictabilities of democratic politics was decidedly lower. Father and daughter had diverged, for instance, over the handling of the communist government formed in the southern state of Kerala in 1957, one of the first freely elected communist governments in the world. In 1959, during a political confrontation between the Centre and the Kerala government, a reporter from a Madras daily, *The Hindu*, interviewed both Prime Minister Nehru and Indira Gandhi (at the time president of Congress). The tone of the conversation is revealing:

REPORTER: Are you going to fight the communists or throw them out?

NEHRU: Throw them out? How? What do you mean? They have also been elected.

INDIRA GANDHI: Papu, what are you telling them? You are talking as prime minister. As Congress president I intend to fight them and throw them out.

In the end, the communist government (headed by E. M. S. Namboodripad) was indeed dismissed, a portent of what later became a regular pattern of central interference in regional politics. Yet the Emergency was much more than an expression of personal quirks. By kicking down the inherited Congress apparatus Mrs Gandhi appeared to enjoy freedom and immediate control: she exuded absolute power. But it was the random, sporadic power of a despot.

The internal decimation of Congress weakened its grip (and by extension the state's) on the provinces' complex politics. Instead of seasoned market-makers in the party, Mrs Gandhi came to rely on a distinctly less savoury network, the Youth Congress: a delinquent boys' club run by her younger son, Sanjay, in whom she confided her exclusive trust. Its members were perfumed young men with shiny attache cases, political yuppies who had turned to politics as a business profession, the best means of upward mobility in a society where access to both the state bureaucracy and the market was restricted. The Youth Congress quickly became the exclusive doorway to the central leadership, and, in a perverse interpretation of a democracy of open access, invited members with quite unusual social backgrounds, often trailing criminal connections.

The old Congress had served as a finely tuned information exchange. By the mid-1970s the PMO had become a solipsistic lair humming with flattery and rumour. The distortion of information was so great that Mrs Gandhi was led to call elections in 1977, in the misplaced conviction that Indians would vote for still further doses of authoritarian bullying. Popular resistance to the Emergency did indeed help to restore democracy that year, though ultimately a blithely deluded leadership gifted it back to the people. The votes went against Mrs Gandhi, and for the first time a non-Congress government was formed at the Centre: the Janata coalition, an alliance of right-wing, Hindu and farmers' parties. The coalition could not bend the political and economic order to its doctrinal enthusiasms and after two years had exhausted itself in domestic bickering. New elections in 1980 returned a chastened, more nervously superstitious Mrs Gandhi to office. Commentators at the time by turns congratulated and then admonished the Indian electorate, first for its 'maturity' in voting her out and then for its 'immaturity' in scampering back to her. But these electoral swings were not wayward pubescent awakenings; rather, they showed how deeply elections had engraved themselves on the popular imagination as ready means to express annoyance at the immediate evidence of political misconduct.

The single most important consequence of Mrs Gandhi's actions was manifest by the end of the first decade of her rule, and the rest of her career was spent trying to balance herself in the whirlwind: she had transformed the meaning of democracy for both the Indian state and its society, and it now signified, simply, elections. Within the state, constitutional decorum and balance were subordinated to what the political leadership interpreted as the will of the people expressed in electoral majorities. The drift was unmistakably towards a Jacobin conception of direct popular sovereignty. Poor and oppressed groups had become more aware of the significance of elections, and an amorphous radicalism was concocted to court them, as politicians tried to trump each other's rhetorical generosity. Mrs Gandhi, invoking her huge parliamentary majorities especially after 1971, tried to portray the Constitution as a conservative obstacle to her radical ambitions. This resort to populism

or, authoritarian democracy

strengthened a certain democratic momentum within the political order, but it weakened others – the observance of rules and procedures designed to instil the moderation which democracy needs. These rules of rule, these procedural constraints which had previously been delicately observed, were set aside. Electoral volatility foreshortened the horizons of political time: the mere capture of power rather than its responsible exercise became the exclusive aim of politicians. New entrants saw electoral triumph as the necessary means to gaining power of patronage over the resources accumulated by the state through several decades of state-regulated economic development; their main intention was now to draw rapid profits from such access.

As elections gained in importance, levels of democratic participation in both national and provincial politics climbed (turnouts in the five general elections between 1967 and 1984 averaged 60 per cent). So, too, did levels of violence, and the connection was not random. According to commonly available understandings of democracy, individuals rationally choose political parties as instruments to pursue their interests. But representative democracy – in India as elsewhere – does not operate through a simple instrumental relation between representative and represented. The relation between politicians and their supporters includes a larger cultural connection, a felt sense of identification and trust. Democratic politics seems to require that identities and perceptions of interest be stable; but political identities and interests do not have a pre-political existence – they have to be created through politics. Thus, paradoxically, democratic politics must itself produce the very identities and interests which it presupposes in order to function in the first place. And this process of identity creation is a dangerous business, more akin to conflict than competition. This was India's situation from the 1980s, when the violence that began to seep into public life was expressive of conflicts related to the rising levels of democratic participation. Liberal pieties that claim democracy to be a pacifying force can be no more reassured by India's experience in this regard than by the evidence provided by long periods in the history of the United States of America or France.

The new political entrants considered themselves – and acted as – members of groups and communities, rather than liberal individuals. These collective identities in some cases began viciously to attack one another: in regions like Bihar, upper castes, their power threatened by the destruction of the vote banks they had controlled, waged wars on those below them. Violence between society and the state also escalated. Conflicts were arising among social groups whose identities could be activated for political ends: religious, urban or rural, caste, language, class, or ethnic origin. The potential agencies of political representation were also plentiful: political parties, trade unions, religious and caste associations, business federations and chambers of commerce, women's and social movements, tribal organizations, and armed insurgents. India's political parties are a good index of this diversity: there have been parties mobilized around religious nationalism (the BJP), caste and class (the Lok Dal), caste alone (the Bahujan Samaj Party), tribe (the Jharkhand Mukti Morcha), religious separatism (the Akali Dal), cultural identity (the Tamil Dravida parties) and nativism (the Shiv Sena).

Democracy quickened the attraction of these social identities in various, often contradictory ways. The potentialities of religion, language and caste inspired parties to devise strategies that respectively appealed to the Hindu religion, the Hindi language or lower-caste status, in order to mobilize for power at the Centre. Regional politics also came violently alive, and very differently from the way it had in the 1950s. The claims of regional autonomy Nehru faced were reactions against the legacies of British rule, which had bequeathed the Indian state administrative territories containing different linguistic groups now discontented by their opportunities. The regional demands of the 1980s, by contrast, were explicitly directed against the central state, which since the late 1960s had meddled incessantly in regional affairs, repeatedly invoking President's Rule – another Emergency power inherited from the Raj and maintained in pristine condition, which allowed a province to be brought under the direct rule of the Centre – and undermining the federal division of powers. Between 1947 and 1966 the powers of President's Rule had been invoked ten times; between 1967 and 1986, seventy times. The steady pilferage by the Centre of powers that constitutionally belonged to the regions welded national and regional politics together. In the past, local issues had been kept local, resolved by chief ministers and regional fixers with autonomous powers. This freed the central government to pursue longer-term ends and protected it from becoming a target of routine dissent. But the new pattern routed all regional power through New Delhi.

Sometimes the effects were grimly comic. In the first two years after her return to power in 1980, Mrs Gandhi inflicted four chief ministers of her choice on the people of Andhra Pradesh: the most bewildered of these flunkeys, trying to make sense of his meteoric passage through office, confessed, 'I came in because of Madam, and I am going because of her. I do not even know how I came here.' Sometimes the effects were tragic, as in the Punjab. This troubled region, torn by Partition and subsequently subject to constant territorial disputes that forced several internal re-partitions, had a firmer sense of its own regional identity than some other parts of the country – derived in part from British imperial myths about the 'martial' Sikh whose home it is, in part from the conjunction there of the Sikh religion and the Punjabi language. During the Emergency, the regional Sikh party, the Akali Dal, had been a strong opponent of Mrs Gandhi's rule, and it participated in the governing Janata coalition of 1977–9. Mrs Gandhi and her son, Sanjay, desperate to break the coalition, tried to weaken the notoriously faction-ridden Akali Dal, and to this end encouraged Jarnail Singh Bhindranwale, a young *Sant* or religious preacher, hoping to use him to plant discord. Once he had done this, and after her return to power, Mrs Gandhi presumed he was dispensable: she re-established control at the Centre and proceeded once more to ignore the regions. But Bhindranwale, his earnest lilt recorded and widely disseminated on cassettes, had by now captured the imagination of a small but energetic constituency of young men in Punjab (as well as in London's Southall and Acton). He encouraged them to question the always potentially tenuous authority of the Indian state over its territorial ownership, and began to flourish the language of self-determination for the Sikhs, the dream of their own Khalistan. This fell on grateful ears, yet the central government justified its neglect of the regions and of the Punjab by invoking a putatively democratic argument: it had a national mandate, and recalcitrant regional governments were, it declared, a threat to national integrity. Groups who could muster support at the regional level and who would have found a voice in India's earlier federal structures were now condemned to permanent exclusion by virtue of minority status in the national electorate.

This comprehensive absorption of powers by the central state occurred when the effects of several decades of unevenly directed policies of economic development began to have visible effects. Resentments about these policies differed widely. Regions that had done well, like Punjab, wanted greater autonomy, while those that believed the Centre had neglected them, like Assam, called for greater redistributive intervention. But all the grievances were expressed in similar political form. Unable to be heard in federal, representative politics, the regions had little incentive to play the democratic game. This, essentially, was the underlying structure of the subsequent crises in Punjab, Assam and Kashmir, which swept local conflicts to the heart of the Indian state, on to the lawns of the prime minister's residence.

Political assassinations in independent India have generally occurred in public places, in the presence of crowds. The Hindu extremist who shot Mahatma Gandhi killed him at a prayer meeting in 1948; Rajiv Gandhi would be killed by a Tamil suicide bomber at an election campaign meeting in 1991. Assassinations have not taken place in the grounds of the palace, in the rooms and corridors of political power, as in so many other new states. They have not been instigated by people authorized by the state to bear arms. The one profoundly disturbing exception to this was Mrs Gandhi's assassination in 1984 by two of her own bodyguards, Sikhs seeking vengeance for the Indian army's assault earlier that year on the sacred Golden Temple in Amritsar, which had led to the death of Bhindranwale and to extensive damage to the shrine.

The organized violence directed against the Sikhs that followed Mrs Gandhi's assassination was the most serious communal violence in India since Partition. This time, however, not only was the state unwilling to act quickly to protect its citizens, but members of the Congress Party were actively involved in instigating and directing the violence against Sikhs. More than a decade after the killings of well over 2,000 Sikhs, mainly in New Delhi, in carefully targeted 'riots' – for several days, gangs moved through the city with electoral rolls, identifying Sikh homes and businesses for attack – no one had yet been tried, let alone convicted, for any of these murders (in 1996 judicial proceedings were finally begun against two senior Congressmen accused of organizing the violence).

India's national imagination was slowly but decisively reshaped in the last years of Mrs Gandhi's rule. The state's failure to conduct itself in a manner that would not provoke its citizens to question its territorial authority led to regions making full-blown secessionist claims. The central government responded in two ways. First, military force was deployed with greater intensity – certain regions were defined as 'disturbed areas', and a series of draconian constitutional ordinances and acts were passed that put them under effective military rule. Areas of Nagaland, Kashmir and Punjab effectively came to be held as occupied territories, and conditions there were stark reminders of the limits of democratic government in India, points at which the state's authority to rule seemed all too similar to the claims of its imperial predecessor. Secondly, definitions of India's political community were subtly altered: Mrs Gandhi flirted with religious sentiments and appeals, hinting that the categories 'non-Hindu' and 'anti-national' overlapped. It was the secular, modernist Indian elite who dragged this language of religious affiliations into the arena of national politics: it entered public life via the state itself, not from the supposedly primordial margins of the political culture.

By the end of Mrs Gandhi's life, the political landscape she had inherited had been transformed beyond recognition. The most decisive change, oddly enough, was that democracy, in the form of electoral participation, had become indelible: no one was willing to give it up. New groups had entered politics as voters and as politicians: rich farmers, the poor, the lower castes. The social and cultural backgrounds of India's political actors had changed. The centrality of elections, and the desperate value staked on winning them, made for engrained political corruption in the public arena: the scandals that tumbled over one another in the 1980s and 1990s were evidence of this. In previous decades, the Congress leadership could safely leave fund-raising to local 'briefcase' grafters: the routines were dispersed throughout the many branches of the party, and had a degree of publicity, so that people believed they knew what was going on, and did not give them detailed attention. But with the concentration of power, the procedures of money-making were also centralized, they became more invisible, and they also attracted more attention: their inflated scale had produced 'suitcase' politicians. The increased electoral participation encouraged politicians to make communal appeals, and they had to become more ingenious in mustering political support.

Meanwhile, the expanded central state commanded considerable resources, for access to which there was intense competition. But it had also now become an easy target for every frustration, resentment and disappointment. Operationally, it was deviating from its earlier constitutional manners. Democracy as a regime of laws and rights, as a set of procedures that moderates the powers of the state, had been damaged. Rules had become subject to political fiddling and routine twisting. Finally, there was a striking decline of intellectual self-reflection, both within the state and among its critics, about what was actually happening, what India's state and society were doing to one another. The self-confidence that had defined the Nehru era and that had allowed India to position itself grandly in the face of the future, had collapsed into the numbing short-term expediency of a political elite desperate to keep its grip on the state. Intellectuals outside the government slumped into despair or catatonia. The sense of a 'crisis' was everywhere: India's original project seemed to have fallen into corruption and degeneration. Politics and the state, once seen as the prophylactic that would invigorate the country, were now seen as the disease.

5

Though during the first fifty years of its independence India was mostly governed at the Centre by one party, Congress, the country's political experience had been neither uniform nor continuous. The effects of the first two critical eras – that of Nehru's state and of Indira Gandhi's democracy – began to manifest themselves in the third, last and most troubled period of Congress ascendancy, the decade beginning in the mid-1980s. Their consequences differed from what, at the time, they had been thought to be. The nationalist elite during the Nehru era had rehearsed the language of democracy impeccably, yet its real historical achievement was to give the state unprecedented centrality. Indira Gandhi had appeared to be the greatest threat to democracy, but in fact the effect of her rule was to throw open the state to popular demands and to brand the idea of electoral democracy indelibly on the Indian political imagination. Since her death, India's politics have been a struggle to come to terms with these historical legacies.

After a record-breaking and freak electoral success in 1984 – in the wake of Mrs Gandhi's assassination – Congress slipped into a slow free-fall in national politics. It still remained the only party able to command some support in every region of the country, but its share of the vote drifted unremittingly towards the threshold at which it would become a parliamentary minority (in India's Westminster-style 'first past the post' system, that means around 30 per cent). Its increased reliance on appeals to caste and religion helped to politicize those social categories and draw them into the national arena, but it also offered opportunities to rivals. The BJP, dedicated to a redefinition of nationalism in exclusively Hindu terms, was a grateful beneficiary of this. In the first four decades after independence, Hindu nationalist parties had never managed to gather more than 10 per cent of the votes in national elections, but in the 1990s the BJP more than doubled this, although its supporters were confined to the northern and western regions of the country.

Even more important than the rise of Hindu nationalism for the future of Indian democracy was the emergence of a new politics based on caste categories. The lowest in the caste order and those altogether excluded from it – who now called themselves Dalits and Bahujans – organized autonomously and withdrew their support from Congress, which had always portrayed itself as the paternal guardian of their interests. Their disentanglement from Congress was encouraged by V. P. Singh, a disaffected minister in Rajiv Gandhi's cabinet who departed in 1987 to establish his own party, dedicated to moral probity, social justice and deposing Congress. He returned to the original commitments of the Constitution and to the recommendations of the Mandal Commission on caste reservations (mothballed since 1980), and promised the lower castes sweeping reservations of education and employment opportunities. The effects were electrifying, particularly in India's two most populous provinces, Uttar Pradesh and Bihar. New lower-caste politicians emerged, for whom Ambedkar was, of all the old nationalist leaders, their only true hero. But unlike Ambedkar, these new politicians did not dress in three-piece suits and speak perfect courtroom English. Figures like Mayawati – a woman drawn from a caste group categorized as 'Backward', who in 1995 became chief minister to Uttar Pradesh's 139 million people – vaunted their social and cultural origins, using them openly to challenge the dominance of the upper castes. These new caste parties were in principle stoutly opposed to the Hindu nationalism of the BJP, and entered into alliances with Muslim and Christian communities against what they saw as a conspiracy of upper-caste Hindus to return to the oppressive *varna* hierarchies of ancient India. Yet in their battles against oppression, they did not invoke universal principles of justice and rights. Instead, they struggled quite explicitly to corner special privileges for their communities.

The breakdown of the federal and coalitional pillars of Congress reinvigorated regional politics. By the mid-1990s proliferating regional parties had set their own stamp on the national political imagination: the national parliament formed in 1996 contained twenty-eight different parties, more than ever before, most elected from the regions. Economic reforms initiated in 1991 by the minority Congress government of Narasimha Rao assigned greater powers to regional governments, and provoked greater competition for control over them. The intensity of political competition produced a generation of regional politicians with remarkable skills and quite novel ways of flattering popular cultural sensibilities: men like Laloo Prasad Yadav, Chief Minister of Bihar, known for stepping out of his helicopter with his parrot on his shoulder and for lacing his speeches with bursts of song from Hindi films.

Regional and caste politics, and Hindu nationalism, embody different potentialities, but they are all direct products of India's first four decades of independence. It is wrong to see them as atavistic forms that repudiate or attack the ideas of the state and democracy; on the contrary, they exemplify the triumphant success of these ideas. That success has been paradoxical. The unstoppable rise of popular engagement in electoral politics, the fact that in a national study conducted in 1996 more than 70 per cent of the electorate rejected the suggestion that India would be better governed without political parties and elections, attests to the authority of the democratic idea. Yet the meaning of democracy has been menacingly narrowed to signify only elections. The compulsion to win power publicly and legitimately has provoked unpicturesque illegalities, old and innovative – violence, corruption and 'booth-capturing', the take-over of a polling station by armed thugs so that ballot boxes may be stuffed with uniformly fake ballots supporting the local darling. Institutions like the Election Commission, responsible for ensuring the legality of elections, have, it is true, reacted impressively: in the 1990s it became, under its hectoring chief, T. N. Seshan, a genuine if sometimes whimsical obstruction to politicians.

But more generally, other democratic procedures have weakened with neglect. In any modern democracy elections are part of a larger set of rules and practices designed to authorize the state, but in India they are carrying the entire burden of society's aspirations to control its opportunities. As the sole bridge between state and society, they have come metonymically to stand for democracy itself; their very simplicity, their conversion since the 1970s into referenda where voters were offered simple choices, have made them universally comprehensible. This expansion of elections to fill the entire space of democratic politics has altered how political parties now muster support. The most recent period of India's democracy has shown a tenacity of community identities, in the form of caste and religion, as groups struggle to construct majorities that can rule at the Centre. But the fact that such identities were less significant for four decades after independence, and then surged into national politics, only shows how much they are creations of modern politics, not residues of the past.

In India, democracy has had to function in a society of peculiar complexity where many different temporal and historical planes coexist. India continues to be a predominantly agrarian society, whose people are not indifferent to religion, and where the individual does not have a strong political or social presence. But towering over that society today is the state. This state is far from supremely effective: it regularly fails to protect its citizens against physical violence, it does not provide them with welfare, and it has not fulfilled its extensive ambitions to transform Indian society. Yet it is today at the very centre of the Indian political imagination. Until little over a century ago, the social order of caste had made the state largely redundant. In 1947 the Indian state dedicated itself – by means of constitutional law and social reform – to the dissolution of the old, oppressive bonds of caste. The past fifty years have trenchantly displayed the powers of the state and of the idea of democracy to reconstitute the antique social identities of India – caste and religion – and to force them to face and to enter politics. But the identities of caste and religion have also bent the democratic idea to their own purposes. The vertiginous terminology of caste belonging in contemporary India – Scheduled Castes, Backward, Other Backward, and More Backward Classes and castes – as also of Hindu religious self-definition bear the heavy burden of modern politics and law. These categories make no sense in the traditional language of caste or religion, the vocabulary of Brahmin and Shudra, vaish-nav or shakta. The conflicts in India today are the conflicts of modern politics; they concern the state, access to it, and to whom it ultimately belongs. And the protagonists are creatures who belong to neither the modern nor the traditional world: they exist in the homeless world of modern politics. Within a very short time, India has moved from being a society in which the state had for most people a distant profile and limited responsibilities, and where only a few had access to it, to one where state responsibilities have swollen and everyone can imagine exercising some influence upon it.

Conflict is part of what democracy is: a raw, exciting, necessary and in the end ultimately disappointing form of politics, that encourages people to make for themselves that most intimate of choices – to decide who they are and how they wish to be recognized, and to refuse to be ruled by those who deny them recognition. In India the idea of democracy has released prodigious energies of creation and destruction. Democracy as a governmental form will no doubt suffer the vicissitudes to which all human institutions are prey. But as an idea, as a seductive and puzzling promise to bring history under the command of the will of a community of equals – a promise that, given the inevitable gap between intentions and consequences, can at best only hope for partial fulfilment – it has irreversibly entered the Indian political imagination. A return to the old order of castes, or of rule by empire, is inconceivable: the principle of authority in society has been transformed.

society & caste > politics

independence - triumph of democracy
& state though democracy
has been reduced to elections
elevation of political
communal movements (religious, caste, region)

TWO

Temples of the Future

Probably nowhere else in the world is there a dam as high as this . . . As I walked round the site I thought that these days the biggest temple and mosque and gurdwara is the place where man works for the good of mankind. Which place can be greater than this, this Bhakra-Nangal?

NEHRU, 1954

What is a young man's ambition today? . . . They think of becoming economists, because an economist plays a big part in the modern world.

NEHRU, 1948

1

India in the 1950s fell in love with the idea of concrete. Millions of tons were used to construct massive dams like that at Hirakud on Orissa's Mahanadi river and at Bhakra-Nangal in Punjab. The dam at Bhakra was the most awesome of them all, a 200 metre-high concrete wall stretched half a kilometre across a jagged Himalayan gorge. It was begun in 1954, seven years after Cyril Radcliffe's boundary lines, showing where 'India' stopped and 'Pakistan' began, had disrupted the world's most intricate network of irrigation canals (a dozen were assigned to Pakistan, three to India; one was sagely divided in two) and had driven around half a million Hindus and Sikhs from a now Pakistani west Punjab into an Indian Punjab unable to grow the food to feed them. If Le Corbusier's Chandigarh – that other great concrete behemoth of the 1950s, designed as the new capital of Punjab – was to stand as independent India's aesthetic response to the loss of Lahore's beauty (which now lay in Pakistan), Bhakra was a monumental exhibition of the impulse to transform India's economic horizons. Three and a half million cubic metres of concrete were needed to raise the dam – the concrete had to be produced over three years, at the rate of ten tons a minute, sixteen hours a day (mid-century India was also in love with statistics). It was a virtuoso engineering performance. For the men and women who laboured to build Bhakra, the motivations were straightforward enough. 'Why are you doing this work?' Nehru asked one; 'Sahib bahadur, that man tells me to take these stones over there. At the end of the week he gives me money. That is why I do it.' But to those who imagined them into existence, these dams – like the gleaming steel and power plants at Bokaro and Bhilai which the Soviets, Germans and British were all crowding in to help build – embodied the vision of modernity to which India had committed itself. They were the spectacular façades, luxurious in their very austerity, upon which the nation watched expectantly as the image of its future was projected. It was a big, audacious image. India, it promised, would become an industrial giant.

Nothing ages worse than images of the future, and half a century later that image, many agree, seems to have been mistaken: grandiose, irrelevant and even destructive. The economy created in the name of the intellectual blueprint of the 1950s, state-directed and regulated, founded on heavy industry and isolated from international competition, has not delivered its promises. The great dams, sluicing through forests and villages, have come to be seen as the emanations of a developmental fantasy insensitive to ecological limits and careless of turning its citizens into refugees in their own land. Poverty in the countryside and the city continues to destroy the lives of hundreds of millions. And, as the example of the East Asian economies has dazzled the world, the dusty failures of the Indian state to devise anything like an effective policy of trade – fundamental to the *raison d'etat* of any modern state – appear increasingly inexcusable. Gandhians and socialists, environmentalists and free-market liberals, all agree that something has gone wrong.

Assigning responsibility for India's economic experience, like evaluating it, involves intricate technical issues and counterfactual judgements about the domestic and international economies. To a large extent, though, responsibility must lie with Indians themselves. In contrast to Latin America or Africa, both foreign aid and foreign private capital played a relatively small role in the first fifty years of independent India's economic life: the agents of creation as well as destruction have been mainly internal. But which Indians? The Indian state was hardly unusual in setting itself colossal developmental ambitions; but it was virtually unique among new states in deciding to pursue these by democratic means. The relationship between the project of development and India's democratic politics tells no simple lesson: it has been a complicated, shifting duet between the arguments and ideas of intellectuals, and the pressures and urgent claims of democratic politics.

For most of the last fifty years, the electoral dominance of the Congress Party and the availability of a sophisticated and extensive public bureaucracy gave the ideas and theories of intellectuals a stable platform, and granted the direction of the Indian economy a remarkable continuity, if not fixity. But these ideas and theories had to be implemented in a society where democracy steadily extended its empire, and where the state became selectively responsive to interests that secured political representation. Unlike its giant northern neighbour, China, India did not dispense with democracy in order to make a brutal revolutionary leap into industrialization; nor did its leadership and intelligentsia intentionally veer to the market, as China's post-Mao leadership did. Liberalization and market-oriented reforms did come to India in the 1990s, but their proponents were impelled to consider them by a self-created fiscal crisis which, in tandem with the arguments of intellectuals, pushed the Indian state towards reform. What has moulded India's visions of economic possibility? And how well have they served Indians?

2

It was by no means a foregone conclusion that, after 1947, India would embark on a path of planned industrialization. Its huge agrarian economy was one of the most impoverished in the world; from Gandhi it had inherited a vision deeply opposed to the project of industrial modernity; and, although it possessed powerful industrial capitalists (at the end of the Second World War, India was the tenth largest producer of manufactured goods in the world), they did not form a united class strong enough to push through a project of industrialization against a society of rentiers, farmers and traders. Historically, the pre-1947 state had not taken on responsibility for developing the Indian economy, and the Congress Party which inherited this state had arrived at independence uncommitted to any decisive economic strategy. There was broad agreement about the problems that faced free India: poverty on a staggering scale and the recurrent threat of famine, the need to maintain economic independence, and inequalities within the society. The proposed solutions, however, varied.

The typical concerns of Indian nationalism rarely encompassed detailed reflection on wealth and power, or the practical arrangements thought necessary to secure these under modern conditions. The historical experience of modernity was usually interpreted as a cultural predicament. Most Indian intellectuals accepted – and strove to twist to their advantage – the colonialists' point that India's distinctive identity and strength lay in its spiritual attributes. Indians could not compete in the 'outer' domain of economic prowess and material production; their control over their own destinies was to be had in the 'inner' domains of religious and family life. Most also accepted the intuitively plausible assumption that with the end of colonial rule, India's economic deprivation would of itself cease. But as independence approached, some looked more closely to the West's history for an image of India's own future. The most impressive aspect of that history was the unexampled prosperity and security that industrialization had delivered to the peoples and states of the modern West.

The West's history recounted no uniform story. The idiosyncrasies of Britain and France were nothing like the trajectories of late developers like Germany and Russia; and all could be read through the contrasting lenses of socialist or liberal theory. For Indian intellectuals in the mid-century, the hope was to condense in rapid simultaneity the different processes that had unfolded in slow sequence in the West: secularization and the rise of a society of individuals, the creation of democratic political institutions, and industrialization. The ambition was encouraged by the emergence after the end of the Second World War of the world-wide phenomenon of 'development economics', which promised to reduce the manifold variety of the West's pasts into a single, universal set of policy lessons and to place them at the disposal of new states, so enabling them to replicate the Western trajectory. For poor and underdeveloped states, the chance to produce their very own industrial revolutions, to achieve economic 'take-off', had never seemed more possible: it merely required sedulous application of these theories. Swiftly, the subtle, protracted arguments that had circulated within the pre-independence nationalist movement about India's future progress were replaced all but exclusively by the language of economic development.

Yet the intellectuals who advanced these arguments were without any social or economic base. They were drawn from the educated, upper-caste elites in India's cities – professionals with status and voice but little power. The policies of British rule, which had divided the urban elites from those who held economic power in the countryside, confirmed a fundamental separation in Indian society between status and economic power. The precise nature of agrarian power varied across India's regions, climates and soils, and it was by no means unified, but throughout it rested with those who controlled the land and its produce, men who were themselves in more or less direct ways creations of colonial rule. The colonial land settlements, introduced first in Bengal in the 1790s and then extended in haphazard fashion across the country, which assigned ownership to local grandees in return for rents paid to the 'Company Raj', had established the power, notionally and usually in practice, of the rentier notables, the *zamindars* in the east and north and, in the south and west, the smaller tenurial cultivators, the *ryots*. On the whole, these men had profited well under the colonial dispensation and had little quarrel with British rule. Their view of their own interests did not converge with those of their compatriot intellectuals in the cities. The stirrings of the intelligentsia had an urban energy, with few effects in the countryside; and despite the later moment of the Gandhian bridge between the countryside and the cities, positions were never reconciled.

The British Raj thus kept Indian economic interests divided, but it was also the first authority to unite India into a single economic field. It provided a common currency, and it developed abilities to conduct policies that were put into effect across the subcontinent. In practice, however, the Raj's scope of economic action was restricted: its motivations were narrowly commercial, with no developmental and certainly no redistributive ambitions. But, unlike the East India Company which it had succeeded, the British administration made its money mainly through indirect methods. It did not rely on direct taxation or rents: with the memory of the 1857 uprising still fresh, the first Viceroy, Lord Canning, had declared that 'I would rather govern India with 40,000 British troops without an income tax than govern it with 100,000 British troops with such a tax', a preference unchanged throughout the time of the British Raj (except during war, revenues from direct taxation never rose above 7 per cent of national income). Wealth was primarily accumulated by manipulating the Indian currency and the balance of payments. In general the British – apart from a few entrepreneurial Scots – had little interest in making productive investments in India or burning its resources in industrial workshops. British rule fostered what economic historians of the Empire have called a 'gentlemanly capitalism', a spirit well-attuned to the manners of local Indian society, pervaded as it was by the tastes of rentier landowners and substantial money-lenders.

The British justified their own desultory developmental efforts by citing the many climatic, social and cultural obstacles, all resistant to reform through policy: divided between malarious and arid regions, united by the slothful and cunning peasant, how could India be developed? They left no model for such purposes. But the Raj did leave its successor one narrow – but for any state, essential – practical legacy. Its commitment to cheap government became entrenched as a finicky administrative concern about sound finances: a tropicalized Gladstonian rectitude that sustained a civil service ethos of fiscal conservatism.

Equally important was the British decision to initiate the collection of statistics about economic conditions, a practice that introduced an idea of 'progress' to their Indian subjects. The officers of the Raj were required to submit regularly to Westminster reports on the 'Material and Moral Progress of India', and colonial administrators, men like William Hunter, began from the 1880s to insist that 'No government has a right to exist which does not exist in the interests of the governed. The test for British rule in India is not what it has done for ourselves but what it has done for the Indian people.' These ideas, facts and arguments were assimilated by sharp-eared urban Indian intellectuals. The 'economic nationalists', as they came to be called, detected hypocrisy in the claims of their rulers, especially when these claims were spoken against the background of the bleak famines of the late nineteenth century. They began, therefore, to learn and turn the language of political economy against the British. This was always a thoroughly parliamentary, loyal style of opposition, and it is inappropriate to see its practitioners as precursors of later nationalism (in fact it is their loyalism that is historically interesting). Poverty in the countryside caught their attention, but poverty stalked their arguments in metaphorical guise: what it referred to remained vague. The language used to describe the poor was the purplest of late Victorian prose, while the actual existence of poverty was proven by the simple expedient of citing the observations of British administrators about the conditions of the Indian poor: terms were used that the poor themselves could make no sense of; they were, and would continue to be, spoken for. Figures were tabled, and invariably used to compare India with other countries, but not Indians with Indians.

The causes of India's poverty lay, according to these critics, partly in colonial revenue policies but above all in a steady decimation of Indian manufactures under British rule, a policy of 'de-industrialization'. Dadabhai Naoroji, a loquacious Parsi and the first Indian to sit in the House of Commons at Westminster, pressed this argument with some flamboyance in his account of what he termed 'un-British' rule, that 'drained' wealth from India to the City of London. Unlike previous imperial looters, who had at least had the decency to spend their plunder within India (so preserving the hydrostatic character of the local economy), the British regularly decamped with their cargo. Evidence of this flow – and of its scale – could be found in a simple statistic: the persistent surplus in India's current balance of trade account. Naoroji's own feelings about this un-British conduct were at best ambivalent ('if India is to be regenerated by England, India must make up its mind to pay the price'), but the simplicity of his demonstration helped to publicize what came to be known as the 'drain theory'. It engrained a fear about the fragility of Indian economic interests in an open, international economy. The solution to the problem of poverty in the villages which the economic nationalists proposed did not encompass changes in agriculture itself: for instance, increasing production through the incentives of higher prices and international trade. Instead, it recommended plugging the drain and redirecting resources to private initiatives in industry, whose benefits would not only revive and enrich the countryside but unite the country even more powerfully than a sense of common political interests. The point was made by one of Naoroji's fellow political economists, Mahadev Ranade: 'The agitation for political rights may bind the various nationalities of India together for a time. The community of interests may cease when these rights are achieved. But the commercial union of the various Indian nationalities, once established, will never cease to exist. Commercial and industrial activity is, therefore, a bond of very strong union and is, therefore, a mighty factor in the formation of a great Indian nation.'

This general inclination towards industry yielded no strategy or precise institutional model. Its rhetoric circulated in the annual sessions of Congress and in the pages of the nationalist press, but little further. By the late 1920s, though, nationalist politics had changed. Under Gandhi, Congress had metamorphosed out of the bespoke worsted of the urban educated elite into a homespun mass movement that drew in support from the countryside. Nationalists were debating more actively the issue of industrialization and its function in shaping India's future, and they did not agree on whether this would indeed remove the miseries of rural poverty. A schism had opened between those who favoured some version of industrial modernity and those who rejected it.

Among the former were three currents, each with its own idea of India's future. Indian industrialists had perhaps the most practical outline for an economic policy. In the mid-1940s, a roll-call of leading businessmen and industrialists (including Sir Purshotamdas Thakurdas, J. R. D. Tata, G. D. Birla, Sir Shri Ram, and Kasturbhai Lalbhai) put their names to *A Plan of Economic Development for India*. Popularly and appropriately known as the 'Bombay Plan', it was very much a perspective from western India: it saw India's future progress as driven by the further expansion of the textile and consumer industries already flourishing in cities like Bombay and Ahmedabad. The industrialists, keen to influence Congress to support their strategy, proposed a paternal role for the state in a future India: the state would provide infrastructure, invest in expensive industries like steel, and guard Indian industry from the predations of foreign capital. They agreed that poverty was a fundamental problem, but they envisaged neither a substantial segment of the economy in public ownership nor extensive redistributive responsibilities for the state.

An overlapping, if rather more technocratic, argument was advanced by men outside the nationalist movement, within the Indian Civil Service or connected with progressive princely states like Mysore and Travancore: civil servants such as Sir Ardeshir Dalal, who headed the Planning and Development Department set up by the colonial government towards the end of the Second World War, and visionary engineers like Sir Mokshagundam Visvesvarayya. Committed to the idea of planned modernization, they favoured a purely pragmatic view of the boundaries between state and private action. Visvesvarayya, who served as Dewan to the Maharaja of Mysore, was already in the 1920s pointing to the success of Japan and insisting that 'industries and trade do not grow of themselves, but have to be willed, planned and systematically developed' – an argument he expanded in the mid-1930s in his *Planned Economy for India*. The task of planning this industrialization, Visvesvarayya urged, was best entrusted to a central intellectual 'brain': an economic council of expert economists and businessmen that would coordinate and direct policy for the whole of Indian society.

A third argument came from the small but articulate left wing of the Congress Party. This too imagined India's future in terms of industrial modernity, but was distinguished by a broader view of the political conditions necessary to sustain Indian independence. Initially, it simply pressed for more explicit redistributive commitments in both industry and agriculture, and it was able to extract this from a temperamentally cautious Congress in the form of the famous Karachi Resolution of 1931, which for the first time appeared to commit Congress to radical reforms. This declaration expressed a desire to speak a political message comprehensible to other Indians: 'This Congress is of the opinion that to enable the masses to appreciate what "*Swaraj*", as conceived by the Congress, will mean to them, it is desirable to state the position of the Congress in a manner easily understood by them. In order to end the exploitation of the masses, political freedom must include real economic freedom of the starving millions.' But it hardly contained an economic programme. During the course of the 1930s, though, these intellectuals tried to shape this well-meaning phraseology into a more confident statement about economic production.

The Congress left's two most rousing voices, Subhas Chandra Bose and Nehru, arrived at an understanding of political economy through an analysis of imperialism, which they understood as an economic form propelled by imperatives of capitalist production, not as a project of racial domination or civilizational supremacy. It would therefore be foolish to conceive of Indian independence merely as a political condition, as many Congressmen did. Political independence would not remove India's vulnerability to economic imperialism. This pre-independence perspective on the international system and India's place in it profited by its echoes of Naoroji and his generation, and it set the outline for Nehru's later strategy of planned economic development. In contrast to the industrialists' suggestions, the future Indian state should commit itself to establishing what Nehru and Bose referred to as 'key' or 'mother' industries: heavy industries that were essential both to build other industries, and for Indian self-defence. Support for light or consumer industries was a distraction from the larger task of pushing India towards an independent industrial future. And these heavy industries had to be in public ownership, for both redistributive and security purposes. Like all who subscribed to the vision of an industrial future, these intellectuals of the Left believed that industrialization and, they added, policies that redistributed land away from the big landlords, would eliminate rural poverty.

The voices in favour of industrialization temporarily converged in the late 1930s under the umbrella of a National Planning Committee. Created at the instigation of Bose, it brought together fifteen very different men – industrialists, advisers to princely states, scientists, economists and a lone Gandhian – under Nehru's chairmanship. Retrospectively, it came to be celebrated as the embryo of Congress's commitment to planned industrialization, but at the time its own divided views were by no means representative of the party, and it was merely one of the many committees within Congress, hardly commanding attention. Bose himself was on the verge of leaving the party to make his own phantom way into history as a general without an army, while Nehru complained incessantly about the constraints his committee faced: lack of data and statistics, and little cooperation from the provincial and colonial governments. The committee disbanded in 1940, when Nehru went into prison for his eighth spell, and it was not revived until the end of the war. Its earnest councils produced no agreement about the role of the state and of a public sector, or about a strategy for industrialization and for balancing heavy, light, and what the Gandhians called 'cottage' industries.

If the brokers of industrialization were divided among themselves, the deepest rift in visions about India's future progress lay between industrializers and Gandhians. This split threw Congress itself further into confusion, as it slid between resolutions that committed it to a policy of state ownership of 'key industries and services' and declarations that it would only support village and cottage industries. The Congress leadership talked murkily around it, as with so many other fundamental subjects of potential conflict, leaving it unresolved by the time of independence.

At the root of the conflict was Gandhi's sweeping dismissal of industrial modernity. To Visvesvarayya's technocratic battle-cry 'Industrialize – or Perish!' Gandhi replied, 'Industrialize – and Perish!' The trivial seductions of commercial and industrial society, with its glittering baubles and trinkets, were exactly what had first enslaved Indians to the British. The purpose of winning *swaraj*, self-rule, Gandhi daily insisted, was to emancipate Indians from the compulsion to imitate the imprisoning, destructive and iniquitous forms of industrial modernity dumbly cherished in the West. The solution to India's poverty was not a matter of state policy, tractable in terms of Western economics; indeed, 'imitation of English economics' would spell India's ruin. Poverty could be banished only through the handiwork of each individual Indian, in their quotidian habits of production and consumption. Gandhi was committed to an ethic of austerity. His obsession with accounting for each *anna* might lie, as he himself joked, in his *bania* blood; it also manifested a shrewd and deeper ecological sense and a prescient grasp of the relationship between modern man and nature. The focus of Gandhi's attention, however, was always relations between his fellow compatriots. Here, he saw the deepest injury of Indian society lying not in poverty itself (which Gandhi assumed would decline after the withdrawal of the British) but in the humiliations of caste. Gandhi saw caste as a dispensable adjunct to the productive systems of village society. By emphasizing caste's status as a symbolic practice of ritual humiliation rather than its functions as a system of economic production, he assumed that the village could continue as a productive unit in its absence: a debatable judgement at the very least. It also led him to believe that caste could be dissolved through pressure of moral argument and example – in contrast to Nehru, for whom industrialization and the social relations it set in place were both essential practical solvents of the bonds of caste.

As independence approached, the contradictions between these different visions sharpened. The nationalist elite addressed itself through a flurry of 'plans'. But the manifestos of the intelligentsia and the industrialists were at some remove from the kind of party that Congress had by now become. By the late 1930s, it depended more than ever on the powerful in the countryside, who were uninterested in industrialization or in the redistribution of wealth and power. The entry of Congress into the provincial electoral politics of the Raj would henceforth practically constrain the imaginative visions of the progressive intellectuals. It bound the party to alliances and commitments that came to dominate India's politics until at least the 1960s. To win, Congress had to carry the support of the upper-caste rural landlords and richer farmers; and after 1947 it continued to rely on them to deliver the votes of those lower in the social order. And to keep the support of the rural rich, Congress had in practice to soften its redistributive intentions and agree to leave decisions about the rural property order in the hands of the men who dominated it. This mixed identity of Congress, joining the high-status urban elite to the wealth of the countryside, made it an unbeatable political machine. It also conferred on Congress its distinctive temper, so different, for example, from the Chinese

Communist Party: a mass party with strong roots in the country-side yet given to political conservatism. The basic dilemma of independent India's pursuit of economic development was presaged here: in a country where the great weight of numbers, and considerable wealth, lay in the countryside, there were relat-ively few pressures to industrialize, still less to redistribute or to effect social reforms.

3

At independence, then, the direction of India's economic future remained undetermined. Nehru found himself leader of a party divided in its views about economic development, with no single group weighty enough to impose its vision. The disruptions of Partition had further blurred things: the refugee crisis and severe food shortages, followed by military interventions, called for immediate *ad hoc* responses. In the Constituent Assembly, the interests of the rural rich were secured by removing land reform and agricultural taxation from the control of the central govern-ment and putting them in the hands of the provincial legislatures, more closely subject to the imprecations of the landlords. Within Congress, Patel, who spoke for the landed classes and for the industrialists, orchestrated the departure of the socialists in 1948. This left Nehru isolated, and with Gandhi gone, it made Patel the most powerful figure within the party. Economic planning – which Patel had never favoured – slipped from attention, and by early 1950 Nehru despaired of being able 'to see the overall picture'. Commentators concluded that the enthusiasm for plan-ning had been a short-lived fashion, now over: the idea had 'failed'. But Patel's death at the end of 1950 put Nehru in com-mand of the state.

Any assessment of Nehru's project of economic development must distinguish between assessing the design's coherence and evaluating its performance; and both again must be kept distinct from judgements about subsequent, purely nominal appropriations of his ideas. Nehru's economic thinking is commonly traced to an over-impressionable liking for the Soviet model of planned industrialization. Yet this is a crude reading of his purposes and practice. Not merely was Nehru from his very earliest encounters with the Soviet experiment critical of its political consequences (a judgement he made very clear after a visit to Moscow in 1927, well before Stalinism); his own practice after 1947 was more improvisatory than ideological, and aimed to unite into a single, coherent strategy quite diverse intentions.

The bright arc of the West's history illuminated for Nehru a silhouette of India's future economic possibilities. It encouraged him to believe that an independent India could follow three ends simultaneously: industrialization directed by a state, constitutional democracy, and economic and social redistribution. This project was rather distant from Soviet practice, and much closer to post-war European social democracy. Indeed, by the late 1940s, Nehru had shifted to a recognizably social-democratic position that would not have been out of place in the radical mood of the post-1945 Labour Party. But it was always his own conception, which joined his views about the international economy with a model of the domestic one and related both to a democratic political order.

The one insight from Nehru's intellectual engagements of the 1930s that he never abandoned was the Marxist analysis of imperialism, which had convinced him as accurate about the economic relationship between colonizer and colonized. Given the structure of the world economy, it would be only too easy for a new state like India to surrender its political sovereignty by slipping into dependence on foreign capital in its effort to industrialize. Within this international perspective on the constraints faced by the Indian state, Nehru proposed a view of the state's domestic responsibilities that had parallels with

Keynesian ideas. The state had actively to create conditions for economic expansion: not through wholesale nationalization, but by investment in and direction of a public sector that would function alongside private enterprise in a mixed economy, acting as a counterweight to the cyclical swings and fashions of private investment. Given the Indian state's inherited tradition of being a low taxer, and given that constraints on agricultural taxation were enshrined in the new Constitution, if it was going to have any resources to redistribute for welfarist purposes, it would have to generate these through a productive public sector in its own control.

The ancestry of this argument for a public sector is therefore not correctly traced to the Soviet model of a command economy, nor did it derive from an ideological conviction in the virtues of collectivism. Rather, in its redistributive ambitions, it had obvious resonances with the policies adopted in many western European countries in the post-war period. That it became associated in the public eye with Soviet practices was largely fortuitous. In the 1950s Nehru had assumed that assistance and support for India's economic development would come from the Western powers. There was indeed very large-scale American financial and food aid: but the Americans more and more insisted that India develop essentially through investment in agriculture and consumer industries, a strategy they believed promised higher immediate rates of growth.

But for Nehru, a rapid growth rate was not an end in itself. It had to be reconciled with independence and with democracy. Higher levels of output might have been achieved by directing investment towards consumer industries, but this, it was believed, would weaken economic independence, which needed a base of heavy and defence industries. As it happened, external support for the strategy of investment in heavy industries came most consistently and generously not from the West but from the Soviets, eager to extend their sphere of influence. Yet Nehru was equally clear that given the Indian commitment to democratic politics, growth rates in heavy industries could not be forced, in Soviet or Chinese style. In contrast to present-day, instrumentalist attitudes to democracy, which puzzle over whether or not democracy is conducive to economic growth, Nehru assumed that democracy was a value in itself. He did not believe in a trade-off between the two, the 'cruel choice' postulated by some economists. Economic development and democracy were intrinsic virtues of the modernity to which he was committed, and both had to be pursued simultaneously. This perhaps obvious point was so elementary to Nehru's view of economic development that it bears restatement.

Nehru's economic design was unquestionably more coherent than any of its Indian rivals in the 1950s. But it had to be built in real and particular circumstances, and inevitably intentions did not match outcomes. The difficulties were rooted in the land: a very unequal distribution of land-ownership, defended by a powerful social order; and very low levels of productivity. These constraints forced Nehru to rely on the state bureaucracy to realize his aims, ultimately a self-confounding tactical choice. The drive towards industrialization, Nehru saw, presumed changes in the agrarian property order. Since the benefits of industrialization were bound to accumulate only slowly, in the intervening period agricultural growth would have to absorb some of the slack in rural employment, as well as provide cheap food. Given his aversion to raising food prices – which was considered unfeasible in a society where most people were poor – the redistribution of land was believed to be the way both to reduce rural inequality and to give incentives to farmers to produce more, so helping India to become self-sufficient in food.

This linchpin of Nehru's plan, legislation concerning land, was put in the hands of the provincial legislatures, yet if the rural property order was to be altered, it seemed that it could only happen through Congress's commitment to the ideas of its national leadership. And on the face of it there was no more likely opportunity than the first decade after independence. Until 1957 Congress ruled in all the states, and in principle it might have been possible. But in fact Congress had never been a strongly ideological party, dedicated to announcing and then enacting political programmes. It was a broad political coalition, itself dependent on what some have described as India's 'ruling social coalition' of commercial and industrial capitalists, rural land-lords, and the bureaucratic and managerial elite (in later decades, newly enriched farmers and unionized public-sector workers would clamber aboard this coalition raft).

The provincial Congress leaders and their party members and supporters, whom the central leadership relied upon to deliver the 'vote banks' at election time, were precisely the groups who stood to lose most through land reform. During the mid-1950s it became evident that the legislative approach to altering the property order had reached an impasse. There were hopeful attempts by the national leadership to pass the burden of reform down to the lowest village levels, through 'community develop-ment' projects and local democracy, *Panchayati Raj*, or rule by village councils. But the measures were rather half-hearted and ineffective, and the district and village councils were sequestered by the already powerful through a blend of cajolery, terror and usury. Land reform was pushed further in certain regions, in communist-governed states like Kerala (which anyway began with less stark inequalities, partly a result of its own cultural forms of matrilineal property inheritance) and later in West Bengal. But overall it ground to a halt, and the great inequalities of the social order were largely preserved. Also, the one effort to address the chronic problem of low productivity on the land had failed. India did not become self-sufficient in food, during the 1950s there were regular shortages and food riots in various parts of the country, and the nation came to depend heavily on American food aid. In contrast to Japan, South Korea, Taiwan

*Failure
to implement
land reform*

and China, all of which successfully implemented land reform programmes, the Indian record was similar to that of the Philippines, one of the least successful growth economies in East Asia.

Nehru was thus trapped by what observers variously called a paradox, contradiction or dilemma. His government was observant of the procedures of constitutional democracy and enjoyed democratic legitimacy, based on its nationalist aura and sustained by winning three general elections between 1952 and 1962. It was also dedicated to establishing an independent industrial base and to reformist and redistributive ends. But neither Congress as a whole nor the democratic weight of numbers, controlled in the countryside by those who stood to lose through reform, could be mobilized in support of these commitments. In principle – and after Nehru – in practice, the choice came to be posed simply: either democracy had to be curtailed, and the intellectual, directive model of development pursued more vigorously (one of the supposed rationales offered for the Emergency of the mid-1970s); or democracy had to be maintained along with all its cumbersome constraints, and the ambition of a long-term developmental project abandoned. The striking point about the seventeen years of Nehru's premiership was his determination to avoid this stark choice. Any swerve from democracy was ruled out; the intellectual arguments had, however, to be upheld. The claims of *techne*, the need for specialist perspectives on economic development, were lent authority by the creation in 1950 of an agency of economic policy formulation, insulated from the pressures of routine democratic politics: the Planning Commission.

Discussions of national progress were by now being formulated in the technical vocabulary of economics, which made them wh. lly unintelligible to most Indians. The task of translation was entrusted to the civil service, and as the algebra of progress moved down the echelons, it was mangled and diluted. The civil service itself provoked deep ambivalence among nationalists:

mistrusted because of its colonial paternity, but respected for its obvious competence and expertise. In the 1930s Nehru had called for a radical transformation of the Indian Civil Service in a free India, though by the time independence actually arrived he had become decidedly less belligerent towards it. It was Patel who had stood up for the civil servants after 1947, speaking thunderously in their favour in the Constituent Assembly. But by the early 1950s Nehru had himself turned more wholeheartedly towards them: he hoped now to use them against the obstructions raised by his own party. The colonial civil-service tradition of fiscal stringency was preserved during the Nehru period, but the bureaucracy was now also given explicitly developmental responsibilities. The result was a leap in its size and power: an expansionary momentum that by the 1970s had become unstoppable, driven by a regime of proliferating licences and regulations. The public bureaucracy duly installed itself as yet another parasitic claimant on the state's resources. Yet Nehru had turned to the bureaucrats for quite specific political reasons, not out of any special affection for them.

4

Nehru's intention had been to subordinate the civil servants to the superior rationality of scientists and economists: the men who glided through the gates of New Delhi's Yojana Bhavan, headquarters of the Planning Commission. During Nehru's government, the Planning Commission came to enjoy an extraordinarily powerful position within the political system, a political position that remains underestimated today (in contrast to its economic proposals, which have been exhaustively dissected). Its power flowed directly from Nehru's own patronage, a dependence that, equally, left it vulnerable and institutionally insecure. Economic development was entrusted by Nehru to a small group:

over a decade, the membership of the Planning Commission was drawn from a pool of only around twenty men, and only about half that number were consistently prominent.

The most spectacular example of this public ascent of the intellectual was marked by the arrival in New Delhi in 1949 of Prasanta Chandra Mahalanobis, the Professor (as he signed his correspondence). Edward Shils, the American sociologist, who had come to India in the 1950s to study its intellectuals, noticed Mahalanobis lurking 'in a somewhat sinister way' behind the planning project, one of the grey eminences of Indian public life. Mahalanobis's recruitment was unexpected. As he himself confessed in 1954, 'I had only a very vague idea of planning when I first came to Delhi. From 1950, when I first started handling national income data, I began to learn.' Yet he was to become the single most important individual in directing Indian development planning and transforming a vision of India's progress into a technical model that directed state policy. Mahalanobis never held a political position, but he was chief advisor to the Planning Commission and a *de facto* member from 1955. Most importantly, he had the complete trust of the prime minister. The decisive Second Plan, drafted in 1954–55, which allocated investment and resources to heavy industry, was in its technical aspects his work.

Born in 1893 of a Bengali Brahmin family, Mahalanobis took a First in mathematics and physics from King's College, Cambridge in 1915 and returned to Calcutta to teach physics. His exuberant intellectual energies quickly led him in directions that made him a seminal figure in the intellectual and cultural history of modern India. He was the perfect exemplar of the mid-century Indian intellectual: he combined in a way possible only at a certain historical moment immense cultural prestige with dazzling scientific virtuosity. Mahalanobis moved easily in a variety of circles. Rabindranath Tagore, for instance, was a close friend. When in Calcutta, the Poet (as he was known) stayed with the

Mahalanobises in their rambling Barrackpore house, and the Professor was a frequent visitor to Tagore's Visva-Bharati University at Santiniketan. (He was with Tagore in 1919 when, after British troops opened fire on unarmed demonstrators in a walled area of Amritsar – the Jallianwala Bagh – and killed at least 300 people, the outraged Poet wrote to the Viceroy, Lord Chelmsford, returning his knighthood.) Mahalanobis was intimately familiar with Tagore's work: the historian E. P. Thompson, in a memoir of his father E. J. Thompson's friendship with Tagore, concluded that Mahalanobis 'knew more about the canon of the poet's early writings than the poet could himself recall', and he provided Thompson with minute guidance – linguistic, literary and personal – in the latter's translations and studies of Tagore's work. Indeed, so admiring was E. J. Thompson of Mahalanobis's literary and cultural judgement that he enlisted him in the preparation of a never-published *Oxford Book of Bengali Verse*.

Mahalanobis combined fluency in Sanskrit philosophy and Bengali literature with acrobatic ability in physics and statistics. Intellectually, he was an awesome polyglot, the kind of man for whom Nehru was guaranteed to fall. In 1931 he annexed a set of rooms in Calcutta's Presidency College and founded the Indian Statistical Institute, and in 1933 launched a journal, *Sankhya* (the title meant both 'number' and 'determinate knowledge'), which went on to become the house journal of Indian planners in the 1950s and 60s. Mahalanobis extracted from Tagore a rather bewildered benediction for the journal, in the form of a prose poem that purported to celebrate the truths of science: 'What we know as intellectual truth, is that not also a perfect rhythm of the relationship of facts that produces a sense of convincingness to a person who somehow feels that he knows the truth? We believe any fact to be true because of a harmony, a rhythm of reason, the process of which is analysable by the logic of mathematics.' In more clipped tones, the launch editorial stated that the journal was 'devoted to statistics . . . the numbering of the people and the collection of the resources of the country'. In its pages the Professor published during the 1930s and 40s a series of articles on a curious assortment of subjects: 'A Revision of Risley's Anthropometric Data Relating to the Tribes and Castes of Bengal' (Mahalanobis's first published work, in 1922, was an anthropometric study on the physical stature of Anglo-Indians in Calcutta), 'A New Theory of Ancient Indian Chronology', 'Distribution of Muslims in the Population in India', and an 'Enquiry into the Prevalence of Drinking Tea Among Middle Class Families in Calcutta 1939'. He was not, clearly, working on the theoretical foundations of a planned economy. What united these technically striking but intellectually rather listless performances was simply their display of statistical virtuosity.

Mahalanobis incarnated a deep rationalist streak in Indian intellectual life, a conviction that qualitative problems could find quantitative resolution, that uncertainty in all walks of life could be reduced and mastered by the use of statistical models. After his return to India in 1915, he studied the work of the British statistician, socialist and eugenicist Karl Pearson, and refined his own statistical techniques. He introduced himself to Nehru in 1940, sending him a paper that outlined some potential uses of statistics in economic planning. The technical approach, although it caught Nehru's attention, had no connection with the very general ruminations on planning within Congress at the time. But after independence Nehru saw the utility of someone who could formulate political aims in the technical and scientific language of economic policy. Initially given the task of collecting statistical data on national income, Mahalanobis soon acquired a more central position in the formulation of policy. He was the dominating intellectual presence behind all three five-year plans of the Nehru era.

Mahalanobis was keenly aware of the absence in India of both economic theory and of economists whom he could induct into his plan-making: hence his search for intellectual support abroad. He travelled to the Soviet Union in 1951, and again in 1954 to Europe, America and the Soviet Union, meeting an array of leading economists, including Ragnar Frisch, Jan Tinbergen, Oskar Lange, Charles Bettelheim, Richard Stone, Joan Robinson, Simon Kuznets and Paul Baran. Many of these were invited to visit India to advise on the planning experiment, and by the mid-1950s India had become a destination for economists the world over; as one of them, looking back on this period from the later era of liberalization, put it, 'honey attracts flies, gold attracts diggers'. Such encounters with initiates of the new discipline of growth economics certainly bolstered Mahalanobis's belief in his own abilities, if nothing else. 'To be quite frank,' he wrote to his protege Pitamber Pant (another physicist-turned-planner) in 1954, 'I am so ignorant about academic economics and my Indian colleagues have been so cocksure about their own infallibility that I had a little bit of an inferiority complex about economic matters. My frequent visits to the West have not only given me greater breadth of vision but have given me increasing self-confidence.' But he also saw in such collaboration a useful political weapon: 'trained and experienced economists can help us a great deal in speaking their own language to Indian economists (which we are unable to do); and in carrying conviction to administrators and political leaders'.

The speed with which professional economists and technocrats came to fill the entire space of public discussion about India's progress was remarkable. The Planning Commission became the exclusive theatre where economic policy was formulated. The subject was removed from parliament and the cabinet – they were now merely informed of decisions taken by the small cohort of experts. The members of the Planning Commission were by no means all economists, but they were chosen by Nehru for their broad agreement with his political project: committed to 'socialistic' and reformist ideals, in the Indianized version of social democracy, and above all to a scepticism about the market and a belief that the state had to take responsibility for allocating resources in the economy. The Planning Commission's work relied on being insulated from wider public deliberation about India's future. The Second Plan, for instance, with its decisive re-channeling of investment towards heavy industry, assumed a theory about the preconditions for industrial growth but gave little public reason for this shift. In its mathematical formulae, it concealed a choice about consumption (less now for the promise of more later) that was undoubtedly a matter of political debate. The Mahalanobis model was used to impart technical gloss to decisions about investment that had been determined by political criteria and specified by Nehru. Amartya Sen had noticed the narrow instrumentalities of the economic model, and its exclusion of alternative policy choices, in 1958: 'It really depends upon what you are after. If you are asked (by, say, Pandit Nehru or Khrushchev) whether a particular target, which the government wants to achieve, can be achieved, you can answer the question with a model of the Professor Mahalanobis sort.'

The Planning Commission and its activities left a lasting imaginative imprint on Indian perceptions of economic development, but the moment of its actual ascendancy was brief – at most a decade. By the mid-1960s the idea of a Planning Commission directing India's economic development within the framework of constitutional democracy was declared by the professionals to be in 'crisis'. 'Perhaps,' one of the closest and still hopeful students of Indian planning wrote in 1968, 'the Commission itself needs a spring-clean.' But even the Professor had to admit that the experiment was actually in deeper trouble. In a revealing but forgotten essay on Gunnar Myrdal's influential account of the failures of development, *Asian Drama*, Mahalanobis expressed 'agreement with Myrdal's main contention that "India's promised social and economic revolution failed to materialize"'. India had not achieved 'take-off', 'self-generating growth', 'the industrial revolution': all those utopic conditions that the science of development economics had enticingly promised in the 1950s. But where Myrdal traced this failure to the persistence of institutional obstacles and the absence of serious social reforms, Mahalanobis's diagnosis reiterated the importance of science and technology to economic growth: his response was to retreat from rather than to take the argument into politics. The rise of modern science had created a third 'domain of decisions', superior to the existing authority of tradition and the liberty of individual choice: 'The tradition and outlook of science requires, and in fact consists of, the acceptance of a new third principle of objective validity of scientific knowledge which has its foundations in nature itself, and which cannot be changed by any authority however high its status, nor by personal choice or preference.' *potentially fascist*

Science was the key to improved rates of economic growth: essential for a 'self-generating economy' in industry as well as in agriculture. 'How to increase agricultural production without increasing the price of food grains,' Mahalanobis insisted, 'is perhaps the most difficult problem of Indian planning.' The solution lay in 'industrial and technological inputs' which, to be effective, required that 'village habits and psychology ... be transformed into the industrial outlook with interests in tools, gadgetry and new innovations, and desire for acquisition of skill in using them'. But advancing the progress of science was a lonely task, since not only the society but the state bureaucracy itself seemed blind to its virtues: 'the number of civil servants and managerial personnel is increasing but the proportion among them with a proper understanding and appreciation of the scientific outlook is probably decreasing, especially at lower levels'. It was therefore imperative to 'liberate science from the authoritarian control of civil servants'. Until that happened, he concluded, 'the future looks dark'. The reliance on the bureaucracy to translate the plans of the intellectuals, to fulfil a cultic role as bearers of Reason's flame to the society, had led to disappointment.

5

'The heart of the problem,' Mahalanobis had written, in what was perhaps the most succinct statement of the way Nehru also saw the issue, 'is to make changes in all necessary directions at the same time, in a balanced way, so as to bring about structural transformation as quickly as possible.' From 1950 until 1964, there was an intellectual logic to the massive complexities condensed in this deceptively prosaic formulation. That logic was battered by political and social circumstances, but Nehru returned constantly to its restatement and adjustment. The views of the economy that emerged over the next two and a half decades wrapped themselves in the language of Nehru's political economy, but they rescinded its intentions and failed to restate a developmental argument coherently. One effect of the Nehru period had been to disseminate the idea that the economy was subject to conscious human control and action: the intellectual elite was itself optimistic about its ability to meet its intentions, to improve society. Democratic politics from the 1970s gave still greater currency to this optimism: it altered popular perceptions of the economy in relation to society and the state. The economy and its management ceased to be seen as the cordoned sanctuary of a technocratic intelligentsia and a benevolent nationalist elite. It was drawn into electoral politics, and became at once a site of more active promise and of contest.

In practice, Nehru's developmental strategy had delivered moderate growth, preserved its democratic legitimacy even though it was insulated from direct claims, and maintained economic stability through prudent fiscal management. By 1991 these three essential pillars were broken. As economic policy lurched from one difficulty to the next while professing allegiance to the earlier strategy, it was difficult to see the accumulating decay. But in retrospect, it is clear that the long-term problems all had their origins in the very first post-Nehru years. Planning lost its status as a productive enterprise – a brief 'plan holiday' was declared from 1966 to 1969, and this began a shift in economic decision-making powers to the Finance Ministry. The Planning Commission continued to solicit official veneration, but it had been toppled from its throne, and in due course it settled into being a sophisticated accounts office and a retirement home for the socially benevolent. The Congress Party, the common arena where demands and interests had been articulated and negotiated, succumbed to the centralizing fetish of its leader: demands were no longer mediated through the party, but pressed directly on the state. And the independence and self-confidence of the civil service was weakened, as senior positions were put in the gift of the political leaders. The loosening of the fiscal belt, combined with stagnation in the state's productive capacities, led to a painful fiscal crisis in 1991. POST-NEHRU

Early crisis had also affected this second phase of independent India's economic experience and put a sharp check on the ambitions of the Nehru period. The rapid political successions after the deaths of Nehru and then Shastri created obvious problems of continuity. The needs of national security, in the wake of the incompetent Indian defence of disputed Himalayan territory against Chinese capture in 1962, followed in 1965 by a more successful war against Pakistan, forced a doubling in military expenditure. The final trigger was the failure of two successive monsoons, in 1965 and 1966, along with longer-term inadequacies in food production: the economy was left hopelessly vulnerable to pressures from the World Bank and the International Monetary Fund (IMF) to devalue the rupee as a condition of further emergency aid. In these trying circumstances, Mrs Gandhi had to acquiesce – with deeply damaging political effects on both Congress and herself. The devaluation confirmed all the old fears about India's vulnerability to the outside world, and fed what now grew into a paranoiac concern with protecting national sovereignty. It left a deep mark on Mrs Gandhi's own thinking about economic matters, and encouraged protectionist policies even when international trade opportunities might have been turned to India's advantage, as was the case in the 1970s.

Mrs Gandhi's initial response to this baptismal crisis was conservative: she tried to reduce expansionist policies, hoping this would end India's reliance on external aid. But, unlike her father, Mrs Gandhi had no intellectual analysis of the domestic economy or of its place in the international arena. Her strength was her political intuition, and unsurprisingly she saw her difficulties as overwhelmingly political, requiring political solutions. To secure her authority she began to use economic policy as an active instrument for mustering political support – in utter contrast to Nehru, whose premiership had been a battle to argue his case against the inclinations of Indian society. After a few years in office, Mrs Gandhi had become a symbol of economic redemption for many different groups in society, which had not suddenly changed or become more radical; rather, she was addressing it in different ways, using a new rhetoric to incite its desires and connect its frustrations to the promises of the state.

In the fading years of the Nehru government, and during the Shastri interregnum, agricultural policy had moved from the earlier emphasis on institutional and structural reform of the property order towards the technological solutions of the 'Green Revolution'. It directed investment heavily towards selected regions (especially Punjab and the north) and social groups (farmers from the intermediate castes with middle-sized landholdings). The results were impressive, and by the mid-1960s these new 'bullock capitalists' began to form their own regional

institutional structural   *technical* 90   *psychological emotional* political parties (the beginning of a phenomenon that by the 1990s would transform national politics). These groups demanded entry with full honours into the 'ruling social coalition': they threatened to withdraw support for Congress unless they received tangible returns. The consequences were apparent in the Congress reverses in the 1967 elections. In response, Mrs Gandhi moved forward to accommodate these rural groups into national politics. She invited their leaders into positions within her Congress, and devised a menu of state subsidies to satisfy the farmers they represented. Electrical power, water, fertilizers and credit all were supplied by the state on concessionary terms, while agricultural incomes and wealth remained untaxed – the largest bounty of all. Besides the prospering farmers, other new interests also laid claim to the state's resources. The managerial elites and unionized labour in the public sector pressed for their 'dearness allowances' to keep ahead of inflation, loss-making enterprises were kept afloat, and overstaffing, in the form of swelling regiments of peons, clerks and petty bureaucrats, became customary practice. Small businessmen and traders thrust forward as another group demanding tax favours and protections for their small enterprises. India's 'fiscal sociology' was altered, as the state made itself more sensitive to the demands of those successful enough to get themselves represented.

Mrs Gandhi also set out to woo the largely unrepresented poor, by taking the rhetoric of economic populism to previously unattained heights. The pale memory of the princes was momentarily revived – it was implied that they were a source of the country's ills, and the constitutional undertaking to provide them with state stipends was abolished. (Nehru had hardly been fond of princely India; but he had resisted parliamentary pressures to renege on constitutional principle.) The banks were nationalized, providing the government with access to cheap money, followed by the insurance and coal industries, and 'sick' enterprises –

especially in the textile industry – were taken over, so bloating the public sector; in the 1970s there was even a brief and entirely disastrous attempt to nationalize the wheat trade. Impenetrable restrictions were placed on foreign investment in the name of defending national sovereignty.

All this was tonic to members of the scientific and left intelligentsia, who in an exemplary display of negative capability interpreted Mrs Gandhi's zeal as a continuation of Nehru's project to modernize and redistribute. Mrs Gandhi herself had a slightly different view of the significance of her actions. As she candidly admitted to one journalist, she now spoke socialism because that was what the people wanted to hear. No effort was made to push through basic structural changes in land ownership, nor had the state suddenly enhanced its productive capacities. Yet she intoned socialist phrases, made extravagant promises, and injected into national politics an evocative – because vague – imagery of redistribution. In time, her rivals and opponents were to adopt these ideological stencils for themselves. The rhetoric fed the most blatantly populist practices – mortgaged festivities such as 'loan melas' at which free milk, saris, food and credit were offered by politicians as inducements to communities and groups in return for their bloc votes.

The subordination of longer-term economic policy to electoral exigencies did not, however, succeed even in securing immediate political legitimacy. The dizzyingly high electoral support for Mrs Gandhi in 1971 soon dissipated, and within four years the country had in her own description become ungovernable. The Emergency accelerated the destruction of Congress's federal grip, and forced Mrs Gandhi to rely on the civil service to administer and govern. She politicized the service, surrounded herself with 'committed' bureaucrats, and retired the less pliant or exiled them to the districts. The Emergency was a parodic rendition of the wish to return to a technocratically directed push towards industrial growth; in the 1950s this had rested on democratic legitimacy, not its contrary. But by now the sun of the intellectuals was in eclipse. Economic policy had been too thoroughly politicized, and Mrs Gandhi's intellectuals – men like P. N. Haksar, D. P. Dhar and Mohan Kumaramangalam, all highly intelligent, urbane, and with past communist associations – stood little chance. The diversion to authoritarian politics did not produce a consistent economic vision. Economic policies were actually intended to effect some mildly liberalizing initiatives, not by introducing more competition but by easing restrictions on foreign trade – which benefited a small lobby. Simultaneously, draconian methods of human husbandry were deployed upon the poor.

There were economic successes for the state during this long second period. It reacted smartly in defensive response to the oil shocks of the 1970s, and, most importantly of all, the agricultural policies of the Green Revolution managed to break India's dependency on food imports. The considerable diversification of India's industrial base begun by Nehru's policies was consolidated. But the larger horizon presaged threats to what had been the most distinctive feature of the Indian economy since independence. Although perceptions of the Indian economy were subject to odd cyclical swings of sentiment between enthusiasm and despair, the economy itself maintained a remarkable stability. To some this was actually an unshakeable inertia. Yet the achievement was unusual: from the 1950s until the late 1980s, India managed to avoid high inflation as well as serious industrial recessions, and did not build up high levels of debt. Few new nations, and almost none which have been democracies, managed this: the usual pattern was for new states to pursue inflationary strategies (usually for populist reasons) and to accumulate high and unmanageable levels of debt. The clue to India's avoidance of this lay in the tradition of prudent fiscal management, inherited from the Raj and maintained even during the most expansionist phase of the Indian state during the 1950s.

This tradition, which accorded with the austere style of the nationalist leaders themselves, Gladstonians in *khadi* caps, slipped into decline in the 1980s.

Between the mid-1960s and the late 1980s, both government expenditure and revenues rose, but the source of the latter was telling. Increased revenues came not from higher takings from direct taxation: the emergence of a huge and mercurial parallel 'black' economy of 'no.2' transactions had ensured an actual fall in taxation revenues (in the mid-1980s, this black economy was estimated to be as much as one third of recorded national income). Nor had there been an increase in revenues to the state from public sector enterprises (those moneys remained stagnant). The increase had in fact come from indirect taxes, from tariffs and duties, which had more than doubled during the period. In the post-Nehru decades, the state had come to rely on a protectionist regime of controls and regulations simply to sustain itself, not for developmental reasons.

Yet despite this increase in revenues, the political pressures to spend still produced fiscal deficits: by the end of the 1980s these were around 10 per cent of national income. Until then, governments had managed to avoid being overbalanced by the steady weakening of fiscal restraint. Whatever poise they could muster rested on two contingencies: the availability of cheap – by market standards – foreign finance in the form of concessional aid and 'soft loans'; and the government's control of domestic banking, which allowed it to set low interest rates for its own borrowing. But this happy combination could not continue in perpetuity. Increased government borrowing during the 1980s coincided with a change in the international climate: rising interest rates brought an end to the supply of cheap money, and international donors became more confident of attaching 'conditions' to aid. By early 1991 the Indian government found itself with enough foreign exchange reserves to cover only two weeks' worth of imports. It was on the edge of a serious fiscal crisis and faced the possibility of defaulting on its borrowings. It had to turn to the IMF, who loaned on condition that a range of comprehensive 'structural' reforms were carried out. The <u>era of liberalization had arrived.</u> 1990s   *& can surprise nationalist populism followed or vice versa*

6

The economic crisis of 1991 came in the midst of political difficulties. India's electoral politics had moved into a phase of fragmented outcomes and coalition or minority governments, as support for Congress haemorrhaged and split between parties of caste, region and Hindu nationalism. The most sweeping realignment of the state's relation to the economy was thus initiated by a minority Congress government, the weakest ever to rule the country. At its head was P. V. Narasimha Rao, who succeeded to the party leadership after the assassination of Rajiv Gandhi in May 1991. Few gave Rao – a backroom fixer thrust into the limelight and visibly acting at the behest of international aid donors – much of a chance. But he was to be the first Indian prime minister drawn from outside the Nehru family to remain in office for the duration of his five-year term. The political weakness of the government worked both to his and to the technocrats' advantage. The Finance Ministry was put in the hands of Manmohan Singh, a distinguished economist who had written a thesis at Oxford in the 1950s on trade policy, and was known to favour a more liberal economic regime. A kind of Mahalanobis for the 1990s, Singh lacked a political constituency, either within or outside Congress; but he had the support of Rao and was the one minister who remained in the same office throughout the tenure of Rao's government. This temporary reprise of powers by intellectuals and technocrats was now turned to goals quite different from those set in the 1950s.

The shift in domestic policy was partly an effect of wider international developments. The collapse of the Soviet Union and the socialist economies had removed the only alternative ideological model to the capitalist market; it also disrupted an advantageous barter trading system for Indian goods (which had allowed India to buy from the Soviet Union without spending precious foreign exchange), and diverted Western aid and concessionary finance to new destinations – the former socialist economies. In Europe, social democratic policies had been abandoned or were in deep difficulties, and governments were everywhere putting their faith in the market. Contingencies like the Gulf War, which had stalled the flow of remittances from Indian migrant workers in the region, put further pressure on the Indian economy. But essentially the crisis which forced liberalization was produced by the state's own actions.

Within India, business and industrial interests as well as some among the political parties had arrived at a disillusioned consensus that state controls of the economy needed to be pruned. The profusion of controls had failed to create a productive public sector, squeezed out private enterprise, and given the state access to resources used not for welfare but as pools of patronage. Some efforts at reduction in controls had been introduced by the Rajiv Gandhi government in 1985, and this had given currency to the idea of economic reform. But in the early 1990s, the most vocal intellectual arguments for liberalization came from abroad – from the ranks of dispersed intellectuals and economists lodged in the international economic agencies and universities. There was no clearer proof of the stunning rise of Indian professional economists since the 1950s: they had become, along with mystics and godmen, India's best export. Their arguments were directed at the basic design of economic development that, they held, had been adopted in the 1950s.

In the most succinct and pointed statement of the liberalizers' argument, Jagdish Bhagwati claimed that India's clever economists of the post-independence years had devised 'a model that couldn't'. The problem, as he saw it, lay in India's rigid pattern of low growth. Its causes lay not in low savings, as had been feared in the 1950s, but in 'disappointing productivity performance', with which the planners had been unconcerned. Their model ignored matters of efficiency and focused purely on allocative choices: capital investment was directed towards industries protected from competition. This had required extensive bureaucratic controls, inward-looking trade and foreign investment policies, and the creation of an unwieldy public sector. The result was a 'control-infested system' that smothered private initiative and encouraged the proliferation of inefficiencies and corruption within both the state-controlled economy and the political system as a whole. Distrust of the market and faith in central control nurtured misconceived economic policies that were continued because of an obstinate political fixation on 'Indian socialism': a doctrine to keep concentration of economic power out of private hands, to protect the small-scale sector such as handloomed textile production, and to avoid regional imbalances across the federal system.

India's economic difficulties, liberalizers like Bhagwati held, were rooted essentially in intellectual misconception and error. 'The central role of the economists, and their responsibility for India's failings cannot be lightly dismissed,' he insisted. 'It is not entirely wrong to agree with the cynical view that India's misfortune was to have brilliant economists: an affliction that the Far Eastern super-performers were spared.' To Bhagwati, himself a distinguished member of this line of brilliant economists, the problems and the solutions to India's economic sluggishness lay in the realm of economic theory. The clarity of this intellectualist diagnosis relied on a certain political naivety: a faith in the power of ideas to shape India's economic destiny that precisely mirrored and inverted the presuppositions of the conception it attacked. India needed 'merely an appropriate policy framework to produce the economic magic that Jawaharlal Nehru wished for his compatriots but which, like many well-meaning intellectuals of his time, he mistakenly sought in now discredited economic doctrines'. And, Bhagwati announced, 'we finally have this elusive policy framework within our grasp'. Yet this skated over the changes in India's democratic politics, which had altered the place of economic policy and subjected it to the imperatives of the electoral cycle. Others, more sensitive to these changes, were less convinced of the capacity to revive the power of ideas and give them directive force. They saw little alternative but another crisis – and the externally imposed conditions it would imply – that would spur the country to correct its economic predicament: neither democratic politics nor the technocratic and intellectual resources of the state could be relied upon to instigate the necessary changes.

Thorough reform of what had become an absurd system of bureaucratic controls was unquestionably essential. The measures introduced in 1991, centred mainly on trade and industry, did bring about significant changes, but by a gradual process of political negotiation rather than through 'shock therapy'. Six years into the process, however, the results were at best mixed. The creditworthiness and reserves of the state were restored, tariffs had been lowered and trade liberalized, foreign investment had risen, and productivity showed signs of improvement. But government borrowing remained high, most of it being used to subsidize and placate, and not for productive or infrastructural purposes. A reduction in the large fertilizer subsidies was vitiated by an increase in prices of foodgrains for farmers; and in the face of trade union resistance, there was no move to privatize public enterprises. Inflation hovered around 10 per cent, high by previous Indian standards, and this despite the absence of external shocks and a sequence of record harvests. If anything, liberalization seemed to nourish still more magnificent scales of corruption: mutually beneficial transactions on the stock exchange and in the sugar, power and telecommunications industries left the wardrobes of cabinet ministers bursting with cash, and Narasimha Rao himself stood in court accused of corruption.

After the initial burst of reforms, the absence of any overall economic design or strategy, and the consequent inability to explain the logic of government actions to the citizenry, became uncomfortably clear. The long twilight of the Rao government was spent in trying to pacify the many groups now voicing their demands in the management of Indian public finances, and in scurrying through economic legislation by means of executive ordinances that precluded parliamentary debate. The lack of any strategy of development was still more acutely manifest in the meanderings of the thirteen-party coalition of left, 'social justice' and farmers' parties that replaced Congress in 1996. Its leader and India's then prime minister, H. D. Deve Gowda, concluded his addresses to potential foreign and Indian investors with plaintive requests: 'Please help me, I am not an economist, give me concrete solutions.' The men with the money were not impressed.

From the early 1990s, the discourse of liberalization came to monopolize economic discussion, just as planning had done in the 1950s and 60s. The standard argument against liberalization, advanced by a stoic Left as well as by old-style and newer Hindu nationalists (the latter, sensing a political opportunity, now painted over their earlier slogans that had favoured liberal economic policies, and gave them a *swadeshi*, protectionist gloss), invoked the fear of losing 'national economic sovereignty'. But this nostalgic yearning for an autarkic purity was sadly beside the point. The real issues lay in two other directions. What kind of participatory opportunities would economic growth actually provide — or fail to provide – for most Indians? Any agreed understanding of economic development, and what it required and entailed, had faded from view; yet all the fundamental problems – poverty, illiteracy, deprivation, ill health, social inequalities – persisted. And how could the state recover its capacities to manage public finances? This last issue had become especially acute because democratic political competition had intensified and more and more interests were organizing, usually around identities of region, caste or religion, to press their claims against the state.

The liberalizers argued that India must create conditions for growth, since indisputably this was necessary for any alleviation of poverty. This exclusive focus on growth encouraged a new faith in the discovery of the 'elusive policy framework' that would enable India to break with what some economists had mockingly dubbed the 'Hindu rate of growth', the steady 3 per cent or so characteristic of the economy between the 1950s and the early 1980s. An excited sense that India had now reached the point of 'take-off' gripped policy-makers, politicians and industrialists. One economic adviser to the government concluded his argument for liberalization with a fly-past of extrapolatory confidence: if the appropriate policy was followed, 'the growth rate of the economy can be accelerated and sustained at an average level of 7–8 per cent per annum. If the economy continues to grow at this rate, per capita income can be quadrupled by the year 2020.' (The authors of the Bombay Plan had in 1944 imagined only a 'doubling of the present per capita income within a period of fifteen years'; inflation was obviously not confined to prices.) The rather restricted focus on growth rates gave the argument for liberalization a definite rhetorical bite; but ironically some economists were now advocating a far richer concept of economic development, which they tried to explain with phrases like 'well-being', 'quality of life', 'capabilities' and 'standard of living' rather than by simple growth indices.

Centrally at issue in the debate about economic reforms was not growth rates but the kind of society in which the growth was expected to occur. If, as in India's case, it was scarred by poverty, illiteracy, poor health and sharp gender inequalities,

Sounds familiar

then the likelihood of tramping the 'Brazilian path' – the Brazilian economy had in the 1970s seen impressive growth rates but little reduction of poverty – would be high. Growth produced by 'unaimed liberalization' – which was not specifically targeted at improving the conditions of the worse-off – could surely be expected to increase inequalities in three ways: across the country, it would widen the gap in social opportunities available to rich and poor; it would sharpen the divide between rural and urban India (urban incomes are around three times the size of rural ones, while female literacy rates in cities are more than double those in the countryside); and it would increase the already pronounced imbalances and differences among the regions, which gave the richest of them per capita incomes three times higher than the poorest ones.

There continue to be, fifty years after India got her freedom, many who break stone, and they have long since ceased to cheer the nationalist heroes. India is one of the few countries where the numbers of those below the poverty line have steadily declined, but there are still around 400 million Indians, mostly in the countryside, who are excluded from the channels of economic circulation and market exchange created since independence. For them little has changed, and nothing in what the liberalizers have to say offers them much prospect of betterment in their lifetimes. So far, these hundreds of millions have been relatively inert politically; but as the idea of democracy seeps through Indian society, and as economic opportunities expand rapidly for some social groups in some locations, one thing that is guaranteed is the absence of a quiet idyll in Indian politics. Indians will have to face directly what the coming of democracy means for their society. The issue – which Ambedkar had seen so lucidly in 1949 – goes to the heart of one of the oldest debates about democratic politics. Does democracy depend for its viability on simply excluding a part of the population from the political

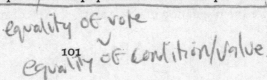

equality of vote
equality of condition/value.

community, the metics and slaves? And if not, what will happen when the very poorest enter the democratic process?

7

In the 1990s Indians look not to the West but to the East for an image of their own tigerish future (a future in which there are unlikely to be any tigers). In the 1950s there had been a general consensus about the availability of instruments and policies to replicate the Western example, but today even the specialists disagree about how the East has won. What is undeniable is that states have been decisive in establishing the conditions for East Asian economic success. Equally, basic education and institutional reforms in land have been essential. India's literacy rate, at around 50 per cent of the population, is today lower than those of China or South Korea when they *began* their economic rise. Education may not be sufficient for economic success, as is clear from the example of Kerala, which can claim near-total literacy but has long had a disappointingly stagnant economy, yet it is obviously necessary, and it can only be achieved by determined state action. This might take various forms, including market-oriented policies such as higher salaries for teachers in rural areas.

Advocates of liberalization are correct to highlight the areas in which the Indian state has shown an inclination to do too much, but that is only half the story, for the state has also done too little. Liberalization in India will not free the state from demands being made upon it. On the contrary, demands, often contradictory, will increase. They will take the form of pressures for and against redistribution to groups and regions; for and against the control of internal migration; for access to resources such as river waters; for control of environmental hazards; and for the regulation of stock markets. Yet, despite this foreseeable range of responsibilities, the Indian state finds itself both without agreed principles and mechanisms to adjudicate claims, and without resources. Planning, apart from its developmental aims, was also intended to be an instrument for correcting regional imbalances. The internal federalism of Congress was another means by which demands by regions and groups could be bartered. Neither is available today. Meanwhile, the problem persists that the creation of a public sector was intended to address: the state's financial resources for redistributive purposes are constricted. The capacity to tax society directly is small. Personal income tax – the most common form of redistributive taxation – is paid by only 2 per cent of India's urban population, and the economic reforms have continued to evade the issue of taxing agricultural wealth and incomes. The failure of public enterprises to produce wealth, and the loss of revenues through the reduction of controls, will worsen the state's position.

Nor have economic reforms shrunk the chronic large deficits run up by governments in the past decade. The argument for liberalization promised immediate remedies for this through the sale of public enterprises and a reduction in the size of the state. Yet six years into the reform process, the enterprises remain in the state's hands, and governments have been unable to reduce deficits substantially. The absence of fiscal prudence is certainly not a monopoly of planned or regulated economies, nor of autocratic regimes, but its presence is an essential precondition for the formulation and pursuit of *any* type of economic policy, liberal or state-regulated.

These two fundamental, and interrelated, responsibilities of India's state – the management of public finances and the formulation of coherent long-term economic strategy on allocation of resources – are in turn related in intrinsic if by no means transparent ways to the operations of India's democracy. In both the developmental and more purely statist aspects of economic policy, democracy has played an important role. The prospect of regular elections has encouraged governments to avoid sharply inflationary policies, since politicians must campaign in a largely poor country where most wages are unindexed. The exercise of democratic rights has averted any recurrence of that terror of British India, famine. The last famine to devastate the subcontinent was in 1943, when distributional failures and inaction on the part of the British Raj killed three million people in Bengal. Independent India has acted decisively to forestall food emergencies, and an uncensored press and free parliamentary opposition have been vital to concentrating the minds of governments to this end. (China, where information was suppressed by a one-party state during the famines of the late 1950s – in which it is estimated up to thirty million may have died – is a telling comparison.) Democratic politics in India has also enabled individuals and groups to debate and contest state policies of economic development, even if on vastly unequal terms. It has brought new values, priorities and interests into the discussion, and has done much to politicize subjects such as the environment. Developmental projects destructive of human and natural habitats have been challenged and sometimes checked by citizens who have used the Supreme Court and the powers of judicial review to press their rights against state policy.

This has led to an optimistic faith in the powers of 'public action' which has two aspects. First, some insist, public pressure groups must continue to politicize issues such as gender inequalities, illiteracy and endemic hunger, and should aim to influence the state to act in these areas. Secondly, economic development might also be usefully advanced by a variety of social movements, non-governmental organizations and self-help organizations that constitute what now tends to be called, fashionably and elusively, 'civil society'. These groups – and a wide array have emerged, from well-known examples like the Self-Employed Women's Association in Ahmedabad (which advances small loans to women to start their own micro-

local efforts not scaleable

enterprises), to the popular science movements in Kerala (which have taken science education to village streets and squares) – they suggest and hope, acting more confidently for themselves, might take on the responsibilities that the developmental state was unable to fulfil and that a liberalized one will be unwilling to accept. There is force to such arguments. But they presume the possibility of a more universalist type of politics for India, which escapes the 'sectional politics' of interests expressed in community and group identities and takes on 'broader concerns that affect most people in the deprived categories'. There are few signs of this emerging. The domain of public action is vibrant in India today; but, by definition it is at its strongest and most effective when most local and particular in its concerns. It certainly cannot provide any perspective from which to envisage an economic policy for India as a state.

Fifty years of state action upon the economy imagined as a single field has resulted in a huge national economy with powerful integrative tendencies. Policy has to be formulated for this economic space as a whole. India's democratic politics has released a multitude of voices and interests, which make the effort to maintain fiscal prudence and to devise and conduct strategies of economic development more complicated than ever before. With the decline of the old lines of conversation, the end of the bespectacled planners and the *khadi*-clothed Congressmen, new forms of bargaining and negotiation have indeed begun to emerge both within and among the regional parties. The economic reforms set in motion since 1991 have led governments at the Centre to concede more power to the regions and their parties. The paradox is that central power now rests on a coalition of parties from the regions, and this could unravel in one of at least two ways. It might encourage an abdication of fiscal responsibilities, as its members decide to reward their own particular interests, the farmers and the poor, who supported them. Or it might encourage leaders from the regions to appreciate and learn the necessities of managing the Indian economy more shrewdly and maturely. The first fifty years of India's economic experience do not reveal an especially impressive learning curve on the part of the country's politicians and intelligentsia. Now, a more rapid collective learning through the deliberative practices of democracy is in the long run the only hope, for a country where democracy has become the oxygen of the society. The absence of a commanding national party that can stipulate decisive economic goals may temporarily return power to the technocrats, but voice is passing from the intellectuals to the *demos*: to the powerful, the aspiring, and the excluded. There are now more arguments, more interests, more conceptions of what development is and what it means for India. It will not be easy.

And rise of populist nationalism

From Nehru planning (moderate, low growth, state control) to Indira Gandhi populism to crisis

1990s liberalization & more democratization precursors of Modi

THREE

Cities

Do not write letter/ Without order refreshment
Do not comb/ Hair is spoiling floor
Do not make mischiefs in cabin/ Our waiter is reporting
Come again/ All are welcome whatever caste
If not satisfied tell us/ Otherwise tell others
God is Great.

NISSIM EZEKIEL, 'Irani Restaurant Instructions'

1

In that eternal city of the imagination, R. K. Narayan's Malgudi, things began to happen after 15 August 1947:

For years people were not aware of the existence of a Municipality in Malgudi. The town was none the worse for it. Diseases, if they started ran their course and disappeared, for even diseases must end someday. Dust and rubbish were blown away by the wind out of sight; drains ebbed and flowed and generally looked after themselves. The Municipality kept itself in the background, and remained so till the country got its independence on the fifteenth of August 1947. History holds few records of such jubilation as was witnessed that day from the Himalayas to Cape Comorin. Our Municipal Council caught the inspiration. They swept the streets, cleaned the drains and hoisted flags all over the place. Their hearts warmed up when a procession with flags and music passed through their streets.

But the nationalist enthusiasm of the Municipal Council was not so cheaply expended. No sooner had the celebrations ended than the chairman decided more had to be done to make Malgudi truly free and patriotic.

He called up an Extraordinary Meeting of the Council, and harangued them, and at once they decided to nationalize the names of all the streets and parks, in honour of the birth of independence. They made a start with a park at the Market Square. It used to be called the Coronation Park. Whose coronation God alone knew; it might have been the coronation of Victoria or Asoka. No one bothered about it. Now the old board was uprooted and lay on the lawn, and a brand-new sign stood in its place declaring it henceforth to be Hamara Hindustan Park. The other transformation, however, could not be so smoothly worked out. Mahatma Gandhi Road was the most sought-after name. Eight different ward councillors were after it. There were six others who wanted to call the roads in front of their houses Nehru Road or Netaji Subhas Bose Road. Tempers were rising . . . There came a point when, I believe, the Council just went mad. It decided to give the same name to four different streets. Well, sir, even in the most democratic or patriotic town it is not feasible to have two roads bearing the same name. The result was seen within a fortnight. The town became unrecognizable with new names . . . a wilderness with all its landmarks gone.

The Municipal Council's appreciation of the principles of rational urban cartography was undoubtedly impaired by an unusual excess of commemorative zeal, but similar second baptisms were sweeping through cities across the country. For, despite the ambivalence of nationalists towards the city – it was, after all, the theatre where India's subjection to the British colonists was most graphically and regularly enacted – they could not turn their backs on it. They had to move into and inhabit the colonial cities, and dedicate them to their own desires and historical remembrances – it was here, in the streets of the city, that the memory of even that most stern censor of the modern city, Gandhi, was immortalized.

Since the nationalization of the streets and parks began in 1947, India's cities have changed utterly. They have become the bloated receptacles for every hope and frustration reared by half a century of free politics and exceedingly constrained and unequal economic progress. More than a quarter of all Indians live in cities, some 250 million people, and it is estimated that by 2010 the figure will exceed 400 million, giving India one of the largest urban populations in the world. In legend and in fact India may still be a land of villages, but no Indian can today avoid the cities. Their very exclusivity, and the spreading rumours of their opulence, have made the cities universal objects of desire – all who dream of the ransom of modernity, who peer at its spectres on television and cinema screens, dream of some connection with the city.

What has brought Indians to the cities, or what has at least brought cities to their attention, is their economic dynamism. The nationalist state took up residence in the city, and it was here too that the Nehruvian ambition to modernize and develop Indian society was scripted and broadcast, radiating outwards across the villages. The modernity created here exemplified fully the life of contradictions that India embraced the day it became a democratic republic. India's cities house the entire historical compass of human labour, from the crudest stone-breaking to the most sophisticated financial transactions. Success and failure, marble and mud, are intimately and abruptly pressed against one another, and this has made the cities vibrate with agitated experience. All the enticements of the modern world are stacked up here, but it is also here that many Indians discover the mirage-like quality of this modern world. This experience has altered beliefs, generated new politics, and made the cities dramatic scenes of Indian democracy: places where the idea of India is being disputed and defined anew.

The major cities of contemporary India are either directly the creatures of colonialism or ripostes to it. They are discontinuous with India's own rich history of urban life, for the British, even as they sometimes plagiarized this history, saw India as a *tabula rasa* where they could reinvent the city, both internally and in its relation to the rest of society. Within the cities, the British Raj governed public space according to its own quite alien concepts. It created a masquerade of the modern city, designed to flaunt the superior rationality and power of the Raj, but deficient in productive capacities. The modernity of the colonial city had a sedate grandeur to it, but it remained external to the life of the society – few bothered about it.

After 1947, Nehru's dominating nationalist ambition in turn set out to recreate the city for its own purposes: to make it not only the symbol of a new sovereignty but an effective engine to drive India into the modern world. The urban world created by this nationalist imagination is certainly no façade – some may still choose to see India's politics or economic development as a pale imitation of a Western paragon, but they can hardly do so when confronted with the country's vibrant and sometimes excessively palpable cities. Yet India's cities have not quite fulfilled the nationalist expectations. Their modernity is not of a pure and happy kind, but a split and discontented one, full of darker, mixed potential. They have become spawning grounds for contrary conceptions of what India is: on the one hand an hyperbolic parochialism, a bleached cosmopolitanism on the other, both far distant from the tolerant Indian cosmopolitanism that the nationalist elite had proposed. As it did in the first half of the twentieth century, the city continues to make the politics of India, but the politics it is making, and the Indias it is coming to believe in, have wandered far from what was intended and imagined in the early days when the street signs were so exuberantly and confusingly nationalized.

2

The colonial city arrived in India in two distinct stages. The foundation during the seventeenth century of the ports of Madras, Calcutta and Bombay, dedicated to commercial extraction and the exhibition of wealth, linked India more intensively than ever to the globally expanding economies of northern Europe, and established an enduring relationship of subjugation and uneven exploitation between these economies and the subcontinent itself. If the Fort and Government House were one central axis of these cities, another ran through the wharfs and docks. The second stage began in the later nineteenth century, when the British built the more schematic cantonment cities, laid out as military encampments but made of brick and stucco rather than canvas, and it culminated in the building of the grandest of modern imperial cities, New Delhi – a monument to the display of power and order. Throughout, the British colonial city kept its distance from – and looked askance at – India's existing cities: places like Murshidabad, Fyzabad or Patna all might have picturesque architectural merits, but otherwise were best avoided. To the colonial eye, they were places of melancholy decay and flabbergasting squalor. The British desire to announce new-gotten wealth through conspicuous and freshly painted buildings, airy confections set in emerald parks ('an entire village of palaces' was how an awestruck visitor described Calcutta's Chowringee early in the nineteenth century), found no match in the crumbling masonry, miasmatic air, and labyrinthine disorder of India's urban neighbourhoods and bazaars. This view of the pre-colonial city was in time formalized into a more elaborate, academically glorified contrast between the Western and the Indian, or 'Asiatic', city. The latter, with its superstition, primitive and uncertain commerce, despotism, religious passions and caste-ridden bonds, became a foil against which to contrast the virtues of European rationality, industrial capitalism, civic government, secularism and individuality.

But set aside for a moment the rigid evolutionary trajectories of the traditional and modern, pre-industrial and industrial, Eastern and Western city, and one can find in pre-colonial India vivid examples of cities that do not quite fit the easy dichotomies. The commercial centre of Ahmedabad to the west is an exceptionally intriguing and neglected case. It was here, in the shadow of industrial smoke-stacks, that Gandhi launched his Indian political career – on his return from South Africa in 1915, he built his 'Satyagraha Ashram' on the banks of the Sabarmati river. This is perhaps the only example of an Indian city modernizing on its own terms, without being dragooned through a phase of colonial modernity. Ahmedabad had a long history of self-generated prosperity, reliant neither on the patronage of a court nor on the exploitation of the surrounding countryside, but on a tradition of textiles and manufacturing. Its history also showed considerable independence in the management of its affairs. Ahmedabad was not an independent city-state (no Indian city ever was), nor did it have formal authorities like a municipal government with territorially defined powers. Since its foundation early in the fifteenth century it did, however, possess powerful mercantile and artisanal corporations and guilds. These corporations, or *mahajans* (their membership crossed lines of sect and caste, sometimes even of religion), used their commercial powers – and the threat of exit – to constrain interference by external political authorities in the management of city affairs. Hindus, Jains and Muslims lived within Ahmedabad's walls, but there was little history of violent religious conflict. The city's prosperity, as well as its religious pluralism, was manifest in an architectural tradition of public buildings: fine mosques and mausoleums, Jain and Hindu temples, all sustained a civic tradition that continued into the twentieth century. Ahmedabad has no colonial architecture of note, but it was the only Indian city where Le Corbusier was commissioned to build by private initiatives.

Most striking of all was Ahmedabad's response to the commercial challenge of British rule. Unlike other wealthy commercial cities on the subcontinent (nearby Surat, or Murshidabad and Dacca in the east), it did not decline with the emergence of the new port cities of Bombay and Calcutta. It flourished in the nineteenth century, and its textiles easily competed with European rivals in the international market. The city maintained its local cultures, language and dress, and showed little taste for European products: although this slipped slightly in the late nineteenth century, when some *seths*, rich merchants, began to wear socks and moved out of their carved wooden *havelis* in the old walled city to large English-style stucco mansions set in the greenery of Shahibagh, north of the city. Uniquely, Ahmedabad turned its mercantile wealth into industrial success. It industrialized under its own steam, without noticeable British investment, in its own language and with little disturbance to its existing cultural habits. Unlike the new city of Kanpur, in the north, which also began to industrialize from the 1870s, Ahmedabad did not depend upon a strong European presence or on the order books of the British Indian Army. The early Ahmedabadi industrial elite was rooted in the city and was regarded as belonging to it – it had not risen as a result of British patronage – and this helped to sustain a sense of an urban identity. Ahmedabad had its own sources of commercial capital, sophisticated banking and insurance techniques, routines for settling disputes that did not depend on colonial law and courts, and high levels of social trust. Above all it possessed a breed of entrepreneurial risk-takers like Ranchhodlal Chhotalal, a government servant who after several essays succeeded in setting up the city's first spinning mill in 1861 (ten years after the first Indian mill was established in Bombay, but just before the railway, generally seen as a crucial prompt to industrialization, reached

Ahmedabad). Such men, supported by the local financial elite, were willing to risk investment in the cotton mills; unlike their more 'gentlemanly' rentier counterparts in Bengal, for example, where the deeper and more overbearing British presence blocked opportunities for industrial ventures and encouraged investment in land. That Ahmedabad, in its own unflashy way the first modern city created by Indians, could generate new productive wealth through its traditions of textile manufacturing and maintain its cultural character, were exactly the reasons that led Gandhi to adopt it as a home – and vital source of funds – for his new nationalist politics. (It was an Ahmedabadi *seth* who once muttered about how much it cost to keep the Mahatma in poverty.)

For all the 'untraditional' aspects of a commercial and political centre like Ahmedabad, cities in pre-colonial India were undoubtedly very different from their European analogues. In eighteenth-century India, large cities could be found in all regions, linked to the countryside through smaller towns – *qasbahs* or *ganjs*, as they were called in the north – which acted as cultural and economic conduits. The intensity of contact among the cities was subject to varying historical rhythms: greater during periods when regional polities were integrated into imperial formations, lesser when these declined. There was no rising and uninterrupted curve of urban contact and exchange. Pre-colonial cities were specialized: besides commercial and economic centres like Ahmedabad, Surat or Cochin, there were destinations of religious pilgrimage like Benares, Puri and Madurai whose size expanded and contracted in line with the religious calendar; and political and administrative cities like Delhi or Agra, their ascendancy and decline hitched to the fate of dynasties. The conjunction of commercial and economic wealth with political and administrative power, typical of Europe's major cities, was rare in pre-colonial India: colonial ports like Calcutta were the first such examples.

Internally, too, Indian cities were distinctively organized: arranged by neighbourhoods of work and residence, and segregated by small-scale castes, sects and religious communities. The struggling interests and contestants were heavily local – there were few implements available to enlarge social horizons or circles of association (printing presses, railways, and administrative technologies like the census – which sorted disparate individuals into sets whose members were deemed to possess 'identical' attributes – all entered with the British). And the movement of people and goods among cities followed avenues of caste: a migrant arriving in a new city would search out fellow caste members. Merchants, while often trading over long distances and by means of sophisticated accounting practices, would truck with members of their own community: the most notable case was the Marwaris, who from their homes in Rajasthan built extensive networks all over India.

Urban political or social associations were nothing like the 'public' bodies that began to appear in eighteenth-century Europe. These European 'societies' were in principle universally accessible to all individuals with common interests, but in Indian cities association was sanctioned by denser criteria of lineage, caste and religion, and it operated by strict rules of exclusion. Religious conflict was restrained by distinctive methods: not, as later nationalists fondly liked to suppose, on the basis of a genuinely 'composite' culture founded on an active and mutual respect among practitioners of different religions, but on routine indifference, a back-to-back neglect, which on occasions like religious festivals could be bloodily dispensed with. Social relations in these cities were neither impersonal nor governed by contractual models of rights and obligations enforced by an external public authority. Social groups certainly performed duties for one another – for example, the wealthy would bestow charity on the poor and on religious mendicants – but such obligations were not enforced by public law or authority. That really was the crucial difference. These cities were not governed by publicly known rules that applied uniformly to all their residents, and that a single authority could enforce: they had no municipal governments, no state power with defined territorial jurisdiction. Above all, the city itself did not appear as a cohesive and single space, an 'anonymous subject' which could be rationally administered, ordered and improved.

That precisely was what colonialism wished to do. The British Raj lived in the city, in compounds of its own creation external to the society over which it ruled. It was in the city that its imaginative impress was heaviest. The Raj both molested the existing cities, the 'old' or 'Black' town, and constructed new ones; together this altered the meanings of the city in India. The colonial idea of the city was disseminated with new vigour in the second half of the nineteenth century, impelled by the desire for greater security in the wake of the 1857 uprising. The three port cities of Madras, Calcutta and Bombay were already well-developed mercantile centres by the time India was absorbed into the British empire and imperial rule proclaimed in 1858. The distinction between European and Indian 'towns', which had initially been characteristic of them, had softened with time: piecemeal and haphazard commercial growth encouraged urban miscegenation. But by the late nineteenth century a more focused concern with defence, sanitation, order, and above all the display of the new imperial power, forced out other considerations. India's cities fell prey to a fashion sweeping through other metropolises across the globe – Paris, Prague, Berlin, New York, Buenos Aires.

Vast areas of the old cities were demolished. In Delhi, which had retained a strong sense of its pre-colonial habits and styles, the stately Mughal Red Fort was turned into a squalid barracks, its watercourses converted into watering troughs. Railway lines were struck through the central areas of the city. Ghalib, Delhi's greatest poet, observed this in 1865:

Let me tell you the Delhi news ... The gate to Bara Dariba has been demolished. The rest of the Qabil Attar Lane has been destroyed. The mosque in Kashmiri Katra has been levelled to the ground. The width of the street has been doubled ... A great monkey, strong as a lion and huge as an elephant, has been born. He roves the city demolishing buildings as he goes.

New cantonment cities were constructed, more than 170 of them, dotted around the country and linked by railway, roads and telegraph into a new geography of command. Their site-plans varied little, strictly segregated into European and Indian sections, with the former in turn divided between the military and civil lines – where the civilian authorities and notables lived. 'The European station,' wrote one observer who moved through these newly rising cities of the Raj,

is laid out in large rectangles formed by wide roads. The native city is an aggregate of houses perforated by tortuous paths ... The Europeans live in detached houses, each surrounded by large walls enclosing large gardens, lawns, out-offices. The natives live packed in squeezed-up tenements, kept from falling to pieces by mutual pressure.

As a counterpoint to these new cities, the British also invented a new countryside for themselves. Not very keen on the exhaustingly hot, dusty plains and low villages that encircled their new cities, they created the hill station – superb sites in the Himalayas and in the more gentle Nilgiri mountains in the south. Here an image of the English countryside, complete with creaking gates and pruned roses, was tenderly nurtured. The British gratefully retreated to mock-Tudor bungalows and wooden cottages, and indulged in homesick idylls; but they also did business, turning the hill stations into temporary secretariats: Simla, the grandest and most elegant of them all, was for at least part of the year the supreme power in the land.

The civilizing ambitions of the British Raj were routinely

rehearsed in the city. No longer merely a pier whence to freight wealth out of the country, the city become a stage where the regalia of British sovereignty was displayed, where the Indian was ruled, where space was most explicitly governed. The rectangular securities of the European station became a notional norm for the entire society. But the conception of the city embodied in the precise assignments of space within British civil and military lines did not mesh with any Indian conceptions, and Indians played little part in defining its meanings. There was no prolonged duel, as in Britain or France, about what a city and its purposes should be, no jostling between crowds and the state which gave a political sense to the public squares or boulevards. The colonial conception was imposed. Given the scale and numbers involved, the success of this imposition depended less on active surveillance and police, more on the ability to fabricate shared, self-disciplinary meanings: of what a city was, of its public and private spaces, and of the rules of each. But this domain of shared meanings extended only to the Indian elites and middle classes, who by the early decades of the twentieth century had grown to a substantial presence in the cities. They aspired to the glistening fruits of modernity tantalizingly arranged before them – street lights, electric fans, tree-lined streets, clubs, gardens and parks – and they willingly emulated the behaviour and acquired the self-restraining habits of the modern city-dweller. Outside these powerful but small circles, however, assent to metropolitan civilities abruptly tailed off. To the poor, to migrants from the countryside, to the destitute, the British idea of a modern city was meaningless; it never reached them.

This conceptual stand-off was evinced by a trait that has repeatedly struck the eye attuned to the modern city, a fact that nonplussed colonials and that present-day visitors have ceaselessly fretted over: the stance that residents of Indian cities appear to take towards waste – refuse, excreta, death. A city like

Benares, for instance, seemed to the Western eye defective in its reluctance to rationalize social life by quarantining activities in different parts of the city, by assigning them to European definitions of the public and private realms. Death was at the very heart of Benares, not banished to its edges but mingled with its daily business: corpses were cremated on specified *ghats*, the great stone ledges descending to the Ganges, which were the city's most important common spaces. Benares seemed, to the foreign eye, indifferent to the need to constitute itself as a city of public arenas, with distinct borders between public and private acts, the hygienic and the non-hygienic. Not the least of Benares's oddities was its unworried marriage of religious purity and physical filth. In a famed account, *The Sacred City of the Hindus* (1868), the Reverend M. A. Sherring exemplified this way of seeing it:

Threaded with narrow streets, above which rise the many storied edifices for which the city is famous, it is, without doubt a problem of considerable difficulty, how to preserve the health of its teeming population. But, when we reflect on the foul wells and tanks in some parts of the city, whose water is of deadly influence, and the vapour from which fills the air with fever-fraught and cholera-breeding miasma; when we consider the loathsome and disgusting state of the popular temples, owing to the rapid decomposition of the offerings, from the intense heat of the sun; when we call to mind the filthy condition of nearly all the by-streets, due to stagnant cesspools, accumulated refuse, and dead bodies of animals; and, when, in addition, we remember how utterly regardless of these matters, and incompetent to correct them is the police force scattered over the city, the difficulty becomes overwhelming.

By the latter half of the nineteenth century, British perceptions of Indian urban life were preoccupied by its filth; earlier, the British had been most discomfited by the infernal and sickening climate, but now the Indian city itself was threatening – and required control. This way of seeing the Indian city developed into an entire sensory response, and it became the natural nationalist mode of perception, too. Gandhi, describing in his *Autobiography* his first visit to Benares, could not hide his dismay:

I went to the Kashi Visvanath temple for *darshan*. I was deeply pained by what I saw there ... The approach was through a narrow and slippery lane. Quiet there was none. The swarming flies and the noise made by the shopkeepers and pilgrims were perfectly insufferable. Where one expected an atmosphere of meditation and communion, it was conspicuous by its absence. One had to seek that atmosphere in oneself ... When I reached the temple, I was greeted at the entrance by a stinking mass of rotten flowers ...

The British obsession with drainage and sewerage systems was matched by more elevated concerns. An empire, unlike a trading company, had to announce itself to its subjects by grander means than shopfronts. Until the 1870s, the British had not directed much energy to displaying their authority – there had been the notorious 'flag marches', designed in the wake of 1857 to suppress any thoughts of sedition, but otherwise there was little parading about in public squares. The abolition and desanctification of Mughal symbols of power and legitimacy after the 1857 rebellion left a vacuum. The British response was to pirate the Durbar, which in Mughal hands had been a sophisticated, courtly ritual of political exchange and fealty between emperor and subjects. The British versions were not in any sense fully public events, as the state rituals in the European metropolises often were – they were staged for a carefully selected audience of loyalists and toadies. The first Imperial Durbar, held in 1877 at Delhi, formally proclaimed Queen Victoria Empress of India, or 'Kaiser-i-Hind'. This ceremonial pantomime was justified to the more austerely utilitarian mood in Britain with the claim that it pandered to the Indian need for awesome spectacles of authority: as the Viceroy, Lord Lytton, put it in 1876, 'the further East you go, the greater becomes the importance of a bit of bunting'. The site where the beguiling streamers were draped was north-west of the Delhi cantonment, in a purpose-built Durbar city, a five-mile arc of tents accommodating 84,000 people. The Durbar itself was an absurd mixture of medals, manipulation, and teutonic drum-rolls: at its climax, the viceroy arrived on horseback to the 'March' from *Tannhauser*. Such performances changed the ways in which authority was thereafter displayed on the subcontinent, and the idea lives on in the Republic Day parades staged by the Indian state every 26 January, the most vivid – and ironic – ceremonial vestige of the Raj. At the third such Durbar, in 1911, George V with Napoleonic modesty first crowned himself emperor and then announced the transfer of the Indian capital from Calcutta to a proposed site at Delhi.

The new capital at Delhi was the summation of British efforts to hoist the imperial pennant on Indian territory. The coastal presidency cities of Calcutta, Bombay and Madras had not been built by a single driving vision: their fitful styles – Classical, Indo-saracenic, Gothic – reflected wavering ideological and aesthetic intentions. New Delhi was the pristine thing. Delhi's attraction was both its rich historical associations as the seat of past imperial overlords, and its provision of a virgin space on which the marshalled layout of the canvas Durbar city could be engraved permanently into the rocky Indian landscape, the chosen site where a late imperial idea of power could be entombed. But New Delhi had also to illustrate a rational modernity: as Lord Stamfordham, private secretary to King George V, explained, the desired effect was to let the Indian 'see for the first time the power of Western science, art and civilization'. It had to reconcile the two opposed principles of tradition and of reason. The design of New Delhi, plum of all imperial commissions, was entrusted to that architectural Hector, Edwin Lutyens, and the more retiring Herbert Baker. The city they built was spread out as a spacious kaleidoscope of broken hexagons and triangles, pivoting on large roundabouts. The central axis, Kingsway (today's Raj Path), took in the mammoth War Memorial Arch, sloped up to the focal point of the city, the acropolis on Raisina Hill, swept past the Jaipur Column, and came finally to rest at Lutyens's *piece de resistance*, the Viceroy's House. The two blocks of the Secretariat, designed to be 'the place of government in its highest expression', were left to Baker. The Council Chamber, now India's Parliament, an afterthought necessitated by the Montagu-Chelmsford reforms of 1919, which extended the Raj's reliance on indirect rule, was apologetically tucked away in a corner below the hill, after its interior was thoughtfully inscribed with homilies for the natives ('Liberty will not descend to a people; a people must raise themselves to liberty; it is a blessing which must be earned before it can be enjoyed').

New Delhi was a sublime fantasy of imperial control over the boundaries and definition of urban space, the creation and ranking of social structures, and the allocation of the Raj's *nomenklatura* to its designated spaces. Its hexagonal grids were demarcated into segments for 'gazetted officers', European 'clerks' and Indian 'clerks', and distance from the central acropolis was gauged by rank – the quarters for Indian clerks were placed farthest from the centre (this in a city of marooning distances and without public transport). Residential protocol was maintained by that essential document of colonial social decorum, the 'Warrant of Precedence': a kind of viceregal *Mrs Beeton's* that assisted in solving such nice conundrums as whether the superintendent for the opium factory at Ghazipur was to be seated ahead of the general manager of the Rajputana Salt Resources. New Delhi's calibration was not merely horizontal: Lutyens, obsessed with the city's physical elevation, was determined to define what he called a 'line of climax'. The houses of the junior Indians ('thin black') had to be physically lower and sited below the elevation of the houses of junior Europeans ('thin white'), and these in turn were placed below senior Europeans' ('rich white'), lifting the line stirringly to the viceregal dome. This sensitivity to altitude explains something of Lutyens's rage during his famous 'gradient quarrel' with Baker: so eager was he to acquire the actual summit of the hill for his construction that he surrendered the original – and lower – site chosen for the Viceroy's House. The result was a shock: the massive plinth of the building, set further back to Lutyens's instructions, had in fact become invisible from the point at the foot of the hill where subjects were enjoined to gaze expectantly up at it. All they saw was a disembodied dome.

'City' is perhaps too strong a term for what was built. New Delhi was besotted with being a capital rather than a city – it was a grand, capitol complex with an attached residential campus. The modernity that New Delhi was designed to incarnate certainly impressed some. 'The Viceroy's House is the first real vindication of modern architecture . . . It is *really* modern. My admiration for Lutyens is unbounded,' gushed the travel writer Robert Byron, when he visited the city in 1929. But it was a modernity that erased every trace of its location. Lutyens gave New Delhi a single, aloof link, Minto Road, to what was now relegated as the 'old' city of Delhi, and he broke all connection with its river, the Jumna. 'Those who claimed to be modern in Delhi,' Nirad Chaudhuri noted, 'had nothing to do with the river.' The superb ruins, tombs and monuments of Delhi – the *Purana Quila*, Humayun's tomb (doubtless the most perfect Mughal dome after the Taj Mahal), the more florid mausoleum of Safdarjung – all were pinioned by Lutyens's axial layout and turned into follies on the imperial estate: they served as mere ornaments to the viceregal omphalos.

Colonialism, changing the status of the city in India as it did, created new instrumentalities of rule that altered India's urban textures. Greater and more regular contact between elites in the cities, not to mention administrative techniques like a decennial census (first introduced in a limited form in 1871), expanded perceptions of the social scale of communities: individuals and groups living in far corners of the country could now conceive of themselves as being members of a single, large community. This made it possible for the first time to imagine a common nation of Indians. But the enumeration and classification of individuals into categories of caste and religion, and the introduction by the Raj of electorates divided along communal lines, also solidified exclusionary identities. Unlike in Europe, where city air was expected to loosen the stifling social bonds of traditional community and to create a society of free individuals, the cities organized by the Raj's policies reinforced contrary tendencies in Indian society. Hindus, Muslims, Sikhs, caste groups, paradoxically began to emerge as collective actors and to conflict with one another in the city itself, the putative arena of modernity.

The colonial imagination also rearranged urban interior spaces, driven by a desire to create a new public arena where behaviour could be regulated by administered rules. The city henceforth had its 'Instructions for Use', which were successfully communicated to – and championed by – the Indian elites and middle classes, in the face of wider Indian indifference. Men like Nirad Chaudhuri fully and perfectly understood that space within the modern colonial city was arrayed as carefully as the inside of a bungalow or an English garden. But to his daily despair in Delhi, his fellow countrymen failed abysmally in their comprehension:

One ineradicable habit all Indians have is to take a shortcut to their destination whatever the risk to themselves or others. One striking illustration of this habit was provided for me. There was a bus stop just outside Mori Gate, and not more than twenty yards from it was a public convenience. But the passengers never went so far. They urinated on a tree nearby, and the poor tree died at the end of six months. In northern India men are never able to resist a wall or a post.

3

Since the colonial city was both emphatically the site of India's subjection, the place where it was most regularly harassed by its rulers, and also an object of Indian craving, housing the promises of modernity, Indian nationalist attitudes towards it were ineradicably ambivalent. Nationalism was the politics of an urban educated elite that presumed itself entitled to negotiate with the British and speak on behalf of the country's villages. For the early nationalist generations, independence meant being free to emulate colonial city life, it promised the opportunity to take up addresses in the residential sanctuary of the civil lines, to create a world where public trees would flourish unabused. Gandhi disturbed this desire to emulate. He reversed priorities, and embraced the very values the colonial imagination rejected. Drawing upon romantic Western beliefs about the Indian village and the virtues of craft production, Gandhi vaunted the idea of the village as a counter to the colonial city. He composed his own pastorale, and used it both to disrupt the order and regularities of the colonial city and to ridicule the hollow mimicry of the Indian elites and middle classes. He brought the nationalist idea from the city to the villages, and through the long foot marches he took across the countryside, his *padyatras*, he constructed a new topography of India, defined not by the railway tracks that linked cities but by routes that connected villages. But Gandhi himself acted both in the city and in the villages: indeed, until his retreat to the ashram at Sewagram in the mid-1930s, his regular scene of action was the city. His audience was found here, and it was his incomparable ability to mobilize urban classes that explained his initial successes. He recognized the extent to which the British Raj was a creature of its cities, and knew how little they meant to the lives of most Indians. If the cities could be paralysed and brought to a standstill

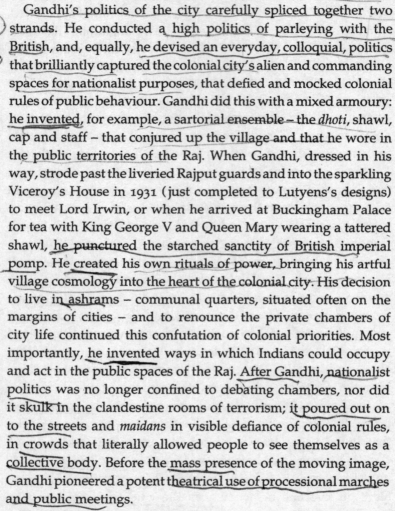

through non-violent *satyagraha*, the Raj itself would be broken.

Gandhi's politics of the city carefully spliced together two strands. He conducted a high politics of parleying with the British, and, equally, he devised an everyday, colloquial, politics that brilliantly captured the colonial city's alien and commanding spaces for nationalist purposes, that defied and mocked colonial rules of public behaviour. Gandhi did this with a mixed armoury: he invented, for example, a sartorial ensemble – the *dhoti*, shawl, cap and staff – that conjured up the village and that he wore in the public territories of the Raj. When Gandhi, dressed in his way, strode past the liveried Rajput guards and into the sparkling Viceroy's House in 1931 (just completed to Lutyens's designs) to meet Lord Irwin, or when he arrived at Buckingham Palace for tea with King George V and Queen Mary wearing a tattered shawl, he punctured the starched sanctity of British imperial pomp. He created his own rituals of power, bringing his artful village cosmology into the heart of the colonial city. His decision to live in ashrams – communal quarters, situated often on the margins of cities – and to renounce the private chambers of city life continued this confutation of colonial priorities. Most importantly, he invented ways in which Indians could occupy and act in the public spaces of the Raj. After Gandhi, nationalist politics was no longer confined to debating chambers, nor did it skulk in the clandestine rooms of terrorism; it poured out on to the streets and *maidans* in visible defiance of colonial rules, in crowds that literally allowed people to see themselves as a collective body. Before the mass presence of the moving image, Gandhi pioneered a potent theatrical use of processional marches and public meetings.

The public meeting was itself new to India's cities. Late in the nineteenth century the urban elites and middle classes began, in imitation of the British, to assemble in public for social and then political purposes. Such meetings – of condolence or congratulation, as well as of supplicant caste associations coveting favours from the British authorities – were held in safe colonial havens: the theatre, municipal hall or university auditorium. They carried no whiff of popular sedition. Men like Bal Gangadhar Tilak took politics on to the streets of Bombay in the early years of the twentieth century, but it was Gandhi – through his mammoth dawn prayer meetings – who radically redefined the public meeting for nationalist purposes. India's colonial cities had few places where crowds could assemble. There were wide streets, *maidans*, parks and monuments, racecourses and sports grounds; but the public square, that essential no man's land of popular gathering and protest in Western cities, had been avoided in the architectural design of colonial cities. Gandhi's mass public meetings became defiant nationalist inversions of the rules and gentilities of the colonial public meeting – they were announced by impertinent flyers urging Indians to attend the next 'Public Meeting and Bonfire of Foreign Clothes'. Mulk Raj Anand's novel of the mid-1930s, *Untouchable*, evokes the excitement of this nationalist desecration of the colonial city in its tumultuous closing scene: the cricket oval, emblem of imperial civilization, becomes a meeting place for a vast crowd, a microcosmic India – 'Men, women and children of all races, colours, castes and creeds, were running towards the oval . . . to meet the Mahatma, to pay homage to Mohandas Karam Chand Gandhi.'

It was obvious to Gandhi that colonialism had to be defeated in its modern fortress, the city, but the point of this victory was not simply to move into the citadels of the departed British. Freedom for Indians meant the freedom to reject the city and to recoup India's enfeebled civilizational powers in the sanctuary of its villages. But, in contrast to the Gandhian insistence that 'the blood of the villages is the cement by which the edifice of the cities is built', other nationalists saw different meanings in the simple opposition between village and city. Ambedkar, for instance, mocked what in his view was the oppressive Gandhian fantasy of a free India based on the camaraderie of the ancient

See Tolstoy's mix

village: 'The love of the intellectual Indians for the village community is of course infinite if not pathetic ... What is the village but a sink of localism, a den of ignorance, narrow-mindedness and communalism?'

Nehru, though marginally less scathing about the village, was equally unambiguous in his commitment to the city. This attachment was not based on a desire to ape the colonial conception: he wrote bitterly of the division of the Indian city between the neglected 'densely crowded city proper' and the placid civil lines inhabited by the English and upper-middle-class Indians, on which no expense was spared because 'nearly all the Big Noises and Little Noises live in the Civil Lines'. And he spoke freely of his dislike for the 'official ridden city of New Delhi' and its spiritless, colossal display of colonial modernity: 'the Governmental structures of Delhi are not all very beautiful to look at, although some of them are obviously meant to impress'. Nor did Nehru intend, in choosing the city, a rejection of India's past. He was drawn, aesthetically and sentimentally, to the old, to Old Delhi rather than New Delhi: 'There is the spirit and the genius of an ancient city, where almost every stone tells you a story, where history is embedded even in the dirty lanes ... it has a definite and positive atmosphere which you can feel in your bones.' Nehru's appreciation of the city came from his understanding of modernity, and from a distinction he drew between inauthentic modernity, represented by the colonial city, and a genuine, productive and universal modernity, which India should not reject. The city was the indispensable hub of a modernizing process that would spread beyond its enclaves and through the whole society.

By the time the British were packing their trunks to leave India, the emulative will of the Indian middle classes had, despite Gandhi's strictures, made the colonial centres very passable editions of modern cities. The Indian elites had carved out their own spaces of recreation and leisure – parks, cricket grounds, clubs – the streets were reasonably clean, coffee-houses and restaurants served English menus. The lower and poorer orders were ghostly presences – they came in at dawn, did their jobs, and melted away into the obscurity of their shacks beyond the middle-class colonies. 'Illegal' hawkers and vendors were regularly and successfully cleared from the streets by officers of municipalities that were often already in the hands of nationalist politicians – a result of the Raj's economizing preference for indirect rule.

Partition introduced the first serious strains into this urban world. It imported a new threat into the public spaces of the modern city. In the past, religious conflict had been restricted to the 'old' parts of the city: now it stalked through every street. And it brought with unparalleled speed large numbers of uprooted people into the cities. In a society where there was very little spatial mobility (in 1931 less than 4 per cent of the Indian population lived outside the state or province of their birth), Partition unleashed the largest transfer of population in human history. Within a very few months, around 15 million people crossed the new borders (in 1951 7.3 million refugees were registered in India, and in 1952 the Pakistan census counted 7.2 million *muhajirs* or refugees), and more than half of the refugees from Pakistan to India settled in urban areas: between 1941 and 1951 the population of India's cities, swollen also by the war and the effects of famine, grew by over 40 per cent. Delhi became a Punjabi city; Calcutta had to absorb hundreds of thousands of refugees from East Bengal; Bombay's Muslim elite was decimated. The problems of resettlement, economic provision and public order posed severe difficulties for both the state and the cities. Refugees were housed in temporary encampments that became permanent, ramshackle colonies. The poorest haplessly took up whatever empty space they could find: along roads or railway lines, on vacant land and in parks. One definitive trait of the future history of India's cities was established: a steady, irresistible flow of political and economic refugees, settling wherever they could, necessarily oblivious to the niceties of the intentions behind pavements, parks or traffic roundabouts.

This was the immediate background to the building of Chandigarh. The need for a new capital for the province of Punjab (the old capital, Lahore, had been awarded to Pakistan) presented an opportunity that matched Nehru's intention to have India break away from the existing cities – stamped by colonialism, soiled by Partition, and in the grip of often corrupt municipalities. Nehru was in search of a way to renew the city, to use it to display an Indian modernity distinct from and free of the colonial version. Like his British predecessors, he was attracted by the possibility of starting again, of constructing on an empty field a generous architectural proposition of the new India. The result was a monumental city, condemned to revolve in an external orbit around the life of its people in Punjab: a glorious stage-set where tableaux of state might be enacted but lacking everyday politics. Chandigarh was a city of politicians, bureaucrats and administrators. Built after the waves of post-Partition migration, it was spared inundation by the poorest and most abject. It became a terminus for the more prosperous: retired civil servants and servicemen, professionals, and a large class of their servitors. But Chandigarh lacked any of the productive capacities of modernity. Le Corbusier, its architect, was insistent that it must be solely a seat of government, not of industry and manufacture: 'one must not mix the two', he stipulated in his eccentric and imperious manual, 'For the Establishment of an Immediate Statute of the Land'. This supremely conceptual city could not generate any shared understanding of its meanings among its inhabitants. There are many middle-class residents who will tell you slightly different, misremembered stories about the city's principles, why it is the way it is; but if you ask the young men who live in the slums about the Rose Garden or about Leisure Valley, they may have only heard of these places and can tell

you little more. For Chandigarh too now has its slums, which
are electorally important – the city's real politics occurs in them,
especially in the populous slum villages that surround it.

If New Delhi belongs in an imperial portfolio of Durbars and
Imperial Progresses, Chandigarh belongs in a nationalist album,
with the Constitution and the five-year plans. Building it was
one of the foundational gestures through which India oriented
and located itself in the modern world: it exemplified at its purest
one impulse in the nationalist imagination of the city. Although
a provincial capital, Chandigarh from its inception had the status
of a national project – Nehru took a personal interest in it, and
it was generously funded by the national government. The site
was desolate but spectacular: 400 kilometres north of New Delhi,
on a plain that sloped slowly, beneath wide blue skies, towards
the Himalayan foothills. 'The site chosen,' Nehru explained, 'is
free from existing encumbrances of old towns', which would
make the new city 'symbolic of the freedom of India, unfettered
by traditions of the past . . . an expression of the nation's faith
in the future'. But Chandigarh was also, and ultimately most
decisively, the fantasy of its architect. Twice in the twentieth
century India has been visited by architectural megalomaniacs:
Le Corbusier began work on Chandigarh barely twenty years
after imperial New Delhi had been completed to Lutyens's plans.
When two Indian civil servants arrived at his Paris apartment
in the winter of 1950 and invited him to design the proposed
city, he was privately ecstatic. 'It is,' he noted in his diary, 'the
hour that I have been waiting for – India, that humane and
profound civilization', which hadn't 'yet created an architecture
for modern civilization' had now turned to him.

In his design, Le Corbusier remained blithely unencumbered
by any understanding of the world he was building for. His role
was that of the prophetic artist, and he played it to perfection.
The initial plan was outlined after a bare glimpse of the site, a
few days after his arrival in India and with Lutyens's redstone

megaliths lodged in his mind (he had come via New Delhi). Maxwell Fry, a collaborator on the project, remembered the moment: 'Corbusier held the crayon in his hand and was in his element. *"Voila la gare,"* he said, *"et voici la rue commerciale"*, and he drew the first road on the new plan of Chandigarh. *"Voici la tete,"* he went on . . . *"Et voila l'estomac, le cite-centre"*.' Devoted to authority, Corbusier saw himself as a modern-day Colbert, and in Nehru he believed he had found his very own Sun King. Whenever he stumbled across some local obstacle to his ideas, the regular refrain in Corbusier's notebooks was a simple injunction: 'Write to Nehru'. Engaged in what he saw as a pharaonic project (working in India seemed to teach him 'the advantages of slavery in high and noble works of architecture'), he preened himself for the role: 'Be implacable, whole, haughty, in charge. Make demands.'

Le Corbusier was, to be sure, an odd choice as democratic India's first architect. But the sheer audacity of his conception, and of Nehru's commitment to it, is revealing. The design of Chandigarh expressed one aspect of Nehru's idea of a modern India: the sense that India must free itself of both the contradictory modernity of the Raj and nostalgia for its indigenous past. It had to move forward by one decisive act that broke both with its ancient and its more recent history. The rationalist, modernist strain in Nehru's thinking here obliterated the attachment to the heritage of an Indianness rooted in the past. Chandigarh boldly divested itself of history, rejecting both colonial imagery and nationalist sentimentalism or ornament. The literal, utilitarian names of its axial avenues (Madhya Marg, Uttar Marg – Central Avenue, North Avenue) recount no nationalist history (no ubiquitous MG Road here). It has no nationalist monuments, because Le Corbusier specifically banned them. The city's radical meaning lay in its cultural unfamiliarity, its proposal of the new. It refused to concede anything to its location, and acted as a kind of shock to India's built environment. In celebrating a wholly alien form, style and material, it aspired to a neutrality, a zero-degree condition that would make it equally resistant to the claims upon it of any and all cultural or religious groups. Just as the English language placed all Indians, at least in principle, at a disadvantage of equal unfamiliarity, so, too Chandigarh could not be seized and possessed by any one group. Even those familiar with colonial architectural idioms, the bungalow and compound, could not immediately usurp this brave new reinforced concrete world.

Chandigarh cheerfully ignored a topic that had troubled both nationalists and some of the British: the idea of an Indian 'national style', endlessly debated in the early decades of the twentieth century by men like E. B. Havell, Ananda Coomaraswamy and the Tagores, Rabindranath and his cousin Abanindranath. Chandigarh's evasion of historical tradition generated its own stories, that struggled to give the place cultural resonance. Hence the forced claims of architects and architectural historians that its design had originated in the figure of the primeval man (*Purusha*), or was based on the principles of the *Vastushastra*, the ancient Indian science of architectural construction; or that its buildings refer to the Dewan-e-Khas at Fatehpur Sikri, or to Hindu temple complexes. These attempts to make it recognizable, to locate it in India, all miss the point. Chandigarh's deliberate renunciation of a national style was itself a gesture of acknowledgement that political authority in India now had to face outwards too, that its sovereignty had to be internationally recognizable: its purpose was to place India in the world. In contrast to New Delhi and colonial architecture, built to force effects upon Indians, Chandigarh was intended to produce an international impact. Like that original monument to modern republican power, Washington DC, Chandigarh chose to speak a certain nationalist poetry in the best cosmopolitan accent it knew.

Yet if Chandigarh echoed anything on the Indian landscape, it was New Delhi. It reproduced the same fetishism of the capitol.

The capitol complex, conceived of as the 'head' of the city, was placed at the highest, northern end of an irritatingly even plain, striving like Lutyens's acropolis for maximum elevation. For Le Corbusier, the capitol had to be defended from the rest of the city: 'Hide all construction of the city', he instructed. He referred to the buildings to the south, where the city stretched, as 'l'ennemi', to be screened off by bunker-like mounds. Today, these serve literally as military fortifications, patrolled by armed guards who defend the embattled symbols of the state in Punjab. The capitol was intended to be a composite of four related buildings, arrayed around a central square: Secretariat, Legislative Assembly, High Court and the Governor's Palace. The latter was Corbusier's response to Lutyens's Viceroy's House, and although it was more restrained, Nehru thought it too delusively grand for a mere provincial officer of a democratic state and it was never built. The immense square plaza, intended as a public space, survives today as a desolate concrete pavement where no one passes, let alone associates.

Its disposition of residential space also mimicked New Delhi's pomposity. The residential area was divided into thirty neighbourhood blocks, or 'sectors', all organized in a repeating pattern. But the egalitarian air was illusory, since the sectors were graded by the strict ranks of administrative hierarchy. The exclusive low-numbered northern sectors, inhabited by bureaucrats and politicians, ranked above the middle-class southern sectors; the high-numbered sectors housed the lowest in the hierarchy. Each sector was internally differentiated: houses were identified by plot number, and the lower the number, the larger the plot; those in the thousands were smallest. Every Chandigarh address thus encoded fairly precise information about its owner's standing in the bureaucratic and economic hierarchy.

Chandigarh never achieved the cosmopolitanism it craved. Instead of ruling, enlightening and modernizing its society, this city of the future became a museum piece in need of protection from its own violently quarrelling citizens and the ravages of the climate. Its vacant, eerily ordered centre was ignored by the teeming and disorganized expansion of the industrial townships of Panchkula and SAS Nagar (which fall within the boundaries of the city, and whose smoky presence no doubt spins Charles Edouard Jeanneret in his grave), whose economic dynamism helped to make it one of India's fastest growing urban regions during the 1960s and 1970s. In that sense, it could claim a certain success. But Chandigarh failed to produce a society of secular individuals or a modernist politics: drawn into the vortex of Punjab's politics, it was turned into a cipher in a battle of communal identities.

4

'It hits you on the head, and makes you think. You may squirm at the impact but it has made you think and imbibe new ideas, and the one thing which India requires is being hit on the head so that it may think . . . Therefore Chandigarh is of enormous importance.' So Nehru explained Le Corbusier's modernist hammer to his compatriots, trying also to reassure himself. Chandigarh spawned further provincial 'concept' capitals: Otto Koenigsberger's Bhubaneshwar, Bhopal and Gandhinagar – the one that most aspired to Chandigarh's image, a cruel concrete homage to Gandhi, which displaced Ahmedabad as the new capital of Gujarat. These new cities were left to the mercies of chief town planners and their engineers at the local branches of the Public Works Department, or PWD as it came to be universally known in India: instituted in the mid nineteenth century and one of the most enduring and ubiquitous legacies of the Raj to Indian public life, with a unique styleless style of its own.

Nehru also animated the construction of industrial cities, steel towns like Bhilai ('a city designed by a pencil stub and a six-inch plastic ruler. It was all parallel lines,' recalled one writer who grew up there), Rourkela and Durgapur, pure utilitarian grids laid out in bleak locations, industrial cantonments that managed to rise to a certain novel provincial cosmopolitanism. They brought together engineers, doctors, technicians from all over India, aching with dietary frustrations, and each invariably had a colony of Soviet, German or British experts, sweatily cursing their exile.

But Nehru was no Ataturk of modernism. If one impulse in Nehru's idea of the city aspired to break abruptly with the past, another was to treasure historical continuity, the layering of cultures, and the mixture and complexity that that nurtured. No colonial Indian city exemplified this mixture with finer sophistication than Bombay. It was also, unlike so many other colonial centres, a city of real productive and commercial wealth, historically the great powerhouse of Indian economic modernization.

Bombay in the years after 1947 was an exception within India as a whole, an island unto itself. It was free from the heavy lumber of government bureaucracy, untroubled by the economic ideas radiating out of New Delhi, devoted to amassing money and to burning it up in extravagant neon signs. It had long been much more than a mere colonial entrepot and, in contrast to Calcutta, boasted a class of native industrial capitalists. Partition shook Bombay's settled cosmopolitanism. The departure to Pakistan of men like Jinnah weakened the Muslim presence; it marked the beginning of the decline of the Parsi community – champions of Indian public life – and it brought tens of thousands of refugees into the city. But Bombay continued to be India's commercial and cultural capital, and soon became permanently lodged in the popular imagination as a totem of modern India itself.

What put it there was cinema. Most Indians had some visual image of it: its cavernous tropical Gothic railway station, Victoria Terminus; the seductions and brutalities of its criminal underworld, its pavements, its skyscrapers, the unforgettable sweep of the Necklace, Marine Drive. In the Hindi cinema of the 1950s, Bombay stood for a certain idea of India. A generation of actors like Raj Kapoor and Guru Dutt, and radical scriptwriters like K. A. Abbas, staged and sang a nationalist vision of India that was recognizably Nehru's own. In films such as *Awaara*, *Shri 420* and *CID*, the city was portrayed as at once a place of bewilderment and exploitation, and an enticing and necessary destination brimming with opportunities. They conveyed its brashness and its impersonality, but also its emancipatory anonymity and the kindness of strangers it fostered. The stories were usually told through the eyes and sensibility of a Chaplin-esque 'common man', a vagabond or tramp happily endowed with an educated lower-middle-class sensibility, who struggled against the authority of tradition and the corruption of wealth, picking his way through Bombay's traps and bewitchments. Such films dramatized in a diffuse but evocative way a democratic, outward-looking and secular nationalist sentiment, and affirmed the city as the most likely place to cultivate this.

But Bombay's own history since the 1950s has belied this picture – for this most modern, prosperous and cosmopolitan of India's cities developed a different politics, an inflammatory parochialism in conflict with the nationalist ideal. Its political itinerary has traced the contradictions in India's economic development – which has delivered fabulous wealth to a very few, and has beggared most. Bombay's politics has been woven out of such contradictions, in a society enlivened by democratic sentiment.

Bombay's wealth flowed both from commerce and from its being the earliest industrial centre in India. Its capitalists in the decades before 1947 tried to shape the choices of Congress nationalism and after 1947 maintained close – if, during the era of planning, somewhat tense and ambivalent – relations with the state. With the decline of planning and its conversion in Indira Gandhi's hands into an instrument of selective allocation and pacification based on a regime of economic controls and licences, industrialists and politicians drew even closer together, their relationship based on buying and selling industrial licences. Bombay's industrialists (and film stars) became an essential source of political funds for governments and parties in New Delhi, and from the 1970s contacts between them and New Delhi's political jobbers flourished. Bombay's reputation as a city of industrial free enterprise and competition is shot through with irony. In fact, most of the industrial wealth amassed there in recent decades has benefited from monopoly licences purchased in return for electoral finance and housekeeping money for the high politics of New Delhi, while the city's industry itself has become increasingly inefficient, a perverse monopoly capitalism sheltered from international and domestic competition. The old heart of Bombay's organized industry, textiles, declined steeply in the late 1970s, and the balance of employment shifted towards the uncertainties of the service economy, to the formal world of finance and banking and to informal jobs in the workshops and homes of the city's slums.

Bombay's different types of wealth have colonized different parts of the city. The enclaves of the rich – the old commercial and industrial money set amidst the gardens of Malabar Hill, the opulence of the film world emblazoned on Pali Hill, and the newer professional wealth stacked up in the ugly towers of Cuffe Parade – where all the amenities are concentrated – are set apart from the *chawls* and slums. But Bombay's congestion makes it impossible for the rich to flee the poor, and the contrasts of lifestyle are vividly adjacent (the population density in the city, at around 17,000 people per square kilometre, is about fourteen times higher than that of London), though the congestion is unequally distributed. Far away from the spacious lawns and tea ceremonies of the Willingdon Club and the Bombay Gymkhana – secured on ninety-nine-year leases at one rupee a year – more than half of Bombay's population, between five and six million

138

people, live in slums squeezed into around 8 per cent of the land area. The residents of the slums are workers and the educated lower middle class, not the very poorest, some 700,000 of whom exist as they can on the pavements, in segments of sewage pipes and under flyovers. The slums have received little from the Indian state in the way of even basic facilities, and budget allocations for urban development have always been minute.

The result is a city that blisters with the aspirations, disappointments and anger of the poor and the lower middle classes. Condemned to desperate conditions, they have had to put up with governments and politicians who chatter in the language of equality while acting and conniving in quite opposite ways. In Nehru's picture of Indian politics, democracy would in time enable the disadvantaged to pursue their own interests. Social conflict would centre around a struggle between rich and poor, as the poor came to organize for themselves and press for better terms. Yet this anticipated democratic struggle against poverty and inequality has no more emerged in India's modern cities than in its villages. The poor are now acting in politics as never before. They have understood that elections can be used to chastise and deliver small advantages: an electricity connection, a water tap, an access road. But even in the cities, where traditional bonds of community have loosened, a society of individuals banding together to pursue their several purposes through interest-based associations – the Edenic image of the liberal West – has not emerged. Urban economic inequalities and social diversities have given rise to politically devised communities of religion and caste. These proudly particularistic groups rarely ask the state to accord universal rights and provisions for better treatment for all; instead, they insist on privileges and protections to be given exclusively to their own community, while others are neglected.

Bombay's politics is a product of such twists in India's democratic politics. The frustrations of the poorer groups have not produced durable horizontal solidarities of class, which both economic processes and the organization of political competition have conspired against. The wide register of productive technologies deployed in India's efforts to industrialize, the local economies of labour and reward, and the ties of neighbourhood and residence in a city like Bombay – all have fragmented and differentiated the working poor and have made it very difficult for them to sustain class associations. Nor have strong class ties evolved through consumption patterns. At the upper end of the social scale, a pan-Indian urban elite is able to glide sveltly through any hotel lobby in the land, but the consumption habits of the urban poor do not allow for a nationwide pattern to emerge. People living in a *chawl*, or slum, might club together to buy a television and install a satellite or cable television connection; but this is hardly a sign of secure affluence, contrary to the view from Malabar Hill or Cuffe Parade ('See, how well these servants are doing these days!'). All it represents is the assertion of an equal right to consume images.

Bombay has had its periods of active trade union and labour politics, but the possibilities of interest-based solidarities have been further vitiated by the populist turn in democratic politics engineered by Congress. Whenever hints of such organization arose – as occurred, for example, in the late 1960s, when communist influence increased in the labour unions and in city politics – local Congress politicians swiftly snuffed them out. Provincial Congressmen gave the party an iron grip over the politics of Bombay and Maharashtra by systematically invoking caste and Maratha identity – based on the rural connections of workers – to mobilize the poor and lower middle classes along vertical links of clientage, which secured electoral victories in the high politics of provincial assemblies and national parliaments. But this high politics, limited for most people to the sporadic experience of elections, was indifferent to the daily concerns of poorer groups. They were increasingly restive, undeferential, and unwilling to remain excluded from the politics of the capital city and from some share in the wealth so ostentatiously displayed around them.

The rise in Bombay of a movement like the Shiv Sena should therefore hardly occasion surprise: it expresses a deep potential within modern Indian politics, and employs all its existing idioms. The Shiv Sena, the 'army of Shivaji', took its name from a seventeenth-century Maratha warlord who fought successfully against the Mughals. It was founded in the mid-1960s as an anti-immigrant party, dedicated to protecting employment and educational opportunities for Bombay's Marathi-speakers: about 40 per cent of the population, generally in lower-level jobs. It has learned from the nationalism of high-caste Hindus, from the populism of Congress, from communist and Hindu extremist organizational methods, from the cinema and popular press, and above all from the streets. It too wishes to make the city afresh, and it has internalized the nationalist faith in the magic of names so deeply that it has renamed not merely the parks and streets, but the entire city, Mumbai. The Shiv Sena's initial successes derived from an ability to develop a quotidian politics with local goals, the achievement of which gave its supporters a direct sense of efficacy, but it also mastered the skills of high electoral politics. Its early targets were Tamils from the south – 'all the lungiwallas' who, it asserted, were 'criminals, gamblers, illicit liquor dealers, pimps, goondas, and Communists'. Its real animus, though, was neither moral nor cultural, but, rather, a resentful belief that southern migrants to Bombay, privileged by their command of the English language, had monopolized the better-paid clerical and lower-management jobs. But the objects of its enmity have proved changeable. To build electoral majorities from the heterogeneous material of the poor and the lower middle classes, the Shiv Sena gravitated to a basic line of religious difference, and in the 1980s turned against Bombay's Muslims, who account for 15 per cent of the city's population. It translated into local urban political terms the polemics that were entering the national arena, and it climbed on the back of Hindu nationalist politics by striking an alliance with the BJP in 1984. This parasitic relation to national politics and the central state is characteristic of the regional imagination it represents: it does not threaten the national state but depends upon it.

The regular energies of the Shiv Sena, however, went into routines of mundane politics and it made little pretence to connect to the distant narcissism of New Delhi. It exploited the democratic sentiment released by Mrs Gandhi's electoral strategies, broke open the corrupt corridors of local politics, and encouraged entry by the lower middle classes and the poor. During an era when the organizational structure of Congress was collapsing, the Shiv Sena drew its strength from an extensive network of 'informal' politics, typical of cities like Bombay: it established *shakhas*, or local branches, youth clubs, and *mitra mandals*, or 'friendship associations', male fraternities supposedly inspired by the idea of individuals associating voluntarily on the basis of shared interests. These last were captured by the Shiv Sena and used to propagate an anti-individualist, communitarian language, and a bowdlerized Marathi culture among the young, for the Shiv Sena celebrates youth and action: the party is famed for processions led by posses of young men with attitude on motorcycles. Connections with Bombay's street culture are intimate, and the Sena relies on neighbourhood 'dadas', local toughs and bullies recruited from the slums who use controlled violence. This 'goonda' politics gives its practitioners a sense of everyday efficacy and has made the Shiv Sena familiar to residents of Bombay's slums. But its relations are fraught, since these people are a fluid mixture of communities that threaten ideas of the city's beauty and purity, and the Sena has regularly led 'beautification schemes' intended to demolish the slums. But it has also successfully drafted slum-dwellers to demonstrate in the heart of Bombay, capturing places like Flora Fountain for a heady day –

moments of self-assertion when the poor can gain possession of otherwise alien and exclusive territory.

The Shiv Sena has built its reputation on its provision of real cultural, medical and educational services to Bombay's poor and lower middle classes. But it should not be confused with the Salvation Army. Its services and rewards are distributed with fierce selectivity, and presume the permanent exclusion of segments of the city's residents. Determined to win support by polarizing Bombay's citizens into majority and minority communities, the Sena has perfected techniques of brutal violence: throughout the 1980s it instigated riots in the outskirts of Bombay and in other Maharashtrian cities, always targeted precisely at Muslims and their property. Violence is an essential technique, and it displayed mastery of the riot most explicitly in December 1992 and January 1993, when it carefully orchestrated riots directly after, and related to, the destruction of the Babri Masjid in Ayodhya by Hindu militants aspiring to construct a Ram temple in its place. During the January riots, for instance, Shiv Sena members and activists circulated through Bombay – in another bitter irony of Indian democracy – with electoral registers, that enabled them to identify Muslim households to attack: a pogrom that imitated the actions of Congress Party members in New Delhi during the anti-Sikh violence of 1984. As in Delhi in 1984, so in Bombay in 1993, retraction of police protection for the victims revealed the extent to which this arm of the Indian state had been communalized. w/ police complicity

After independence, Bombay had embodied most richly India's nationalist expectations of the city. Bombay, it was hoped, would fulfil the potentials immanent in – but also distorted by – the colonial city. Freedom would bring rational economic development, a democratic politics of interests, an egalitarian urban form, and a cosmopolitan culture of individuals. 'In Bombay all Indias met and merged. In Bombay, too, all-India met what-was-not-India . . . what was beautiful in Bombay was that it belonged to nobody and to all' – that old nationalist dream of Bombay, and the sense of its end, suffuses Salman Rushdie's lament for the city. That vision has been surpassed by the history that the nationalist ideal itself set in motion, but the challenge to it is not a simple contrary one that rejects the city in favour of some other ideal: for example, the village. The political imagination of a movement like the Shiv Sena shares with the nationalist one the ambition to have a modern, rational, clean and functional city. But it differs entirely in its idea of the India in which such a city can exist. Its provincial, partial idea of India does not envisage a fragmentation or disruption of India's political unity, it does not demand substantially greater autonomy from the centre, and it is committed to the idea of a strong state. Nor does it challenge India's democratic nature: on the contrary, it thrives on the spread of democratic sentiment throughout Indian society. The difference lies in its conception of the cultural substance and units that constitute India. The Shiv Sena visualizes India not as a land of cosmopolitan miscegenation, but as a hierarchical grid that contains internally homogenous communities, each insulated from the others. This idea seeks to efface Bombay's cosmopolitanism, to annex its modernity and distribute the benefits of it to one, closed community.

5

By the 1990s the Indian city had entered a new, post-nationalist stage. The established cities had deviated from what had been anticipated of them. Their economic inequalities and their political opportunities had sharpened contradictions, and had produced more partial, if more intensely held, conceptions of what a political community was. The old contrasts between the city and the village, or the colonial city and the nationalist city, had ceased to hold. The city in India was being reinvented once again, in contrasting models. An aggressive small-town India was surging across parts of the country, impelled by rural economic surpluses: this new urban type, in limbo between city and village, proudly proclaimed its vernacular cultural and political tastes. Simultaneously, the entry into India of new forms of economic capital, owned by transnational corporations, was driving forward a new professional upper class, mobile, ambitious, and in search – as its colonial and nationalist predecessors had been – of unsullied ground on which to set its imprint.

Since the 1960s parts of rural India had experienced considerable economic development and had accumulated surpluses. The sources for this new affluence varied: the 'Green Revolution' in agricultural productivity in the north, a 'White Revolution' in dairy farming in the western regions, and in the south remittances from emigrants working in the Gulf states. Money was invested in small industries, and in properties in provincial cities and small towns. In the north, some of the fastest growing areas in the 1980s and 1990s were provincial cities like Faridabad, Ghaziabad, Ludhiana, Meerut, Muzzafarnagar – built-up sprawls stretching along the national highways deep into the countryside, blurring distinctions between village and city. India has more than 200 cities with a population of over 100,000, and these are the homelands of India's 'new middle classes', who no longer gaze enviously at the distant metropolitan cities, whose horizons are not shaped by ideas of Bombay or New Delhi – cities that, if anything, they resent and disparage. This is the India of ZEE TV and cable television, more rawly and frankly consumerist than the nationalized Doordarshan, which transmit an arresting linguistic hybrid of Hindi and English. Most big-city opportunities for consumption are available in these new towns: Maruti car salesrooms, hotels and fast-food restaurants, shops selling Reeboks and Proline, Titan watches and Videocon electronics. But surfaced roads, pavements, streetlights, parks – all those essential tokens of modernity that excited the colonial and nationalist imaginations – are barely to be seen here. The streets are nameless, absolving those who pass along them of even a gestural historical memory. The conceptual sense of a 'city' is weak. There are few civic amenities, no urban form, no effective police authorities. And their scale – smaller than the metropolis, with its potential to generate anonymity and impersonal relations between strangers – has fostered new and distinct kinds of social relations, neither modern nor traditional. Ties of kin and caste remain strong, but operate here on a more expansive terrain than in the village, and have acquired a thinner, more instrumental form.

The sensibilities of these provincial towns have begun to impose themselves upon India's national politics. These towns are electorally important, and they have become sites of sharp contest as parties try to establish majorities. The absence of any neutral arm of the state to police and to provide protection, especially in regions such as Uttar Pradesh and Bihar, has left this essential responsibility to the discretion of politicians and men who command armed gangs, which gives these towns a culture of violence. The conflicts have taken one of two forms: on the one hand, upwardly mobile intermediate castes, successful middle peasants, and 'bullock capitalists' who maintain properties in and strong connections with their villages, have made these cities the heartlands of a vigorous caste politics, encouraged by the partial implementation of the Mandal Commission's proposals on reservations; on the other hand, they have also become recruiting grounds for the BJP's Hindu nationalists. The BJP's brand of televisual religion is attuned to the desires of these cities' inhabitants, and the mobilization of their votes has become an essential element in the party's strategy. L. K. Advani's *rathyatra* of 1990, for example, a chariot procession that covered more than 10,000 kilometres, took in dozens of such cities. As the *rath*, a tinsel chariot erected on a Nissan jeep, rolled across the plains from town to town – sparking off violence and riots wherever it went – signs were put up declaring that these towns had been 'captured' and were now part of a 'Hindu state'. In a reversal of the Gandhian idea of a *padyatra* linking the villages, Advani's *rathyatra* hoped to spread a sense of Hindu unity across the country by connecting the new towns.

In contrast to the garbled modernity of these northern towns, a quite different trend is represented by the aspiring esperanto of Bangalore. The capital of the southern state of Karnataka and the most anglicized city in India, Bangalore was established as a British cantonment early in the nineteenth century. During the colonial period, Bangalore fell within the princely state of Mysore, and was not given to bursts of nationalist enthusiasm: there was no wholesale repainting of street signs after independence, and Queen's Road, Kensington Road, St Marks's Road, Brigade Road, Cubbon Park, all are still there. It has long been solidly middle class, and the colonial layout has kept its shape well. Bangalore has its slums, but they are fewer and less evident than in other Indian cities. The city is, however, sharply divided between the northern cantonment areas, primarily Tamil, and the poorer Kannadiga areas in the south of the city. Its climate, parks and greenery made it a retirement destination for civil servants and military officers; and in addition to its physical attractions, its educational and scientific resources made Bangalore a choice site, in the 1950s, for several large state-owned defence and communication industries. It became an established centre of scientific research and developed a wide technological base. Since the 1970s it has experienced rapid growth, and a new Indian middle and upper class has emerged. This is based not on the traditional sources of wealth in independent India – control of land, bureaucratic office or industry – but on professional and technical skills. Unable to break into the exorbitantly priced property markets of a city like Bombay, this highly internationalized and entrepreneurial class – many with qualifications from America, not from the old elite educational metropolis of

147

Britain – has adopted Bangalore as the strongest alternative incarnation of Indian modernity.

This new class has been sustained and given substantial economic power by the arrival in India, especially after the liberalization begun in 1991, of foreign capital and multinationals: Hewlett-Packard, Asea Brown Boveri, Agfa and IBM have all been attracted to Bangalore as a source of cheap skills. These companies have transformed the wage structure of the Indian professional world. They are able to offer Indians in their late twenties salaries not reached even at the retirement points of Indian public enterprise salary scales. Bangalore is the gateway for this new international private capital, which until the 1990s played a minute role in India's insulated economy. There is nothing in India that could withstand the economic power of these corporations which are potentially irresistible. But the Indian social classes that depend upon them are simultaneously very vulnerable and without any economic allies: indeed, to bureaucrats, businessmen and industrialists, these professional classes are galling parvenus. Their internationally franchised tastes make them ready targets for moralizing politicians and cultural nationalists. For their part, the horizons of this new class are certainly not constrained by the territorial frame of the nation state. They pride themselves on their international mobility, and are quite prepared to forsake the shopping malls of Bangalore – Big Kidskemp, Fifth Avenue, Barton Centre, all still with a somewhat ersatz air about them – for the real thing in Singapore (or wherever) should the opportunity arise. Bangalore has become the capital of Non-Resident India: like the Indian politicians, industrialists and film stars who choose to use the banking facilities of Vaduz and Zurich, this new class too has a secessionist understanding of the idea of India.

Bombay and Bangalore: each is an avatar of the contrary potentialities of India's modernity, each manifests an exhaustion of the nationalist imagination. They have spawned ideas of India

provincial nationalists v. cosmopolitan

at sharp variance with Nehru's one. To an adherent of the Shiv Sena in Bombay, defining oneself as Maharashtrian, or Hindu, seems to deliver more direct benefits: Indianness has become an instrumental choice, a less advantageous identity. Likewise, to the young MBA or software expert in Bangalore, India is merely one stopping place in a global employment market.

India's cities are hinges between its vast population spread across the countryside and the hectic tides of the global economy, with its ruthlessly shifting tastes and its ceaseless murmur of the pleasures and hazards of modernity. How this three-cornered relationship develops over the next decades will decisively mould India's future economic, cultural and political possibilities. The demographic drift across the world is unstoppably towards the urban: more than half the global population will soon live in its cities. Yet India, in this as in so much else, will remain something of an exception: despite the vast absolute numbers that continue to cram its cities, most will still make their lives on the land. The contradiction runs deep. Will India's cities, bolstered by – but also subject to – the dynamism of global capital, come to direct the country's economy, to manipulate opportunities in their favour, and make the culture in their own image? Or will the countryside be able to turn to its advantage the democratic power of its numbers, enter the state that resides in the metropolis, and bend it to its own purposes and hopes? How much longer can India's cities remain a modern veneer, by turns glittering and blistered, to the contradictory life of its society?

FOUR

Who is an Indian?

Four hundred million separate individual men and women, each differing from the other, each living in a private universe of thought and feeling.

NEHRU, 1946

Unity cannot be brought about by enacting a law that all shall be one.

TAGORE, 1902

1

Towards the end of 1989 the attention of many Indians was focused upon a collection of 167,000 bricks piled up in the northern pilgrimage town of Ayodhya. These were not ordinary bricks. They were *Ram shilas*, 'Ram's bricks', collected from places across the country and outside India. Each was inscribed with its place of origin, and among the most proudly displayed were those dispatched by emigrant communities in the United States, Canada, South Africa and the Caribbean. The bricks had travelled to Ayodhya, in the state of Uttar Pradesh, in ceremonial and often violent processions organized by the 'Sangh Parivar' – a cluster of militant Hindu organizations associated with the BJP. They were to be used, it was claimed, to construct a gigantic temple to mark the cartographically certain spot where Ram, a god central to the worship of many Hindus, was believed to have been born, and where a mosque – the Babri Masjid – had stood since the sixteenth century. The foundation stone of this

150

temple, which Hindu leaders saw as part of the transformation of sleepy Ayodhya into a 'Hindu Vatican', was to be laid at a *shilanyas*, or foundation ceremony. In a bizarre choreography of the singular rituals of Hindu worship, it was announced that at 1.35 p.m. on that day all Hindus, everywhere, should face Ayodhya and make an offering.

But the *shilanyas* was not about worship. It was a political performance oblivious to the rhythms of the sacred calendar and timed to coincide with the electoral one. For the BJP, dedicated to what it called 'Indianization' – its manifestos saw this as the forging of 'one nation, one people, one culture' – it was a further step in a long campaign for electoral success, which by the end of the 1980s had hauled the party to the threshold of political power. The project of Indianization drew upon an historical imagination at odds with the definition of Indianness the nationalist elite had aspired to install after 1947. To Hindu nationalists, Ayodhya telescoped into a single narrative otherwise quite unrelated events: the birth of Ram 'nine lakh [900,000] years ago', the entry of the Mughals into India in 1526, and – to a rather different cue – the rise of the BJP as the chosen party to right immemorial wrongs and put modern India in direct touch with its glorious past. As the subsequent destruction of the Babri Masjid in 1992 by *kar sevaks*, special volunteers of Hindu militant organizations armed with pick axes and shovels, confirmed, Ayodhya had become the site of the most piercing assault ever faced by the Indian state, one that shook its basic political identity.

Not that the fundamental matter of India's selfhood has ever been settled. The truncated colonial territories inherited by the Indian state after 1947 still left it in control of a population of incomparable differences: a multitude of Hindu castes and outcastes, Muslims, Sikhs, Christians, Buddhists, Jains and tribes; speakers of more than a dozen major languages (and thousands of dialects); myriad ethnic and cultural communities.

This discordant material was not the stuff of which nation states are made; it suggested no common identity or basis of unity that could be reconciled within a modern state. Nor was there a compelling ideological doctrine or symbol, a 'socialism' or an emperor, around which to unite. For a few parenthetic decades after independence, Nehru's improvised conception of a tolerable, common Indianness seemed to suggest a basis for India's sense of itself. It was an explicitly political conception, and to sustain itself, it had constantly to persuade. That conception has given way, corroded by more exclusivist ideas of India and of political community. By the 1990s, definitions of Indianness were in fierce contest once again: Hindu nationalists struggled to capture the state and to purge the nationalist imagination, leaving it homogenous, exclusive and Hindu; others fought to escape the Indian state altogether and to create their own smaller, homogenous and equally exclusive communities.

The uncertainties that surrounded definitions of the Indian political community had settled symbolically on the town of Ayodhya, a place with no resonances of colonial humiliation or trace of futuristic monuments, but a stage where a quite different historical drama could be re-enacted. The wrecked site itself poses Indians with a practical dilemma. What should be done with it? Should a new Ram temple be built, as Hindu nationalists urged, and as the armed police assigned to guard the site were only too eager to assure visitors would indeed happen? Or should the destroyed mosque be restored? Or should it become, as some proposed, the ground for a civic monument to the Indian state's secular identity?

2

The puzzle of India's unity and of Indianness raised a variety of contending responses within the nationalist movement that brought India to independence. Nehru's was only one among these, and it was in no sense typical of nationalism as a whole. 'Indian nationalism' is a somewhat misleading shorthand phrase to describe a remarkable era of intellectual and cultural ferment and experimentation inaugurated in the late nineteenth century. The various, often oblique, currents that constituted this phase extended well beyond the confines of a political movement such as the Congress, with its high political, bilingual discourse. The possible basis for a common community was argued with ingenuity and imagination in the vernacular languages, especially in regions like Bengal and Maharashtra that had been exposed longest to the British, where a sense of regional identity only came into being as people tried to define a larger 'Indian' community. The belief that Indian nationalism had subsequently to unite and subordinate these regional identities is thus a curious misreading of the relationship between nation and region in India. In fact, a sense of region and nation emerged together, through parallel self-definitions – and this point is essential to any understanding of the distinctive, layered character of Indianness. The content and styles of these diverse explorations of a common community were neither uniform nor consistent, and the picture painted by nationalist historiographers of independent India, of a rising arc of nationalist self-consciousness from the 'Renaissance' in nineteenth-century Bengal to a culmination in 1947, is at best sentimental.

Similarly, to reduce these wide-ranging intellectual and political inquiries to a simple description of 'nationalism' is to conflate the differing projects of anti-colonialism, patriotism and nationalism, conveniently forgetting just how widespread and enduring were forms of patriotic loyalism that sang the glories of both the Motherland and the Empress Victoria. (In 1911, Gandhi, who only two years earlier had written his mauling indictment of the West, *Hind Swaraj* – an iconic work of Indian nationalism – was himself advising Indians to tender loyalty to their new king at George V's coronation.) Yet if there was one intention threading together these projects, it was to rebut the humiliation inflicted by colonial views, epitomized in John Strachey's lofty declaration, 'there is not, and never was an India, nor ever any country of India, possessing according to European ideas, any sort of unity, physical, political, social or religious; no nation, no "people of India" of which we hear so much'. By the 1920s, at least three distinct lines of reply to this goad had emerged. Nationalist Hindus asserted that Indian unity could be found in its common culture derived from religion; Gandhi, too, settled on religion as a source of interconnection among Indians, but manufactured his own eclectic and pluralist morality from different religious traditions; others, for whom Nehru became the most effective spokesman, turned away from religion and discovered a basis for unity both in a shared historical past of cultural mixing, and a future project of common development.

Nehru no doubt exaggerated the cultural interconnections, and his own picture of the Indian past inevitably was coloured by the image of the future India he desired. Like all nationalists, he was inclined to forget the historical infancy of the wished-for object. After all, before the nineteenth century, no residents of the subcontinent would have identified themselves as Indian. There existed intricate, ramified vocabularies of common understanding, which classified people by communities of lineage, locality and sect; but 'Indian' would not have figured among its terms. Subcontinental society was hardly static, yet most people never ventured beyond their own or neighbouring localities. They knew little about each other and were uninterested in learning more, preferring to remain distant strangers in a land peopled in their imagination by marvellous and absurd 'others'. Inhabitants of the land called India had been of interest only to outsiders: to the Greeks, who first named the land Indica, to travellers, traders and invaders, and then most comprehensively to the British, who in their train-spotting way darted across the subcontinent mapping, tabulating and classifying the territory and people that gradually came into their possession. What made possible the self-invention of a national community was the fact of alien conquest and colonial subjection. It was the British interest in determining geographical boundaries that by an Act of Parliament in 1899 converted 'India' from the name of a cultural region into a precise, pink territory. But to the British, that was all it was. Lord Curzon, for instance, scorned the suggestion that India had 'natural frontiers'- to him, there was no Indian nationality to coincide with nature. The arbitrary precisions of colonial administrative techniques thus brought forth an historical novelty, a unified and bounded space named India.

Yet it is too simple to see India as pure invention, a complicitous by-product of the opportunities presented by the British Raj and the interests of an aspiring nationalist elite. It is less radically novel. The dissimilar agrarian regions of pre-colonial India did share intelligible, common cultural forms, derived from both Brahminic traditions and non-Brahminic sources. The storehouse of shared narrative structures embodied in epics, myths and folk stories, and the family resemblance in styles of art, architecture and religious motifs – if not ritual practices – testify to a civilizational bond, that in fact extended well beyond the territorial borders of contemporary India: to Persia in the west and Indonesia in the east. Across the subcontinent, the single trait that overwhelmingly struck all outsiders was the orders of caste, which imposed themselves on incomers (except the British) and absorbed them into the productive relations of the society. Though hardly suggestive of a political unity, these characteristics – mythic narratives, aesthetic and ritual motifs, the typology of caste – did bestow a certain unified coherence on lives in the subcontinent.

Equally significant was India's archive of images of political community, which related culture to polity. In the Brahminic traditions, for instance, the Puranic literature expresses a sense of the subcontinent's natural geographical frontiers, reflected in a sacred geography mapped out by *tirthas*, pilgrimage points scattered across the land, and encompassed by the idea of mythic realms like *Aryavarta* or *Bharatavarsha*. In later periods, during the central Asian invasions from the eleventh to the fourteenth century, epics like the *Ramayana* were infused with political significance and were used by regional kings and courts to represent the political community. These narratives became a key by which one could read contemporary events: the characters were revised and the story rewritten to divinize particular kings and demonize ethnically strange invaders. And of the period immediately preceding the rule of the British, some historians have begun to speak of an 'old patriotism of the homelands' in certain regions – the strongest version being the Maratha kingdoms of the seventeenth and eighteenth centuries, with their acute sense of territoriality, veneration for the land, and a vision of community that transcended bounds of caste and drew upon non-Brahminic traditions such as Bhakti devotional cults. The comparatively brief episodes of subcontinental empire suggested a still different conception of political community – based not on a common culture but encompassing different religious groups, which imperial patterns of power allowed to live in insulated adjacency, requiring simply that they acknowledge the paramountcy of political authority and punctually yield revenue; religious and social habits were left unmolested.

This varied, amorphous historical inheritance was at once a spur and caution to the imagining of a national Indian past. It carried no single message. On the one hand, it was evident that nothing like regional nationalities or nations had emerged on the subcontinent. The gradualness with which first Islam, and then Britain entered India meant that different regions were conquered and incorporated in dissimilar ways, without inciting effective dissent along regional lines. If India was weakly united, it was also weakly divided: there were no politically significant regional identities that could either obstruct unification or direct it – no subcontinental Prussia or Piedmont. On the other hand, it was uncomfortably clear that the moments of actual unification in India's past were achieved under the yoke of imperial rule. Both colonial historians and nationalists, hungrily searching for precedents for their antagonistic projects, seized upon these exceptional historical scraps and gratefully turned them into the essence of India's past.

But past imperial dynasties, no matter how benign or tolerant, could hardly provide much assistance to the nationalist idea of a future India united in freedom. Nor was caste, the greatest cultural continuity across the subcontinent, convenient for this purpose: practically, it divided, and morally no nationalist was inclined to justify it. Race and language were equally useless: the idea of an original people subject to invasion was flimsy, since there had been so many 'invasions' that, despite some intrepid efforts, it was impossible to separate out the *ur-* from the new; and while Sanskrit (and then English) gave the elite a common tongue, they could scarcely use either to rouse the masses.

This quandary – the tantalizing possibility of a principle of unity but its evident empirical lack – led some to summon up a common historical past through explicit fantasy: to write, as the Bengali Bhudev Mukhopadhyay did, the history of India as it came to him in a dream. But to bestow upon themselves this gift of an unpossessed past, these intellectuals depended on British histories of India even as they undermined, defied and mangled them. The impulses and interests of colonial histories had shifted widely over time, depending on metropolitan cultural and political exigencies. There is a large distance, for example, between the late-eighteenth-century British discovery of Hinduism by deists like William Jones, who revelled in India's myths and legends as historical sources and who insisted on an original, valuable internal coherence to its civilization, and the distinctly less enthusiastic reactions of nineteenth-century evangelical reformers.

A distillation of these colonial histories of India, the most influential, and by some way the most laborious, was James Mill's *History of British India*. Cavalierly external in its viewpoint ('a man . . . may obtain more knowledge of India in one year in his closet in England, than he could obtain during the course of the longest life, by the use of his eyes and ears in India'), this utilitarian epic dispensed with the resources of language, myth or culture for narrating the Indian past. Instead of fables, Mill curated a history of fact, intended to reveal why Indian civilization was best served by its subjugation to the British. To Mill, dwelling on the antiquity of Indian civilization, or on the fancy that it was once great, was irrelevant to the more pressing governmental problem of calculating the current utility of Indian institutions or laws, and the costs of reform. There are no interpretational prizes to be won for seeing Mill's *History* as an instance of promiscuous, bad-mannered European Orientalism. But it gave Indians new opportunities. By portraying India as susceptible to change and reform, it gave the past a plasticity, and prompted Indians to invent their own alternatives. Stories such as Mill's reinserted India into a single historical narrative of progress, something ruled out by Hegelian and even Marxist philosophical histories, for example, which pictured a static, amorphous India set outside of the march of universal reason.

The exteriority of Mill's vision, his incautious refusal to allow the existence of any internal principle of Indian unity, and his heavy assault on the Hindu past, were sufficient provocation to many. The subjects of the British imperium began to reverse the presumptions of their masters' historical voice, to dispute its validity, and to substitute their own stories, which recounted the adventures of a common 'we'. This urge to write their own history could be bent to blatantly self-regarding ends: the histori-cal genre was used, for instance, to whip up a spate of traditional *jati* genealogies as 'caste histories', supplications by caste elites in terms they thought guaranteed to win boons from the British government. But others were transforming the scope and mean-ing of elusive terms like *jati*, using it to encompass a larger community of shared beliefs and interests: the hesitancies and spirals of this complicated manoeuvre and these difficult choices in the cultural politics of colonial India have been beautifully and definitively traced in recent studies. 'We must have a history', the Bengali intellectual Bankimchandra Chattopadhyay urged, and within fifty or so years, by the 1920s, the ambition of history writing had seized the nationalist intellectual imagination – scholars, politicians, dilettantes, would-be terrorists, all dutifully turned their hand to it. But inevitably the writing of history also confounded and divided nationalism. The substance of the Indian past was so diverse, so discontinuous, and often so downright contradictory that present desire, far from an embarassing intrusion, was actually essential to discerning a pattern and order that could show it to be a 'history'. Future political conflicts among the different elements of the nationalist imagination were rehearsed in the histories it chose for itself.

In this search for an internal principle of unity to the past, religion was given a foundational position by both orthodox and reformist Brahmin intellectuals. In Bengal, a Hindu conception of the Indian past was devised and diffused both in subtle literary essays and in more rough-hewn textbooks. India's history was sliced into Hindu, Muslim and British periods. The originating, defining historical moment was discovered in an ancient Hindu India, the 'classical era' of Vedic culture, and in periods such as the Gupta empire from the fourth to the seventh centuries.

Decline, these histories agreed, thereafter set in and led to the 'Muslim Period', a dark age that corrupted the society from the eleventh century onwards and left it prey to British conquest, a vast stretch of the Indian past that remained unintegrated, a millennial aberration styled as a period of brave but ultimately foundering Hindu resistance against tyrannical and cunning invaders. But even appeals to Hindu religion failed to provide a simple and unambiguous principle of unity: the fact of caste, and the bewildering internal pluralism of Hindu beliefs, thwarted such ambitions. The idea of Hinduism therefore had to be ingeniously tailored to emphasize territorial origin and broad cultural commonalities rather than ritual practices, caste exclusivities or particular gods. Any fixation upon such traits, or solely on Brahminic traditions threatened to lose not only Buddhists and Jains, but also the millions of outcastes.

The most arresting political figure in this search for a seamless Hindu past was Vinayak Damodar Savarkar, from whose writings the BJP would later take their mantric prosody, *Hindutva*. A Maharashtrian Brahmin belonging to the Chitpavan caste, and of the same historical generation as Nehru, Savarkar was himself a non-believer. Self-schooled in the history of European nationalism and an admirer of Mazzini – he translated the Italian's autobiography into Marathi – Savarkar founded a secret society modelled on Young Italy: its members learned bomb-making from a Russian revolutionary in Paris and schemed to assassinate Lord Curzon. And he wrote history: a counter-narrative of what the British termed the Mutiny of 1857, which Savarkar recounted as *The Indian War of Independence, 1857*; and, in 1923, *Hindutva: Who is a Hindu?*

'Hindutva is not a word but a history,' Savarkar expounded. 'Not only a spiritual or religious history . . . but history in full. Hinduism is only a derivative, a fraction, a part of Hindutva', and he used this history to resolve to his satisfaction the indeterminacies that troubled all definitions of Indians and India. In

Savarkar's genealogical equation between the Hindu and the Indian, members of the Indian political community were united by geographical origin, racial connection (rather ambiguously specified), and a shared culture based on Sanskritic languages and 'common laws and rites'. Those who shared these traits formed the core, 'majority' community. Those who did not – Muslims, who constituted a quarter of pre-Partition India's population, 'tribals', Christians – were relegated to awkward, secondary positions. The special frisson of Savarkar's ideas lay in their translation of Brahminical culture into the terms of an ethnic nationalism drawn from his reading of Western history. This created an evocative, exclusivist and recognizably modern definition of Indianness, with rich potentials to sustain future political projects and to induce direct political effects. It was contact with these ideas that in 1925 led another Brahmin, K. B. Hedgewar, to found the Rashtriya Swayamsevak Sangh (RSS – Association of National Volunteers), to this day the backbone of Hindu nationalist organization, and it also inspired the Hindu Mahasabha, until 1950 the main party of Hindu nationalism. The Gandhian Congress adroitly marginalized the Savarkarite conception of Indian history and Indianness, but its presuppositions were never erased: many nationalists outside Congress, and even some within it, shared them.

The undertow of this modernist Brahminic imagination of the Indian nation, outlined around the turn of the twentieth century and systematized by men like Savarkar, has moulded India's political history more deeply than is usually acknowledged. The official ideology of the post-1947 Indian state effaced it from the histories of nationalism it sponsored; and as a political organization, Hindu nationalism perfected an astonishing ability to mismanage its own self-declared destiny. But its definition of an Indian nation was an ever-present imaginative magnet, the pole against which men like Gandhi and Nehru constantly had to act. Hindu nationalism was a real mover in the agitation for Partition, both directly through the organization and action of Hindu communalists, and through its influence within Congress. Secular and Hindu nationalisms have invariably assigned primary responsibility for Partition to Muslim 'communalism' and separatism. Yet recent historical research has complicated the conventions of this picture. It is true that a Muslim argument for a homogenous Muslim nation, which presumed a different interpretation of the historical past, was made at different times over the past century; this was the view Muhammad Ali Jinnah expressed in his famous speech in Lahore in 1940: 'We know that the history of the last twelve hundred years has failed to achieve unity and has witnessed, during the ages, India always divided between Hindu India and Muslim India'. But this did not amount to a coherent impulse towards an independent nation state for all Muslims on the subcontinent.

The twists by which this came about were heavily contingent on the attitudes and actions of the Hindu majority, as well as those of Congress. The Muslims of British India did not form a monolithic community with a single 'communal' identity or interest any more than the Hindus did. Class and region divided as much as religion might unite, and beliefs about community and interest varied between provinces where Muslims were in a majority and those where they were not. (The terminology of 'majority' and 'minority' was itself an inescapable imposition of the political accountancy of the Raj.) Muslim politics had significant secular voices, most notably Jinnah's own. It is perfectly plausible to construe Jinnah's political project as intended not to bifurcate India and create two territorial nation states, but to safeguard the interests of Muslims in provinces where they formed minorities, an intention which, as it turned out, he failed entirely to realize. In this respect, his fears about democracy in a large state with an undivided electorate and one religious community holding a numerical – and potentially permanent political – majority, has its parallels with anxieties that have surfaced in India's regions during the past decade, when many have become mistrustful of the ability of India's large democracy to represent their interests.

Jinnah saw the Muslims as forming a single community, or 'nation', but he envisaged an existence for them alongside a 'Hindu nation' within a united, confederal India. The core of his disagreement with Congress concerned the structure of this future state. Jinnah was determined to prevent the creation of a unitary central state with procedures of political representation that threatened to put it in the hands of a numerically dominant religious community. As such, this was a perfectly secular ambition. But the contingencies of politics and the convenient availability of powerful lines of social difference pushed it in a quite contrary direction. The Muslim insistence on a separate state crystallized only in the decade before 1947, and there is real force to the point that practical experience of Congress rule in the Indian provinces after the elections of 1937 was instrumental in encouraging Muslim political alienation. Congress governments, subject in many cases to the influence of nationalist Hindus, lost the trust of Muslims and so helped to kindle support for the Muslim League. It was this erosion of trust that fanned a desire to redescribe a 'minority' within British India as a separate 'nation', and to take it outside the boundaries of India. The political and intellectual weight of the Hindu nationalist imagination, with its desire for a clear definition of Indianness based on an exclusive sense of culture and of an historical past, was decisive in imposing an artificial cohesion to the diverse local Muslim identities on the subcontinent: indeed, Jinnah himself protested that the idea of Pakistan was foisted upon him by Hindu public opinion. The instabilities of Muslim nationalism on the subcontinent became dramatically apparent more recently in the secession of East from West Pakistan in 1971 and the creation of Bangladesh, when a Bengali identity was defended against what the Bengalis saw as the domination of the Pakistani state by a Punjabi elite; the instabilities continue in Pakistan's politics, restated in the daily attrition and conflict that has bled the provinces of Sind and Baluchistan.

But Hindu and Muslim nationalisms in India did not exhaust the possible uses of religion to define inclusion or exclusion from the nation's political community. Gandhi refused to separate religion from politics, as modernists and secularists insisted, and strove to refute the colonial charge that religion must ultimately keep India divided. Equally, however, he recoiled from the vision of nationalist Hindus. Where they harped upon an image of Hindus as oppressed, terrorized and victimized both by the colonial present and by past Muslim rule, and promised a remedy in a martial patriotism, a khaki-shorted veneration of the Father-land, Gandhi deftly inverted this image: he resurrected an older language of feminized patriotism (which men like Savarkar had sought to infuse with virility) and made his life and body, his habits and posture, a demonstration of the message that strength was with the victims of history. Gandhi rejected the idea that past history was a source for defining future possibilities or orienting present action. The British fascination with historical dissertations was expressive of their desire to dominate: history was used to justify colonial rule and to show that past dissensions prohibited the possibility of future unity for India. It was only by kicking this British 'habit of writing history' that Indians could release themselves from the cultural harassments of their rulers: 'I look upon Gibbon and Motley as inferior editions of the *Mahabharata*.'

But, lest that suggest any fondness for epic Hindu histories, Gandhi made it equally clear that the mimic narratives of religious nationalists had also to be abandoned. 'I believe,' he wrote, 'that a nation is happy that has no history', and in contrast to nationalists who sought to construct a reliable future out of a selected past, Gandhi expressed profound distrust for the historical genre. He turned to legends and stories from India's popular religious traditions, preferring their lessons to the supposed ones of history. The fact that so many on the subcontinent found these fables accessible, and recognized their predicaments and symbols, itself testified to a shared civilizational bond. In place of an Indian unity based on a common historical past, Gandhi substituted a religious morality that assembled elements from folk and Bhakti traditions as well as from Christian morality.

Gandhi refused the ubiquitous ground of all nationalisms, the discourse of history, and created a distinctive definition of Indian identity. With unique sensitivity, he evoked a patriotic symbolism that allowed him to be visualized not merely as an all-Indian leader among the nationalist elite but as a local saint in the different regions and communities of India. His appeal to pre-existing local beliefs and identities in order to create a larger, Indian one was tied to an idea of *swadeshi*, a patriotism based on a respect for the everyday material world inhabited by most on the subcontinent. His adoption of cloth as a symbol of interconnection exemplified this esteem of the everyday. By spinning and weaving their own cloth, through literal self-production, Indians would regain the economic control and cultural self-respect that colonialism had usurped and battered. They would become linked by common forms of production, and the wearing of *khadi* would unite Indians by removing the distinguishing marks of caste proclaimed in the precise sartorial signatures of traditional dress. This ambition for a self-producing community was strongly moralizing, and dispensed entirely with the idea of a territorial nation state. 'Both India and Pakistan are my country,' Gandhi insisted as Partition approached. 'I am not going to take out a passport for going to Pakistan.'

3

The influence of the Gandhian vision receded with surprising speed during the 1940s, submerged by the swell of Hindu and Muslim nationalisms. In the aftermath of Partition and Gandhi's assassination by Nathuram Godse, a nationalist Brahmin from Maharashtra with links to the RSS, the Gandhian idea was literally effaced. Gandhi's 'anarcho-communitarianism', the non-statist idiom in which he expressed his pluralist definition of Indianness, and his faith in the everyday tolerances of ordinary people, was helpless in the face of the communal mayhem that threatened to sweep the subcontinent following the withdrawal of the Raj's police powers. The new Indian state had to act quickly; and that state was in the hands of a nationalist elite over which Nehru came ultimately to preside. Amidst perilous political balances and lethal religious divisions, Nehru had to devise a workable response to the question of an Indian identity, one that the state could sustain and enforce. His acquisition of the levers of state was fortuitous, and certainly did not represent an ideological victory for his idea of India, nor even a broad consensus over it. Yet he was able to install an intricate, pluralist definition of Indianness that gave, for a time, an illusion of permanence. Nehru's skill in endowing the contingent with a sense of grand historical necessity, and in making his definition of Indianness seem the only possible one, nurtured this illusion. He relied on a compelling, if imaginary, story of the Indian past, told as a tale of cultural mixing and fusion, a civilizational tendency towards unification that would realize itself within the frame of a modern nation state. He located this story of an internal impulse towards Indian unity within a larger story of the movement of world history, a narrative of diverse peoples coming to determine their own futures and to participate in the benefits of economic progress.

Nehru's political practice after 1947 has come to be regarded as the mere application of intellectual arguments that he developed in the pre-independence period. Yet this misses the real originality of his answer to the question of an Indian identity. The definition that he tried to install after 1947 was more shaded and nuanced than anything one might reconstruct from his intellectual statements of the 1930s and 40s. It was also more continuous with the pattern of the Indian past than any of its rivals, then or now. Nehru's idea of Indianness emerged through improvised responses to constrained circumstances: its strength was not its ideological intensity, but its ability to steer towards an Indianness seen as layered, adjustable, imagined, not as a fixed property. While Nehru was attracted by the political and economic examples of the modern West, he was far less taken by its cultural models. It was fundamental to him that Indian nationalism could not fashion itself after European examples. In contrast to the academic analysts who see nationalism as the diffusion of a standard form devised in the industrialized West – whether in the Gallic version of a community of common citizenship or the *volkisch* idea of a shared ethnic or cultural origin – Nehru self-consciously rejected the idea that Indian nationalism was compelled to make itself in one or other of these images. To that extent Nehru agreed with the two men whose influence he acknowledged as most important to his thinking about this matter, Tagore and Gandhi. But unlike Tagore and Gandhi, for whom the state was a dispensable nuisance, Nehru believed that an Indian identity could emerge only within the territorial and institutional frame of a state. A specifically Indian compromise was needed, and he saw strengths in this. That compromise was outlined in the practical adaptation, after 1947, of the state into a distinctive model shaped by Nehru's under-standing of the Indian past: a model committed to protecting cultural and religious difference rather than imposing a uniform 'Indianness'.

Nehru's intellectual response to the perturbations of India's unity and of a shared Indianness was stated with some subtlety in *The Discovery of India* (1946), written in prison on the eve of independence. The title announced India as an indubitable presence, but also wryly acknowledged that it could not be taken for granted by people of Nehru's class and background – its contours had to be actively plotted. For a man who carried with him the burden of an anglicized past, who answered to the name of Joe until his mid-twenties, it was not an easy book to write. Like Tagore and like Gandhi, like all nationalists, Nehru had to make himself Indian. *The Discovery*, even more so than his *Autobiography* (1936), was such a work of self-making – a slow, laborious transformation of the alien critic into an Indian, one who could recognize and embrace the complexity of India's past. *The Discovery* is correctly read as an expression of the nationalist imagination, but a highly unusual one, capacious, accepting, and with no trace of a desire for purification or hardening of boundaries.

Where Tagore reworked the poetic language and Gandhi turned to religious traditions to make their Indian selves, Nehru discovered India and himself through the medium of history. Temperamentally, he saw the world historically: a perspective that at once defined his sense of political possibility and made him vigilant about attending to how the future would look back on his own actions. But his turn to history in *The Discovery* was also spurred by a specific insight into Indian culture: that to Indians the past was as valuable as language or religion; they valued it themselves and saw the world through it. His book was an elaboration of this insight, and there was little evidence of the *Marxisant* and sometimes didactic historical scaffold that had buttressed his two earlier narratives, *Glimpses of World History* (1934) and the *Autobiography*. In telling his story of the Indian past, Nehru relied on the 'Orientalist' histories the British had written: but he entirely reworked them to suit his own purposes.

British histories showed India as a society of self-enclosed communities, always potentially – and, in the absence of an imperial state, actually – in gruesome conflict with one another. Tagore, in his great essay 'The Message of Indian History' (1902), had called this 'foreigner's history':

The history of India that we read in schools and memorize to pass our examinations is the account of a horrible dream – a nightmare through which India has passed. It tells of unknown people from no one knows where entering India; bloody wars breaking out; father fighting son and brother killing brother to snatch at the throne; one set of marauders passing away with another coming in to take its place; Pathan and Mughal, Portuguese, French and English – all helping to add to the nightmarish confusion.

Nehru seized upon Tagore's allusive evocation of what he saw as the authentic message of India's past and elaborated it into an Indian history that defied both the British and the Hindu nationalists' uses of history. Nehru produced for the first time an epic of India's past in which it appeared neither as a meaningless dust-storm nor as a glorified Hindu pageant, but as moved by a logic of accommodation and acceptance. In his imagination, India appeared as a space of ceaseless cultural mixing, its history a celebration of the soiling effects of cultural miscegenation and accretion, 'an ancient palimpsest on which layer upon layer of thought and reverie had been inscribed, and yet no succeeding layer had completely hidden or erased what had been written previously'.

Nehru romanticized the past. He recognized the allure – 'that old witchery' – of his feminized Motherland. He saw too that he was engaged not in 'a meticulous chronicle of facts' but in producing 'living history', an enabling fiction that had to bind together the 'multitudinous past of innumerable successions of human beings' into the shared history of a single political community. But his essential point was not off-beam: that the

residents of the subcontinent were at once distinct and shared a
family resemblance. Nehru's sense of the differences encompassed within the artificially precise territorial boundaries of
India was not the outcome of purely textual or intellectual
encounters: it was arrived at literally through politics, the outcome of the gruelling election campaigns of 1936–7, which he
saw as his pilgrimage across the country. These electoral pere-
grinations left him with his own Indian album, a repertoire of
turning images. It led him also to recognize that every Indian
possessed his or her own portfolio:

If my mind was full of pictures from recorded history and more-or-less
ascertained fact, I realized that even the illiterate peasant had a picture
gallery in his mind, though this was largely drawn from myth and
tradition and epic heroes and heroines, and only very little from history.
Nevertheless it was vivid enough.

The experience gave him what today would be fashionably called
a de-centred view of Indian culture, it substantiated a point he
had made in the *Autobiography*: just as India had never had a
single dominant or capital city, so too 'Indian culture was so
widespread all over India that no part of the country could be
called the heart of that culture'.

The Discovery signalled Nehru's homecoming, not to a single
culture but to this profusion. It settled some of the anxieties that
had wracked him in the late 1930s and that had pervaded the
Autobiography: the sense of being 'lonely and homeless . . . India,
to whom I had given my love and for whom I had laboured,
seemed a strange and bewildering land'. But to know one's
home, one had also to know the world, to find a place on that
wider stage. Unlike many other nationalists who had come to a
sense of their Indianness through the detour of the West, there
is no trace in Nehru of that inwardly turned rage of an Aurobindo
or Vivekananda, political intellectuals who strove to purge themselves of what they came to regard as a defiling encounter with

the modern West – an encounter that had in the first place planted in them the urge to be Indian.

Isaiah Berlin has written of Tagore that 'he never showed his wisdom more clearly than in choosing the difficult middle path, drifting neither to the Scylla of radical modernism, nor to the Charybdis of proud and gloomy traditionalism', and Nehru too had that capacity to keep to the centre, to find a cultural poise that allowed him to accept the presence of his Englishness as one more layer to his Indian self. There was, for Nehru, no return to a past purity, no possibility of historical cleansing. Colonialism was a humiliation, but it also carried the aroma of modernity. And that modernity too would have to infiltrate and leave its trace on the palimpsest. To that extent, the discovery of India was a forward movement through as yet undescribed and unmade history. Mere recovery of the past could not make Indians self-sufficient: the necessary veneration of a rich and unusual history had to coexist with a modernist, more self-critical idiom that acknowledged the immense failings of that past.

The acceptance of modernity as integral to the definition of free India implied the need to turn this grand, complex nationalist imagination into a state form. In *The Discovery*, Nehru arrived at an historical image of the link between culture and political power in India that was at odds with the standard conceptions. It avoided the liberal presumption that individuals could transcend their cultural inheritance and remake themselves however they – or their state – happened to see fit: a view that placed abstracted individual rationality before any sense of cultural identity. Equally, he steered away from the perception of cultures as self-enclosed wholes, hermetic communities of language or belief, a perception which could nurture either a conservative idea of the state as an instrument at the community's disposal, available for its own aggressive ends, or a more benign view of the state as curator of cultural exhibits, responsible for protecting and preserving communities. Nehru saw cultures as overlapping forms of activity that had commerce with one another, mutually altering and reshaping each other. India was a society neither of liberal individuals nor of exclusive communities or nationalities, but of interconnected differences. That insight or – to the more sceptical – belief guided his practice after 1947. Given the environment in which he had to act, it is particularly striking that he could maintain this distinctive conception. Partition had given currency to a simple logic: since a Muslim state had been created in Pakistan, India should now define itself as the state of a Hindu 'majority' and make itself the agent of religious preferences.

Half a century later it is easy to miss the sheer novelty of what was attempted in the two decades after independence. Today the idea of multiculturalism is a familiar if vague one, surrounded by sophisticated and unworldly philosophical and legal arguments. Yet in the late 1940s, it was certainly not a standard way to envisage the construction of a new state. There were few models, from either European or any other history, that could be used to help focus India's assorted diversities into a political structure founded upon a democratic principle. This had to be invented through practice. The minimal precondition for any kind of Indian identity after 1947 was a state, an agency that could in practice enforce a constitutionally defined identity, and this was quickly consolidated. The new Indian state had to rely largely on its inheritance of military and bureaucratic capacities from the Raj. After 1947 these colonial legacies were the sole instruments with effective capacities to impose a political identity over the whole territory. The Congress Party was the only authentically Indian organization that reached across the country; but unlike many anti-colonial nationalist organizations that subsequently emerged elsewhere, it never had the capacity to impose its definition of a nationalist identity. It lacked a military arm, which in so many cases anti-colonial movements turned not only against their colonial enemies but also against their 'own' peoples in order to impose nationhood – think of Algeria, Indonesia,

Vietnam. The army and the civil service gave the Indian state a professional class recruited from an all-Indian base, able to operate and move easily across the country – an elite of 'functionary Indians'. To these inherited instruments, now turned to forging a common political identity, was added the institution of economic planning: essential, in Nehru's conception, to impart cohesion, drawing Indians into a shared project of development. Besides these centripetal elements of the state, the multiplicity of cultural and political voices in the society demanded recognition. No attempt was made to impose a single or uniform 'Indian' identity upon the new nation. This, seen as a potential weakness from the perspective of the Western theories of nationalism which guided the thinking of nationalist Hindus, was actually the most remarkable achievement.

Citizenship was defined by civic and universalist rather than ethnic criteria, which guaranteed a principle of inclusion in India's democracy. Although it was the operations of democratic politics that in later decades were to challenge a single conception of India, democracy was also instrumental in sustaining that conception – through its ability to include new political entrants within a common, Indian frame. Democracy was intended to recognize the claims of Indians as individuals. In practice, it was led also to recognize the claims of groups, and this certainly scattered seeds of future tension. But the claims of Indians as members of particular communities did require some sort of recognition and accommodation.

Language and religion, those elementary markers that are generally used to ease any awkwardnesses of fit between individual and nation, were not given this assignment in India: neither was adopted as an effortless badge of Indianness. The issue of whether or not India should embrace a single national language provoked some of the longest, certainly the most bitter debates in the Constituent Assembly during 1948–9: at times they threatened to split it irrevocably. In the pre-Independence

173

period, in defiance of the mixed administrative units of colonial rule, Gandhi had reorganized Congress into linguistic units, and encouraged the use of provincial languages within them. This initiative made political discussions locally comprehensible and so helped to turn Congress into a mass movement. English continued as the language of the national leadership, but everyone agreed that this was a temporary expedient which in the future would be superseded by a common Indian language. The most likely candidate was Hindustani, a mongrel of two already hybrid languages, Hindi and Urdu – which could be written in either Urdu or Devnagari scripts. Even this, however, was spoken only by a little over two-fifths of the population, all concentrated in northern India. English therefore remained the only tongue that linked the elites in the north with those in the south.

After Partition, the Hindi-speakers – the largest single language group in the country – began to press for the adoption of Hindi as the national language. Their spokesmen in the Assembly, claiming to represent a majority, demanded a purge of Urdu words and English technical terms from the Hindi language (including, with ironically misplaced zeal, what they thought of as 'Arabic' numerals, which are in fact derived from Sanskrit), and the introduction of a standardized, purified and sanskritized Hindi as the national language. People were symbolically and vehemently divided over the issue of what language should be used for the Constitution: chaste English or purified Hindi? Hindi lobbyists produced their own version, brimming with baffling sanskritized neologisms: its advocates optimistically cited the Irish adventure with a Gaelic Constitution. Nehru, however, had to remind them that de Valera had confessed to him that the Irish were finding the Gaelic edition 'hard going' and were veering round to English. The constitutional ambitions were rendered in legal English, equally hard going and still well outside the linguistic universe of most Indians.

In the end and in a highly charged atmosphere, Nehru and

his supporters managed to secure a more satisfactory compromise on the larger issue. Hindi was recognized as an 'official' but not the 'national' language, a dozen other regional languages were accorded similar status as 'officially recognized' (with the possibility of adding others to the list: an arrangement that could deftly accommodate new claimants without threatening speakers of the languages already recognized). It was agreed that English would continue as the language of state, with the option of gradually phasing it out in the coming decades. Instead of ceding to the linguistic nationalism of a substantial segment of the population, a pluralist compromise was engineered, which recognized the use of different languages at different levels, and for different purposes.

This technique of compromise refused to anchor an Indian identity to a single trait – an option which, had it been chosen, would have suborned regional cultures to majoritarian definitions of a national one. It inscribed as a constitutional principle the practical habit that had made Congress successful as a nationalist movement. Indianness was defined not as a singular or exhaustive identity, but as one which explicitly recognized at least two other aspects. Indian citizens were also members of linguistic and cultural communities: Oriyas or Tamils, Kashmiri or Marathi. India's federal arrangements were intended to embody this idea of a layered Indianness, an accretion of identities. Nehru's initial hope had been for India's regional states to continue as the mixed, multi-lingual administrative units established by the Raj. The precise boundaries of these states were artificial colonial creations, but the principle of mixed linguistic cultures that they embodied was continuous with past Indian historical pattern. Nehru therefore saw no need for internal re-partitioning.

But in the mid-1950s, strong demands were raised within the provincial branches of Congress itself to recognize regional cultural groups by creating linguistic states. Nehru finally came round to accepting these claims (except in the case of Punjab, where a linguistic state in response to Sikh demands was not granted until 1966). He saw these new states as a step towards rendering the practices of democratic government more comprehensible, rather than as a challenge to or dilution of Indianness. The principle of regional states defined by linguistic boundaries was adopted, and the use of vernacular languages (rather than Hindi or English) in regional administration was also instituted. Such adjustments recognized the principle that the institutional forms of being Indian could within broad limits be revised. Indianness was not a culturally closed or static condition.

The adjustments around the still more vexed issue of religion demonstrated a similar willingness to improvise and risk the unconventional. It is usual to prune Nehru's complex, changing views on religion into the now withered bush of 'secularism'. But this imparts a misleading ideological fixity to what was always much more an active precept of political prudence. Nehru had no such doctrine, no worked-out constitutional theory that invested a blind faith in legal consistency. In fact the term 'secularism' was inserted into the Constitution only by Mrs Gandhi, during the frenetic amendments of the Emergency period. Rather, he operated with a coherent view about the real and potential political threats of religious identity, now that Indians had their own state. The authority of this new state relied on being able to win the trust of its citizens. Democracy, based on universal suffrage and a single electorate not divided by communities, was the principal means to this end.

But for those who had seen themselves as protected by the segregated electorates of the British Raj, especially India's Muslim communities, new protections would have to be found under conditions of universal democracy. This was especially so after Partition, when the Indian state struggled to secure the trust of its Muslims. Parallel to the federal recognition of Indians as possessing regional linguistic identities, the law would have to recognize Indians as members of religious communities. In particular, Indians who belonged to smaller religious communities had to be protected against the totalitarian potentials of mass democracy. Indian law had to be sensitive to particularity: communities that were judged numerically weak or subject to past oppression were given explicit protections, effectively made wards of the state, through caste reservations and the provision of customary civil codes of law for different religious communities. But given his views about the changeable, transactional nature of cultures, Nehru expected that these provisions would themselves be subject to change. Communities would in time open themselves up to reform; but they had to retain the right to decide when.

The state did from the early 1950s begin to reform the laws that guided customary Hindu practice. In this, it continued and intensified an interest in social reform among Hindu communities that had originated early in the nineteenth century. The spate of legislation after independence on matters such as the abolition of untouchability, the removal of caste restrictions on entry to temples, the ending of interdictions on inter-caste marriage, the prohibition of polygamy, and the recognition that women had equal rights of inheritance, all was continuous with impulses within earlier nationalism. To be sure, Nehru supported such legislative reforms, but it was hardly the case that he initiated all of them, and in fact the initiatives generally came from practising Hindus themselves. On the other hand, Nehru did oppose the strongly supported demand of Hindu conservatives for a ban on cow slaughter. Ultimately he compromised on this, but not without first ensuring that it was removed from the attention of the central government and relegated to provincial state assemblies. He also insisted that any such ban had to be justified by public, secular arguments, for example, economic ones: it could not be justified merely by invoking religious convictions.

To Nehru, secularism was not a substitute civic religion, still less a political project to remoralize society by effacing religion and stamping a secular identity on all Indians. He fully recognized the depth and plurality of religious beliefs in India. It was precisely this that convinced him of the need to keep religious social identities outside the political arena. His energies were directed not towards installing a doctrine of secularism, but against the uses of religion for political purposes, the dangers of what he called 'communalism'. This involved him in a constant political argument with nationalist and traditionalist Hindus, both within and outside his party, and he successfully quarantined national politics from religious demands.

Indianness was constituted out of internal diversity, but in Nehru's vision it was equally an international identity, a way of being in the wider world. In contrast to the sometimes narrowly domestic horizons of most in the nationalist movement (only the Indian communists consistently shared with Nehru an appreciation of the significance of international politics, though of course for rather different reasons), Nehru understood independence as an opportunity to establish India as a presence on the world stage. The international profile of states depended on their economic and military prowess, and India obviously could not make its mark in these domains. A new state like India, weak by international standards, would have to pursue its interests by creating its own opportunities and chances. By speaking the language of morality and justice, it might just be able to surprise and unbalance the more powerful, extracting concessions from their sheer embarrassment. Nehru, in this a follower of Gandhi, turned around the language of victimhood: instead of portraying India as a martyr to colonial subjection which had to turn inwards to find and repair itself, he affirmed India's character as a self-confident actor in international politics. The decision to remain within the Commonwealth, but as a republic, is only one instance of this sensibility, of Nehru's commitment to an idea of a layered past, and of his refusal to purge or purify historical connections.

Equally, it showed an unsentimental determination not to be enthralled by this past but to adjust it to suit India's present interests.

The Indianness outlined in the two decades after 1947 was an extemporized performance, trying to hold together divergent considerations and interests. The result was a highly unusual nationalism that resists summary in clear or simple doctrinal statements. It tried to accommodate within the form of a new nation state significant internal diversities; to resist bending to the democratic pressures of religion; and to look outwards. This experimental response to the question of how to be Indian was not a victory of theoretical consistency. It was a contingent acquisition, based on a coherent if disputable picture of India. It did not reassure itself by relying on a settled image of the culture, nor did it try to impose one. That was its most important trait: it did not monopolize or simplify the definition of Indianness. For all the political vexations visited upon it, it could claim success: India, an ungainly, unlikely, inelegant concatenation of differences, after fifty years still exists as a single political unity. This would be unimaginable without Nehru's improvisation.

4

Within two decades of Nehru's death in 1964, India's layered, plural, political self-definition was in serious difficulties. The extent was apparent from a shift in intellectual climate. India's Westernized intellectuals, on whose support Nehru could always count, had turned against the state that was acting in his name. The object of their criticism was the elusive notion of secularism. These intellectuals were trying to explain a puzzling fact about India in the 1980s. Four decades after independence and the end of colonialism – which, according to nationalist dogma, had been responsible for 'communalist' dissensions – the identities of religion and caste had started to invade national politics with ferocious energy. Why?

To the self-proclaimed 'Nehruvians', devotees of the 'scientific temper', the fault lay with the society itself, limited in its education and shackled by superstition and obscurantism. Yet fewer and fewer were convinced by this diagnosis. The presence and actions of the state, committed to the project of modernization and 'nation-building', seemed to be responsible. Some intellectuals, searching for a sociological explanation, attacked the ambition of trying to create a secular state and a society of liberal individuals. Oddly, they ascribed this project to Nehru. And they saw it as doomed in India: it was, in the words of one of the country's leading sociologists, 'the dream of a minority which wants to shape the majority in its own image, which wants to impose its will upon history but lacks the power to do so under a democratically organized polity'. Nehru, a hapless straw man in such ruminations, was condemned both for trying to impose his modernist will upon a society of deep religious belief and for not being Kemalist or Leninist enough to push through his secularist ambitions. Given the extent of religious belief in Indian society and given that India was a democracy, such arguments proceeded, it followed that the religious preferences of the majority should rule in the state: 'In an open society the state will reflect the character of the society.' The centrality of religion must be expressed in the Constitution, which should be revised to remove 'anomalies' – protective safeguards for communities and regions – in order to produce a uniform, homogenous legal code. Democracy meant, quite simply, the rule of the majority.

More trenchant arguments pointed to the way that secularism had, since Nehru, become an instrumental ideology of the state. It now functioned as a legitimating cloak for the modernist elite, who used it to mask their grip at the very moment when this was being challenged by the surge of mass democracy. The use of secularism as an ideology of state power had engendered a new monster on the political landscape, a Hindu nationalism remotely linked to religion, which merely used it instrumentally to capture state power. Secularism as a doctrine of state was thus responsible for the corrosion of faith in the society. It had instrumentalized and corrupted the capacities for inter-religious understanding and social peace which India had possessed in the past. The intellectual argument here resonated with the anti-statism that had animated the thinking of both Tagore and Gandhi; but in the face of the palpable reality of the Indian state, it remained difficult to see what it could imply in practice.

The intellectual unease was a symptom of wider changes sweeping Indian society and its terms of political identity. The axis of connection between state and society since 1947 had been the Congress Party: it had acted as a kind of translation machine, which enabled communication between two distinct worlds, never creating a common sense but at least maintaining a kind of tenuous mutual intelligibility. For around twenty years after 1947, it successfully organized and aggregated the multiplicity of identities within the society. But it was running into difficulties; and because of its centrality, difficulties for Congress meant difficulties for the Indian state. The problems were partly produced by inevitable historical fatigue – Congress could no longer rely on the nationalist heritage by the 1970s – but also by its own actions, in conditions that were certainly not easy to navigate through.

The steady political mobilization instigated by democratic competition was bringing lower and poorer people into politics, many who were organizing themselves into groups defined by legally ascribed public identities: the Backward and Other Backward Classes, the Scheduled Castes and others. They considered their interests framed by local horizons, and from the 1970s began to find a voice in a multiplicity of regional parties and political formations. Social differentiations were increasingly reflected in a range of political groups. The uneven effects of economic development were meanwhile adding new layers to an already differentiated society. The capacity of Congress to muster and maintain political support across India, to speak for the nation, was in decline. In the era of its dominance, Congress had relied on its internal federalism, and its ability to build support at the national level by means of coalitional bargaining and negotiation between the national and regional leadership. This had successfully restricted the groupings according to caste and religion to local levels. Congress did not appeal directly to the 'nation' or to particular communities that could imagine themselves as national ones. National power was knitted together by its regional party organizations.

But the centralization of power within the party from the early 1970s weakened the regional roots of the party and unleashed disastrous potentials: regional demands were no longer filtered through party channels, but began to be asserted with rising irritation against the central state. In the 1950s the demands had been for cultural recognition in unilingual states; by the end of the 1960s movements in states like Maharashtra were insisting that economic opportunities in each state be reserved for its 'natives'; by the 1980s the demands had escalated to full-fledged regional autonomy and separatism in states like Punjab and Kashmir.

The concentration of power choked the federal layers of Indian identity. The Centre resorted to describing these regional demands as 'anti-national' and as threats to 'national integrity', and used this to justify still further concentration, provoking still more dissent: every move became a further turn of this vicious screw. The populist redefinition of democracy merely made national politics ever more volatile, activated more social identities, and invited them to organize for political ends. To win national elections without the support of the regional 'bosses', Mrs Gandhi had to transform Congress from a federal party into a mass party. This put it in the classic dilemma of every mass political party in a competitive democracy: it claimed to speak for and to govern in the 'national' interest, but to be able to do so it had to appeal directly to people as members of particular communities. The appeal to caste identities had long been accepted as a necessary part of Congress strategy in local and regional politics. But what occurred now was a decisive break with Congress practice. The national leadership had never invoked religious identities for electoral purposes. This taboo fell in the 1980s, and religious and caste sentiments were now routinely invoked in national elections.

The insecurities of different religious minorities were played on: Hindu minorities in Kashmir and Punjab, Muslims in Uttar Pradesh, all were invited to support Congress if they wanted the state's protection and favours. The politics of secularism was interpreted to mean that the state was visibly solicitous of all religions. To prove her ecumenical *largesse*, Mrs Gandhi 'balanced' her appeals to Muslims by frequenting Hindu places of worship, surrounded herself with Hindu insignia, and welcomed mysterious swamis to her retinue. The implications and scale of this deviation from Congress principle became apparent in the anti-Sikh violence that followed Mrs Gandhi's assassination in 1984, where evidence points to its having been instigated in New Delhi by Congress members. Paradoxically, the ability of Congress to sustain itself as a 'national' party had come to rest on its ability to play with parochial affiliations.

The Indian nationalism of Gandhi and Nehru had not only resisted invoking religion, but had also scrupulously avoided defining the nation in terms of a majority community. But the populist turn in Indian politics redefined democracy as majority rule. The operations of this simplified sense of democracy began to unravel the nationalist imagination. This showed itself in two ways. First, the new forms of democracy alienated those in the regions. During the 1980s national electoral majorities were used to justify implicitly the Centre's isolation and neglect of political dissatisfaction in the regions. Given the scale of India's democracy, and the distribution of the electorate and of parliamentary seats across the country (Uttar Pradesh, for instance, sends eighty-five members to the Lok Sabha, the national parliament, while Punjab and Kashmir send, respectively, thirteen and six), national elections could be won by ignoring dissident regions and mustering support elsewhere – so turning democratic procedures into an instrument that left these regions structurally disenfranchised. Secondly, the diffusion of the language of majoritarian democracy gave opportunities to rivals of the Congress in its claim to represent the nation. In particular it began to revive the imagination of the Hindu nationalists. Congress still held title to the nationalist movement and its recognizable symbolic paraphernalia, but the historical immediacy of the nationalist movement was fading and the meanings of its symbolism were less widely shared, especially among a predominantly young electorate. In the 1977 elections, which ended the Emergency and ousted Congress from national power for the first time, three-quarters of the electorate either were born or reached voting age after 1947. The political contest over identities that occupied so much of Indian public life from the 1980s onwards was provoked by the crisis of Congress itself. Centralization and the neglect of federal channels incited strident regionalism; the substitution of a 'national' electorate and the redefinition of democracy forced Congress into inviting local identities into the national arena, which worked to the advantage of those who claimed to represent more directly and intimately these groupings of religion and caste.

5

The crisis of Congress became a crisis of the state itself and hence a crisis in the terms of Indian identity. Congress had functioned as a centrist party, spokesman for no single category or interest, and its coalitional character enabled individuals and groups throughout India to make a nest in it. Its pragmatic political determination in the two decades after independence had managed to confine the scope of the alternative definitions of Indianness which Hindu nationalists proposed. The later intensification of democratic competition forced it to appeal to more exclusive identities: this broke the old pattern of political representation and created opportunities for rival parties both in the regions and at the Centre.

The logic of this process was rehearsed in miniature in the politics of Uttar Pradesh, India's most populous regional state and heartland of Congress since the 1920s (the province has provided seven of India's twelve prime ministers). The party had built its support here through an alliance of upper castes, the lowest in the social order and Muslims. By the 1990s Congress had declined to a sorry rump and the politics of Uttar Pradesh had fragmented. The upper castes had turned to the Hindu nationalists; the intermediate castes – the 'Backward' and 'Other Backward Classes'- in alliance with Muslims formed their own regional parties; and the lowest in the caste order, the Bahujans and Dalits, turned to leaders and parties that kept alive the ideals of Ambedkar, now expressed in new rhetoric. No single group was powerful enough to dominate. By an unexpected inversion, this pattern of regional deadlock and political fragmentation imprinted itself on India's national politics. General elections in 1991 and then again in 1996 gave the country successive 'hung' parliaments, and minority or coalition governments. A single national party could no longer fill all the political space.

A resurgent Hindu nationalism benefited from this opening. Its historical roots are as deep as those of more pluralist Indian nationalisms, and reach back to the late nineteenth-century Brahminic responses to colonial rule. Essential to its rise in the 1980s was a new-found ability to expand beyond its exclusively Brahminic and high-caste membership and to gain imaginative hold over India's middle classes – to whom it offered a religious idiom tailored for democratic times. But this political Hinduism was deeply untraditional. The definition of Hinduism is an elusive academic quest, but one feature all agree on is its intrinsically decentralized structure. Ritual practices have always been differentiated by caste, by region and by sect, and there has never been a fundamental scripture that all must accept. The emergence, under Brahminic auspices, of more singular and unified definitions of Hinduism during the colonial period was a self-consciously emulative reaction to the challenges of Christianity and Islam. In this sense a 'Hindu' identity – as distinct from defining oneself as a vaishnav, shavite or shakta – is as decisively modern as a regional or national identity, or as the juridical identities of caste created by Indian law since 1947.

This culturally unfamiliar Hindu self-definition attracted many of India's expanding and selectively Westernized middle classes. Rising consumerism and the extension of the market during the 1980s did not fuel an individualistic hedonism nor breed liberal individuals. Rather, it was experienced as an opportunity to sample the pleasures of modernity within collective units like the family. (The outstanding hit of the Hindi cinema in the mid-1990s, *Hum Apke Hain Kaun?*, was a film with the barest of story lines, a four-hour celebration of domestic consumption, dining and marriage.) For many in India modernity has been adopted through the conservative filters of religious piety, moralism and domestic virtue. This has spawned a novel Hinduism, where holographic gods dangle on well-used keychains and cassettes of devotional *ragas* are played in traffic jams: instances of a religious sentiment freed from its original defining contexts, from the subtle iconography of materials and the punctual divisions of the day into sacred and mundane time. Besides tapping the sentiments of domesticity and piety, political Hinduism also summons up the energies of the young, many of whom have drifted through India's colleges and universities (for most, an idle rite of passage rather than an education).

These veins of piety and energy were effectively mined by extremists belonging to the organizations of the 'Sangh Parivar', the BJP's 'family'. Out of it have surfaced characters like Sadhvi Rithambhra, an extraordinary orator able both to elicit and to incite collective emotion, to reassure and to enrage. Rithambhra's voice, recorded on cassettes that circulate 'with the ubiquity of a one-rupee coin in north India', blends exhortation and argument in a tone that trembles with a sense of Hindu loss and dispossession – of insult, injury and humiliation inflicted upon Hindus by history and now by a state that refused to acknowledge their presence:

As far as the construction of the Ram temple is concerned, some people say Hindus should not fight over a structure of brick and stone. They should not quarrel over a piece of land. I want to ask these people, 'If someone burns the national flag will you say "Oh, it doesn't matter, it is only two meters of cloth which is not a great national loss."' The question is not of two meters of cloth but of an insult to the nation. Ram's birthplace is not a quarrel about a small piece of land. It is a question of national integrity. The Hindu is not fighting for a temple of brick and stone. He is fighting for the preservation of a civilization, for his Indianness, for national consciousness, for the recognition of his true nature.

The idiom of cultural dispossession reverberates deeply in Indian politics. After 1947 it was the preserve of Gandhian socialists like Ram Manohar Lohia and Jayaprakash Narayan, men who in different ways attacked what they saw as the neo-colonialism of a notionally Indian state ruled by a modernist, English-speaking elite. With the collapse of these badly directed political projects, this idiom passed into the hands of Hindu nationalists. It was used to great effect in rural north India – a region which in the past had been attracted by Gandhian social-ism – and it successfully inducted new groups to its support, allying them to the urban middle classes and the educated young. The aura of cultural injury and martyrdom is a trademark style of the BJP, the most recent incarnation of a Hindu nationalist political party. (It was created in 1980, out of the old Bharatiya Jan Sangh, itself an upgrade of the pre-independence Hindu Mahasabha.) The BJP was a direct beneficiary of Congress decline: it styled itself as the legitimate heir to Congress, and it shared more with the political horizons of the Congress era than with the pattern that began to emerge in the mid-1990s.

But the BJP's definition of Indian nationalism was precisely the contrary of Nehru's. It explicitly declared allegiance to the Savarkarite idea of *Hindutva*, 'Hinduness', and celebrated a glori-ous Hindu past: phrases from Vivekananda – 'It is out of the past that the future is moulded. It is the past that becomes the future' – adorned its manifestos. But Hindu nationalism also embraced the armoury of the modern state. Its ambition was to complete the project of achieving an Indian nation state by piloting it towards what it saw as its logical terminus: a culturally and ethnically cleaned-up homogenous community with a singu-lar Indian citizenship, defended by a state that had both God and nuclear warheads on its side. It was the BJP which kept alive most devotedly the ambition of modernization based on Western experiences of nationalism. The BJP did not propose a return to a traditional Hindu polity, it had no Gandhian picture of a stateless India composed of village republics, nor did it even insist that all Indians must be Hindu. Its ambitions were more purely statist: to eradicate any legal and political recognition of cultural and religious differences. Although it described itself as a positive project of 'cultural nationalism', in fact the BJP was committed to a negative programme, designed to efface all the signs of non-Hinduness that are in fact so integral to India.

Nowhere has this been more apparent than in its determination to reform the Constitution, to remove what it describes as its 'anomalies' and substitute a uniform legal code. The BJP has focused most closely on Muslim customary law which regulates marriage and divorce; and on the special constitutional provisions regarding the Muslim-majority valley of Kashmir, which include the promise of plebiscitary rights on the question of its accession to the Indian Union, and which prohibit other Indians from acquiring real property in the region. To be sure, these issues do raise considerations that are not easily reconciled: the claims of the rights of women and of individuals, for instance, as against those of cultures and groups. They are legitimate subjects of debate – if not quite in the terms suggested by the BJP. Indeed, the political success of a party like the BJP has relied not merely on its ability to translate the piety of the street and *puja* room into a populist cultural democracy, but on its fluency in the high discourse of state legality and constitutional reform. In this it is similar to Congress – which has long monopolized this language – and different from regional opposition parties, which are in touch with the popular pulse but only have a primitive command of Indian constitutionalese.

The BJP's conception of law and of the state's relation to society is entirely its own, however, and quite alien to anything from India's past history: it proposes an even bigger historical rupture than that signified by the emergence of the colonial Raj in the nineteenth century or the establishment of an Indian state in the mid twentieth century. The fundamental debate in Indian political and intellectual life during the 1980s and 90s about the crisis of secularism has tended to skirt around the depth of this proposed change and its implications. The pluralistic nationalism

outlined after 1947 was certainly informed by the language of
Western constitutional theory; it spoke an impeccable legal
language. But its basic intuition about the relationship between
political power and the diverse cultural practices of Indian
society derived from an insight into the operative principles of
the few large-scale political formations of India's past. It saw
that these had been sustained by relatively limited interference
in the society's religious practices. The political proposals of
Hindu nationalism veer away from this historical pattern: they
hope to bring the array of Indian religious and cultural activities
under command of the state, to tidy up the compromises and
accommodations that litter Indian life and bring them into a
regimented design, presided over by a single legal system.

The Hindu nationalist aspiration to redefine Indianness always
presumed the availability of a strong state as the instrument
through which to forge an identity. Yet just when it seemed
poised to capture the state, many of the latter's capacities have
been dramatically constricted. One of the central legacies of the
last period of Congress government, 1991–6, was the restitution
of political decision-making powers to the regional governments
of the Union. This was not based on a punctilious commitment
to the principle of decentralization; rather, it flowed from a canny
realization by Narasimha Rao that it was politically wiser to let
regional politicians appear responsible for implementing
unpopular economic measures linked with liberalization. The
reinvigoration of regional politics, often driven by lower-caste,
Dalit and rural parties, against the impositions of the Centre
was a striking feature of the 1990s – encouraged by economic
liberalization, by the opportunities presented by a declining
Congress, and by the threat that many in the regions feared in
Hindu nationalists capturing central power and wielding it to
impose a singular definition of Indian identity. The political
momentum of these lower-caste and regional parties is the single
most impressive obstacle to nationalist Hindu ambitions.

By definition, the regionalist ideas of India are plural rather than singular or shared, shaped as they are by the legacies of different historical pasts and varied experiences of political rule and economic development. The most spectacular instances of regionalism have been the violent separatist movements of the 1980s and 90s, which proposed a dissolution of the Indian idea. No group turns lightly to the project of separatism, and those who have done so in India have had strong reasons, based on a conviction that the founding principles of the Indian state had lost positive value. Large-scale populist democracy excluded their voice from the Centre. Economic development had failed them: some groups, in poorer states like Assam, claimed it had exploited their resources while leaving them in conditions of deprivation, and demanded more active redistribution; others, in regions that had prospered like Punjab, wanted the government to curtail its redistributive ambitions. And secularism too had failed them: the dalliances of Congress, and the prospect of a government led by Hindu nationalists, were profoundly disturbing to a Muslim in Kashmir, a Sikh in Punjab, a tribal in Assam or a Christian in Nagaland. There is strength to such arguments, and it is hard not to feel that the claims of separatists in Kashmir or Nagaland have the force of justice behind them. But they are remarkably ill-conceived as political projects. The likelihood of practical success for such separatisms is small: the capacity of the Indian state to contain armed insurgency – either through outright suppression or by attrition – and to maintain India's territorial identity against domestic challengers has never been seriously disturbed – a record inherited from the Raj. The recent histories of Punjab and Kashmir, where armed separatists have taken on the Indian state and their own people, are witness to the tragedy of misjudging this capacity. Further, regions like Punjab, Kashmir and Nagaland are landlocked border territories in geo-politically strategic locations, with no military or economic viability as independent states: exclusion from the economic markets and resources of the Indian Union would be disastrous for their people.

A second type of regionalist idea of India has acquired prominence since the devolution of some economic powers from the central state. Its leaders are a band of powerful regional politicians (many of whom have spent much or all of their careers outside the Congress Party) who have refused to be dictated to by the central state and who now have real powers to resist it. This new breed, men like Laloo Prasad Yadav, Mulayam Singh Yadav and the former prime minister, H. D. Deve Gowda, are all drawn from outside the upper castes, and each possesses his own distinct regionalist perspective. None would dream of suggesting that the Union be dissolved, but neither do they propose a coherent idea of an Indian identity. This is manifest in their picture of the economy, which they see essentially as a cluster of regional units – each seeking to maximize benefits at the expense of others – rather than as a unified national economy (in his few months as India's prime minister, Deve Gowda ensured that his home state of Karnataka received a bounty of state and private investment).

For Nehru, the possibility of India depended as much on the project of common development as on the potentialities revealed by past interconnections. Decades of state-directed and regulated development have given India a huge national economy, whose functioning depends on a central supervisory state. That state needs the powers of redistribution to reduce regional inequalities. The unequal effects of liberalization are already clear, as investment is made in regions with more developed infrastructure like Maharashtra, Gujarat and Karnataka, and neglects less developed regions like Bihar, Rajasthan and Orissa. Over the next decade or two, the effects of such market selections will surely place strains on the Union and on the idea of a shared Indian identity. It will require formidable skills and imagination to handle this fundamental issue. Such considerations hold even more forcefully on the subject of a common natural environment in which present and future generations of Indians can hope to exist. It is hardly the case that the Indian state has a distinguished record on environmental matters, but any dissolution of its regulatory powers will certainly create still more hazards, pose even greater difficulties of control, and encourage regional states to act heedlessly.

But potentially the most far-reaching consequences of this new regionalism lie squarely in the cultural realm. India's regional politicians have essentially parochial views, and they are devoted to cultivating their own vernacular gardens. The implications of this are apparent when considered against the background of India's large-scale cultural trajectories. In the past decade India has had two prime ministers who entered office with fluency in only one language, English, or in Deve Gowda's case, the regional language Kannada. (To be fair, one prime minister had command of more than a dozen languages.) The bilingual, bicultural idea of an Indian identity, the idea that animated the nationalist movement, is fragmenting into three cultural segments: a small but powerful anglicized metropolitan elite; a loose, huge group of Hindi-speaking urban middle classes and lower castes; and the vernacular regional cultures. The lines of political connection now run across and among these fragments, and are producing an intricate tessellation of identities. From this, a new image of Indianness may well disclose itself, for what is also striking after fifty years of political freedom is the depth and extent of the commitment to some idea of India. Yet there are good reasons to be sceptical. The developments of the 1990s as an emergent cultural pattern mark a serious rupture with the idea of a layered Indian political identity. And it is hard to see a coherent replacement for it: each cultural fragment is suspicious and resentful of the other, unwilling or unable to learn to speak the other's language. But there is the example of the prime ministerial Hindi lessons.

6

'All the "best" people in India', Henri Michaux wrote in a cranky *feuilleton* of his imaginary adventures through India, 'gave it up, from the beginning, gave up India and the whole earth. The great miracle of the English is that now the Hindus do care about it.' The ideologues of the British Raj trumpeted the claim that India lacked any natural unity as a territorial state. There were no 'Indians' to govern themselves, only subjects of religious belief and imperial rule. But British domination helped to create the opportunities for Indians to acquire a modern self, a political identity guaranteed by a state. In the twentieth century Indians have taken that opportunity and have invented themselves, and they have kept that inventiveness alive. They have shown a kind of care for the idea of India, as well as sometimes an anger.

India, this historical and political artefact, a contingent and fragile conjunction of interlinked, sometimes irritable cultures, has been since 1947 continuously subject to a common political authority. The notions of territorial integrity and national unity, fundamental to both Hindu and Indian nationalism, are, as in all nationalisms everywhere, ideological fictions, fabulous myths – this applies equally to the Indian Union and the idea of *Bharatavarsha*. But it also applies to the more fragmentary imaginations of those aspired-for lands, Khalistan or Tamil Eelam, Kashmir or Bodoland. The demands of culture, the claims for recognition, are against large federal states, but the pressures of economics are towards interconnection and expansion of scale. The idea of India has been constituted through struggles to balance these contrary pulls in a coherent political project, to respect the diversities of culture with a commitment to a common enterprise of development.

After fifty years of an Indian state, the definition of who is an Indian is as passionately contested as ever. What has kept it in contest is the presence of the state whose access to resources makes it a real prize, and the persistence of democratic politics, which has kept most people in the game for this prize. The contest is over economic opportunities and about cultural recognition: it is a contest for ownership of the state. The intensity of that conflict today can be seen in the dizzying assortment of claims upon that state, claims that have been at once agitated and frustrated by democracy and economic progress. Acceptance of this inherited, proliferating diversity and the capacity to live with it are for Indians pragmatic necessities. India's history has shown two broad possibilities of dealing with that diversity: a theoretically untidy, improvising, pluralist approach, or a neatly rationalist and purifying exclusivism. India's history has also, for the first time in all its millennial depth, given the present generation of Indians the responsibility to choose between them. They must decide what they wish to build out of the wreckage of Ayodhya's Babri Masjid.

The Garb of Modernity

You want self-knowledge? You should come to America. Just as the Mahatma had to go to jail and sit behind bars to write his autobiography. Or Nehru had to go to England to discover India. Things are clear only when looked at from a distance.

A. K. RAMANUJAN, 'Annayya's Anthropology'

Annayya, a scholarly Brahmin from Mysore living in Chicago, buries himself for years in the libraries of the University of Chicago. Here, in self-exile, he discovers his own India. 'When he lived in India, Annayya was obsessed with things American, English or European. Once here in America, he began reading more and more about India; began talking more and more about India to anyone who would listen.' One day, while devouring the pages of *Hinduism: Custom and Ritual*, a newly published anthropological monograph by an earnest American researcher, Annayya's eyes alight on a photograph taken by its author during fieldwork in Mysore and now used to illustrate the cremation rites of South Indian Brahmins. Suddenly, eerily, Annayya sees his own past flash literally before his eyes. He recognizes in the photograph the faces of his family: it is the cremation of his own father, news of whose death had not reached him in the library stacks of Chicago. It is an uncanny moment of loss and recognition, like realizing one is looking at light from a long dead star.

Even in their most intimate self-perceptions, Indians over the past century have come to see themselves in mirrors created by the inquisitive energies of the West. Likewise, India's public life is constituted by a host of self-images fashioned out of Western reflections: from the cultural narcissism of nationalist Hindus, lit by the faded beacons of Orientalist scholarship, to the practices of groups like the Dalit Panthers, modelled on the Black Panthers of 1960s America. The traffic has of course moved in both directions. India, the idea and place, has itself shaped the self-images of others. From Megasthenes in the early third century BC, via Alberuni, the Portuguese missionaries, Schlegel and the Romantics, Schopenhauer, and on to the theosophists, Kipling, E. M. Forster, Paul Scott, the Beatles, and Goa Trance, other cultures have recurringly used India as a foil to define their own historical moments: to reassure or to doubt themselves. And Indians have also, on occasion, tried to work out their own 'indigenous' ways of knowing the West. It is impossible to sever these twisted bonds of mutual knowingness and ignorance: the plunder is constant, and neither side can retreat into a luxurious cultural hermeticism. Any discussion of India is thus inescapably forced on to the treacherous fields of the politics of knowledge. These must be navigated, like any political activity, by one's wits. There is no privileged compass, no method or idiom, that can assist.

The idea of India was created by such collisions between cultures and politics. These encounters have left Indians with three questions of practical judgement. What possibilities are available to them? What challenges are they likely to face? And what is the significance of the history they are making? Answers to these questions necessarily invite dispute and revision, but the questions themselves are direct, urgent and unavoidable. In posing them, this book has throughout implied that the categories and terms of Western political thought are essential to all judgements about them. This is not out of a conviction that the ideas of Western politics themselves represent the summit of human thought and feeling. It is simply in recognition of the profound historical impress of these ideas upon the practical experience of India and of the non-Western world in general. The mutually defining contact between Western political ideas and the non-European world goes back a long way. But the intensity and scope of that engagement have achieved an historically unparalleled scale in the twentieth century. The ideas of the state, nation, revolution, democracy, equality, racial purity, economic growth and many more have not only defined the West's own habitat: they have reconstituted the entire world, if invariably in localized accents. It has been a far from universally happy experience. But neither side can escape its consequences. The stories of the entirely unanticipated, often horrifyingly perverse, and sometimes laughably ineffectual consequences of these ideas for peoples and cultures outside Europe is now an essential theme of any reflection on the historical trajectories and the supposedly universal scope of these Western ideas. The future of Western political theory will be decided outside the West. And in deciding that future, the experience of India will loom large.

Twentieth-century Indians have for their part voluntarily adopted many of these ideas and welcomed the opportunities of regular contact with the world beyond their own country. They have voyaged widely in search of livelihood and ideas, and they have discovered themselves through the clarities, oversights and yearnings that distance induces. The exact character of the homelands they have journeyed from has proved elusive, and often imaginary. Where in the world is India? Historical precedent suggests that it is possible to be wildly – if profitably – wrong about its geographical location (remember Columbus). And there is a venerable tradition that has insisted on seeing India as a conceptual rather than a physical space. 'A country', as Rabindranath Tagore put it, 'is not territorial, but ideational'; or, in the more demotic cadence of the tourist board poster, 'India is a state of mind'.

It may well be. But since 1947 India has existed as a precisely mapped, counted, and bounded territory governed by a sovereign political authority, as a state, a recognized member of the international state system. In coming to define itself in the global coin of modern politics – in the currency of state sovereignty – it has had to do violence to itself. Exactly *why* India came to have the territorial shape it does remains a puzzle and an incitement to the political imagination of South Asia. The precise spatial extent and specific human content of every state is, at any particular point in time, potentially open to contest. What has kept this subject so vigorously embattled on the subcontinent is the permanent disturbance of Partition.

For an act so decisive to the lives of hundreds of millions, it remains curiously difficult to characterize just what Partition was. The greatest violation of Gandhi's idea of India as a civilizational unity, it was the last deed of the British Raj: a supposedly rational slicing of the land on the basis of religion. To the departing British, the religious sentiments of the subcontinent were backward and superstitious; yet these were the very principles used to create two modern nations. Partition's ruthless entangling of the rational and the irrational has unnerved historians. Most have opted either to reconstruct the minutiae of elite intrigues, to show Partition's logic according to some intricate political calculus allegedly deployed by the actors involved; or they have dwelt on the sheer horror of it, treating it as an eruption of pure unreason and religious passions. The ensnarement of the rational and irrational is mordantly balanced in the brilliant, bitter absurdism of Saadat Hasan Manto's short story 'Toba Tek Singh'. 'A couple of years after the Partition of the country,' Manto's supreme parable begins, 'it occurred to the respective governments of India and Pakistan that inmates of lunatic asylums, like prisoners, should also be exchanged. Muslim lunatics in India should be transferred to Pakistan and Hindu and Sikh lunatics in Pakistani asylums should be sent to India.'

Partition rustles through the subcontinent's public imagination, a surreptitious and always available motif around which the inevitable disappointments of modern politics can gather. It was a deed born out of fear on the part of all those involved: Hindus, Muslims, Sikhs, non-believers, the British themselves. Its consequence was to heighten, not allay, the fears of those who had to live with its after-effects. There was no poetry in Partition, yet W. H. Auden's lines on Cyril Radcliffe – the man entrusted with determining the boundaries of the successor states to the Raj, India and Pakistan – succeed in rendering something of the haste, danger and ultimate enigma of this incalculably pregnant moment of decision:

> Shut up in a lonely mansion, with police night and day
> Patrolling the gardens to keep assassins away,
> He got down to work, to the task of settling the fate
> Of millions. The maps at his disposal were out of date
> And the Census Returns almost certainly incorrect,
> But there was no time to check them, no time to inspect
> Contested areas. The weather was frightfully hot,
> And a bout of dysentery kept him constantly on the trot,
> But in seven weeks it was done, the frontiers decided,
> A continent for better or worse divided.
>
> The next day he sailed for England, where he quickly forgot
> The case, as a good lawyer must. Return he would not,
> Afraid, as he told his Club, that he might get shot.

What exactly was done? Was it the division of one territory between two 'nations' or peoples? Or the breaking of one civilization into two territories? The larger conceptual enigma of Partition also casts its mystery over the fine details. Radcliffe destroyed all his notes and papers relating to the Boundary awards before he left India. In deciding the borders, his Boundary Commission was instructed to draw its lines on the basis of 'contiguous majority areas'; it was also asked to take into account 'other factors'. But neither these factors, nor the unit of the area to be divided, were ever specified: whether it was the district, or smaller sub-units like the *tehsil, zail* or village, that should serve as the unit in which 'majorities' and 'minorities' were determined, was left contentiously ambiguous. Partition infiltrated into the South Asian imagination that ubiquitous imagery of modern politics: the pornography of borders, an imagery that at once excites actually existing and aspiring nationalisms ('separatisms') with the fantasy of fulfilment, and must always leave them with permanent disillusion, the melancholia of endless corridors of no man's land.

Radcliffe knew nothing about India other than the five perspiring weeks he spent there, trying with maps and pens to fulfil his impossible duty of devising a judicious cartography. A day before the stroke of midnight, when the British Union flag would be lowered finally on the subcontinent, Radcliffe wrote to his stepson:

I thought you would like to get a letter from India with a crown on the envelope. After tomorrow evening nobody will ever again be allowed to use such stationery and after 150 years British rule will be over in India – Down comes the Union Jack on Friday morning and up goes – for the moment I rather forget what, but it has a spinning wheel or a spider's web in the middle. I am going to see Mountbatten sworn as the first Governor-General of the Indian Union at the Viceroy's House in the morning and then I station myself firmly on the Delhi airport until an aeroplane from England comes along. Nobody in India will love me for the award about the Punjab and Bengal and there will be roughly 80 million people with a grievance who will begin looking for me. I do not want them to find me. I have worked and travelled and sweated – oh I have sweated the whole time.

It is the weary, fearful, honest pathos of these private words, not the fine public speeches and pomp that accompanied the British departure, that is the true imperial epitaph.

Partition is the unspeakable sadness at the heart of the idea of India: a *memento mori* that what made India possible also profoundly diminished the integral value of the idea. It conceded something essential in the nationalist vision, the conviction that what defined India was its extraordinary capacity to accumulate and live with differences. Tagore died too soon to experience this loss; Gandhi suffered it, but for a mercifully short while. It was Nehru who had to make his own and his country's life in Partition's shadow, to try to recover some grandeur for the darkened idea of India. There was, he suggested, a way that it might be done.

History has not anaesthetized the original crisis of Partition. Like 1789 for the French, Partition is the moment of the Indian nation's origin through violent rupture with itself. It both defines and constantly suspects India's identity, dividing it between the responsibility to tolerate differences, and the dream of a territory where all are compelled to worship in unison. The deep, valuable diversities of India have kept alive the fear and ambition of future crises of division. It will remain so until Indians begin to come to terms with Partition's political and historical signifi-cance. The most promising among recent interpretations of Par-tition have begun to probe the popular experiences of violence and displacement: the very experiences that were constitutive of this episode yet that find little place in the historical memory of the state. This self-consciously evades the perspective of the state; but in doing so, it misses the point of what Partition was.

Partition emerged out of a conflict over the state: a conflict about whether a single successor state ought to acquire the rightful authority to enforce its judgements over the entire popu-lation and territory left by the Raj. For those who wished to separate and establish their own state, the promise of Partition was the promise of a state made less alien. The impulse ascribed to Muslim 'separatists' was no different from that which animates all modern political sensibilities: a desire to reduce the imperson-ality of the modern state. Since the end of the eighteenth century, all efforts to make the state less impersonal have invoked the idea of the nation: a form of solidarity usually specified in terms of a common religion, language, culture, race or history. It does not require too much historical delving to demonstrate the fictive, spurious character of all nations; and yet no modern idea has managed to summon up stronger, if erratic, feelings of identification with the alien apparatus of the state.

The modern state too is a fictive entity; and it too maintains a stubborn reality. It is by definition impersonal, and it needs to remain that way if it is to be a state at all. In Hobbes's famous, bizarre image of the Leviathan, it is a *persona ficta*, an 'artificial man' that encompasses both rulers and ruled, but belongs to neither. It cannot be reduced to, or identified with, any one element in the society. Conceptually and practically, the state is an alien, unnatural entity, often an active menace to its own subjects. But it also offers them protections. The citizens or subjects of a state themselves regularly pose mutual individual or collective hazards. The greatest cruelties are often those inflicted by neighbours, by those who have lived alongside one another and who in some sense are all too intimately familiar with each other's ways. Every state carries within it traces of what Hobbes called the 'state of nature'; but to live with these traces is on balance less damaging than the constantly fearful existence of those condemned to survive without the protection of a state. The risks in modern politics are not simply those posed by the state to its citizen-subjects. Every citizen body is itself divided by religious, class, gender, ethnic and other interests. The hazards embodied by the state can pale before those that may arise from conflicts along such lines of social division.

The ambition to rid oneself of the state, to escape it by retreat to the village or to wish its elimination, is a forlorn ambition. Equally misdirected is the desire to blend the state with the identity of all or some over whom it rules: to make it the state of a singular religion, culture or *ethnos* – the torrid, empty dream of partition. The only tenable normative aspiration in modern politics can be to make states more trustworthy to all who must live under them: to make them more graceful and civilized in their dealings with their citizens, and with one another. In that project of civilizing political power, the model of constitutional democracy has proved the most reliable instrument available to modern populations. It is not the finest product of the desiring human intellect. But it is certainly more practicable than other, more promethean conceptions. It has proved reasonably effective in the struggle to create and sustain a degree of identification between states and their citizens. Allegiance and identification in the modern world are profoundly political relationships. Religion, language, culture, economic interdependence: these all can help to foster the sense of belonging. But ultimately, identification with or allegiance to a state must be sustained, if it is to be sustained at all, by constant renewal through consent.

That is what has made the idea of democracy so widely accepted today: vital both to political leaders, who must struggle to sustain their acceptability in the face of the shifting opinions of those over whom they rule; and to citizens, who desire to live free from fear, to judge and choose for themselves. This desire of the citizenry resounds in Aung San Suu Kyi's direct and irresistible evocation of the popular demand for democracy in her stifled country : 'When asked why they feel so strong a need for democracy, the least political will answer: "We just want to be able to go about our own business freely and peacefully, not doing anybody harm, just earning a decent living without anxiety and fear."' People do not, as the Burmese 'democracy songs' put it, want to be mere 'rice-eating robots'. Opponents of this desire have resorted to arguments from culture: to claims about 'Asian values' and the 'Asian way', hoping by such means to exorcise democracy from their states. But the definition of a culture – especially a 'national culture', let alone that of a continent – invites contest. The decision to select and highlight certain traits, to be conveniently amnesic about others, to see culture as a self-enclosed whole and to turn it to the legitimation of particular ends, all are eminently political strategies.

Part of the purpose of a state must be to protect not merely the physical and material security of its members but also their identities. All too often this has involved a tortuous simplification of internal cultural diversities into a uniform political identity, a tidy template singularly distinguishable from those of surrounding states. India's public life is today riven with conflicting arguments about the appropriate contents of a cultural nationalism; and it will certainly be essential for Indians to create some version of this. This is especially true during a period when so many aspects of India's varied cultural ecology are being severely tested by their greater exposure to the entrepreneurial talents of domestic and international operators, to forms of ingenious, often callous exploitation. But there is little need to retreat into an anxious and inward exclusivism. India's past has bequeathed an immensely rich, varied and flexible repertoire out of which an expansive cultural nationalism might be created.

What has made democracy viable in India is not simply the appeal of the idea, or pre-existing cultural and historical predispositions. Nor, until now, has democracy's survival been conditional on economic success. Ideologically unwelcome and paradoxical as it may seem to inhabitants of the 'virtual' world of post-modernism, it is in fact the continuous stability of the state that has been essential to India's democracy. Democratic states, like all other states, survive through their ability to withstand external threats. Today, such external threats are principally of two types: military challenges, and the pressures of the global economy. Both militarily and economically, the international conditions in which the Indian state will henceforth have to make its way have changed significantly. The disintegration of the socialist project removed a linchpin of the Indian model of military security: the Soviet Union. In the altered strategic situation of west and central Asia, the new and older states in this region have begun to sense the mutual benefits in stressing their cultural and religious connections. Meanwhile, politically India remains a lone democracy surrounded by an arc of non-democratic states: Pakistan to the west, China to the north, Burma to the east.

The collapse of the socialist empire has also altered the range of economic alternatives. The argument that filled so much of the political and intellectual space of the twentieth century, between socialism and the market, is for the moment decisively settled in favour of the market. But markets are instruments, not values; and the language of equality remains as pointed as ever a standard by which to evaluate societies. The economic disputes in India, as elsewhere, now centre around contending views about India's entry into global competition and trade. Is international trade a public good for all participants? Or is it more accurately seen as a zero-sum game, where certain nations and groups prosper at the expense of others? The last 200 years have generated a variety of confident answers to this question. But, from Adam Smith to the current catfights of GATT, the question itself remains wide open. It is not even clear who is best entitled to answer it: transnational experts, 'world economists'? Or those who directly and most immediately experience the effects of the intrusions and withdrawals of global capital – members of trade unions, supporters of political parties, the organized citizenry?

Judging between the relative claims of military security as against economic security, deciding which risks to invest against, can never be easy. None of the existing traditions of political reflection – conservative, liberal, socialist, Gandhian – has faced such issues very frankly. In modern democracies, judgements about military security are almost exclusively the preserve of professionals. Judgements about the economy, however, resist continuous insulation from the pressing demands, beliefs and actions of the citizenry. Unlike the threat of war between states, which nowadays is usually intermittent or sporadic, the challenge of the global economy is ceaseless. The routine viability of India's democracy will therefore come to be tied more closely to its economic performance, assessed in terms of stability, growth and distribution. Rulers and those who elect them will together have to devise effective practical responses to the opportunities and hazards of the international marketplace. How they respond, what decisions they take about how to exploit or protect India's natural habitat, will also determine the prospects for future generations on the subcontinent.

But ultimately, the viability – and most importantly, the point – of India's democracy will rest on its capacity to sustain internal diversity, on its ability to avoid giving reason to groups within the citizen body to harbour dreams of having their own exclusive nation states. Such dreams of partition and domestic purity are animated by the fantasy that all problems begin and end at the border; they do not. There is no ideological or cultural guarantee for a nation to hold together. It just depends on human skills. That is why politics, as an arena where different projects are proposed and decided for and against, has never been more important for Indians. *The case for politics*

In entering the world as a state, India has had to cut its own modern garb. For Indians, this self-fashioning has brought discomforts, pain and risks. But it has also brought them new liberties. India's experience reveals the ordinariness of democracy – untidy, massively complex, unsatisfying, but vital to the sense of a human life today. It establishes that historical and cultural innocence do not exclude Asian cultures from the idea of democracy. But it does not mean that these cultures – or any other, for that matter – are tailor-made for democracy. It will always be a wary struggle. For opponents of democracy in Asia, the history of this experience is a warning of what can be done. For its advocates, it is a basis of hope. The uproarious laughter that suffused the afternoon meetings held in Rangoon after

Aung San Suu Kyi's release from house arrest in 1995 expressed something of that hope. It was the laugh of freedom – that dissolves fear and says, however quietly, there is no longer a divine right to rule.

Aaaugh – given the change

REFERENCES

EPIGRAPHS

p. xxxix Jawaharlal Nehru, *The Discovery of India* (Calcutta, 1946), pp. 30–31

p. xxxix Ved Mehta, *Portrait of India* (New York, 1970), p. 279.

INTRODUCTION: IDEAS OF INDIA

p. 1   'it is necessary to fight . . .', V. S. Naipaul, *India: A Wounded Civilization* (Harmondsworth, 1977), p. 8

p. 6   'One way of defining diversity . . .', A. K. Ramanujan, 'Where Mirrors are Windows: Towards an Anthology of Reflections', *History of Religions*, vol. 28, no. 23 (1989), p. 188

CHAPTER ONE: DEMOCRACY

Epigraph

p. 15   B. R. Ambedkar, Speech in the Constituent Assembly (25 November 1949), *Constituent Assembly Debates*, vol. 12 (New Delhi, 1950), p. 979

p. 15   'Given the fact . . .', *The Hindu*, International Edition, vol. 22, no. 34 (1996), p. 11

p. 16   'the strangest of all', Thomas Babington Macaulay, 'Government of India', Speech in the House of Commons, *The Works of Lord Macaulay*, vol. viii, edited by Lady Trevelyan (London, 1866), p. 122

p. 18 'When they divided the Man . . .', Purusha-sukta (The Hymn of Man), *The Rig Veda*, trans. Wendy Doniger O'Flaherty (Harmondsworth, 1981), p. 31

p. 22 'a class of persons . . .', Thomas Babington Macaulay, Minute on Education, 2 February 1835, in *Macaulay: Prose and Poetry*, selected by G. M. Young (London, 1952), p. 729

p. 31 'Life here continues . . .', Jawaharlal Nehru to K. P. S. Menon, *Selected Works*, second series, vol. 4 (New Delhi, 1986), p. 585

p. 33 'We wanted music of Veena . . .', cited in Granville Austin, *The Indian Constitution: Cornerstone of a Nation* (Oxford, 1966), p. 325

p. 35 'On the 26th of January 1950 . . .', B. R. Ambedkar, as epigraph

p. 40 'I attach great importance . . .', Jawaharlal Nehru to K. N. Pannikar, *Selected Works*, second series, vol. 15, pt 1 (New Delhi, 1993), p. 433

p. 40 'I will fight them . . .', Jawaharlal Nehru, cited in S. Gopal, *Jawaharlal Nehru: A Biography*, vol. 3 (London, 1984), p. 227

p. 42 'it would create . . .', Indira Gandhi (Nehru) to Jawaharlal Nehru, in Sonia Gandhi (ed.), *Freedom's Daughter: Letters Between Indira Gandhi and Jawaharlal Nehru 1922–39* (New Delhi, 1989), p. 389

p. 47 'Are you going to fight . . .', *The Hindu*, cited in Uma Vasudev, *Indira Gandhi: Revolution in Restraint* (Delhi, 1974), p. 276

p. 51 'I came in . . .', T. Anjiah, *India Today* (1–15 March 1982), p. 24, cited in Henry C. Hart, 'Political Leadership in India', in Atul Kohli (ed.), *India's Democracy* (Princeton, 1988), p. 54

CHAPTER TWO: TEMPLES OF THE FUTURE

Epigraphs

p. 61 'Probably nowhere else . . .', Jawaharlal Nehru, *Jawaharlal Nehru's Speeches* vol. 3, 1953–57 (New Delhi, 1958), p. 3.

p. 61 'What is a young man's . . .', Jawaharlal Nehru, Speech at 19th Annual Meeting of the Central Board of Irrigation, New Delhi (5 December 1948), *Jawaharlal Nehru's Speeches*, vol. 1, 1946–49 (New Delhi, 1949), p. 86

p. 62 'Why are you doing', Jawaharlal Nehru, cited in Henry C. Hart, *New India's Rivers* (Bombay, 1956), p. 186

p. 67 'I would rather . . .', Lord Canning, cited in B. R.Tomlinson, *The Economy of Modern India 1960–1970* (Cambridge, 1993), pp. 151–2

p. 67 'No government . . .', William Hunter, *England's Work in India* (London, 1881), cited in Pramit Chaudhuri, 'Changing Perceptions of Poverty in India: State and Poverty', *Sankhya: The Indian Journal of Statistics*, special vol. 55, pt 3 (1993), p. 311

p. 69 'if India is to be . . .', Dadabhai Naoroji, cited in Bipin Chandra, *The Rise and Growth of Economic Nationalism in India* (New Delhi, 1966), p. 638

p. 69 'The agitation for political rights . . .', Mahadev Ranade, cited in ibid., p. 69

p. 70 'industries and trade . . .', Mokshagundam Visvesvarayya, *Reconstructing India* (London, 1920), p. 133

p. 71 'This Congress is . . .', Resolution of the Indian National Congress on Fundamental Rights and Economic Policy, Karachi, in Maurice Gwyer and A. Appadorai (eds), *Speeches and Documents on the Indian Constitution, 1921–47*, (2 vols, Bombay, 1957), vol. 1, pp. 248–9

p. 82 'I had only . . .', P. C. Mahalanobis to Pitamber Pant, 23 June 1954, *Pant Papers*, Nehru Memorial Museum and Library, New Delhi

p. 83 'knew more . . .', E. P. Thompson, *'Alien Homage': Edward Thompson and Rabindranath Tagore* (Delhi, 1993), p. 58

p. 83 'What we know . . .', Rabindranath Tagore, *Sankhya: The Indian Journal of Statistics*, vol. 2 (1933), p. 2

p. 85 'honey attracts . . ., Jagdish Bhagwati, *India in Transition: Freeing the Economy* (Delhi, 1994), p. 74

p. 85 'To be quite frank . . .' P. C. Mahalanobis to Pitamber Pant, 23 June 1954, *Pant Papers*, Nehru Memorial Museum and Library, New Delhi

p. 85 'trained and experienced economists . . .', ibid.

p. 86 'It really depends . . .', A. K. Sen, 'A Note on the Mahalanobis Model of Sectoral Planning', *Arthaniti*, vol. 1, no. 2 (1958), pp. 31–2

p. 86 'Perhaps the Commission itself', A. H. Hanson, in Michael Lipton and Paul Streeten (eds), *The Crisis of Indian Planning: Economic Planning in the 1960s* (London, 1968), p. 45

p. 86 'agreement with Myrdal's . . .', P. C. Mahalanobis, ' "The Asian

Drama": an Indian View', *Sankhya* (series B), vol. 31 (1969), p. 445

p. 87   'The tradition and outlook . . .', ibid., p. 446

p. 87   'How to increase . . .', ibid., p. 444

p. 87   'the number of civil servants . . .', ibid., p. 448

p. 88   'The heart of the problem . . .', P. C. Mahalanobis, 'Social Information for National Development', *Sankhya* (series B), vol. 25 (1963), p. 50

p. 97   'The central role . . .', Jagdish Bhagwati, *India in Transition: Freeing the Economy* (Delhi, 1994), pp. 53–4

p. 97   'merely an appropriate . . .', ibid., p. 98

p. 98   'we finally have this elusive policy . . .', ibid., p. 98

p. 99   'Please help me . . .', H. D. Deve Gowda, *Financial Times* (19 November 1996), *Survey: India*, p. 1

p. 100 'the growth rate of the economy . . .', Bimal Jalan, *India's Economic Policy: Preparing for the Twenty-first Century* (New Delhi, 1996), p. 177

p. 100 'doubling of the present . . .', Purshotamdas Thakurdas *et al.*, *A Plan of Economic Development for India*, pt 1 (London, 1944), p. 14

p. 105 'broader concerns . . .', Jean Dreze and Amartya Sen, *India: Economic Development and Social Opportunity* (Delhi, 1995), p. 92

CHAPTER THREE: CITIES

Epigraph

p. 107 Nissim Ezekiel, 'Irani Restaurant Instructions', *Collected Poems 1952–1988* (Delhi, 1989), p. 240

p. 107 'For years people . . .', R. K. Narayan, 'Lawley Road', *Malgudi Days* (London, 1984), p. 111

p. 111 'an entire village of palaces', George, Viscount Valentia, *Voyages and Travels to India, Ceylon, the Red Sea, Abyssinia and Egypt in the Years 1802, 1803, 1805 and 1806,* (3 vols, London, 1809), p. 236, cited in Norma Evenson, *The Indian Metropolis* (Newhaven and London, 1989), p. 20

p. 117 'Let me tell you . . .', Mirza Ghalib, letter to Amin-ud-Din Ahmad Khan, in Ralph Russell and Khurshidul Islam, *Ghalib: Life and Letters* (Delhi, 1969), pp. 316–17

p. 117 'The European station . . .', W. H. Russell, *My Diary in the Years 1858–9*, 2 vols. (London, 1860), cited in Anthony D. King, *Colonial Urban Development* (London, 1976), p. 125

p. 119 'Threaded with narrow streets . . .', Rev. M. A. Sherring, *The Sacred City of the Hindus: An Account of Benares in Ancient and Modern Times* (London, 1868; reprinted Delhi, 1975), pp. 181–2

p. 120 'I went to the Kashi . . .', M. K. Gandhi, *An Autobiography or The Story of My Experiments with Truth* (1927; reprinted Ahmedabad, 1990), pp. 201–202

p. 120 'the further East . . .', Lord Lytton to Lord Salisbury, 11 May 1876, cited in Bernard S. Cohn, 'Representing Authority in Victorian Britain', *An Anthropologist Among the Historians and Other Essays* (Delhi, 1987), p. 661

p. 121 'see for the first time . . .', Lord Stamfordham, cited in Robert Grant Irving, *Indian Summer: Lutyens, Baker and Imperial Delhi* (Newhaven and London, 1981), p. 73

p. 123 'The Viceroy's House . . .', Robert Byron, *Letters Home*, edited by Lucy Butler (London, 1991), p. 151

p. 123 'Those who claimed . . .', Nirad Chaudhuri, *Thy Hand, Great Anarch! India 1921–1952* (London and New York, 1987), p. 710

p. 124 'One ineradicable habit . . .', ibid., p. 714

p. 127 'Men women and children . . .', Mulk Raj Anand, *Untouchable* (1935; reprinted London, 1940), p. 136

p. 127 'the blood of the villages . . .', M. K. Gandhi, 'Talk with Press Correspondents (28 May 1946)', *Harijan*, 23 June 1946, in *Collected Works of Mahatma Gandhi*, vol. lxxxiv (Ahmedabad, 1981), p. 226

p. 128 'The love of . . .', B. R Ambedkar, *Constituent Assembly Debates*, vol. 7 (New Delhi, 1949), p. 39

p. 128 'nearly all the Big Noises . . .', Jawaharlal Nehru, *An Autobiography* (London, 1936), p. 143

p. 128 'the Governmental structures . . .' Jawaharlal Nehru, *Selected Works*, second series, vol. 17 (New Delhi, 1995), p. 313

p. 128 'There is the spirit . . .', ibid.

p. 131 'The site chosen . . .', Jawaharlal Nehru, *Construction of the New Capital at Chandigarh: Project Report* (no date), cited in Ravi Kalia, *Chandigarh: The Making of an Indian City* (Delhi, 1987), p. 12

p. 131 'It is . . .', Le Corbusier, cited in Ravi Kalia, *Chandigarh: The Making of an Indian City* (Delhi, 1987), p. 87

p. 132 'Corbusier held the crayon . . .', Maxwell Fry, 'Le Corbusier at Chandigarh', in Russell Walden (ed.), *The Open Hand: Essays on Le Corbusier* (Cambridge MA, 1977), p. 354

p. 132 'the advantages of slavery . . .', Le Corbusier, *Sketchbooks vol. 3 1954–1957*, edited by Françoise Franclieu (Cambridge MA, 1982), pp. 16–17

p. 134 'Hide all construction . . .', Le Corbusier, cited in Lawrence Vale, *Architecture, Power, and National Identity* (Newhaven and London, 1992), p. 109

p. 135 'It hits you . . .', Jawaharlal Nehru, Speech at the Seminar and Exhibition of Architecture, New Delhi, in *Jawaharlal Nehru's Speeches*, vol. 4, 1957–1963 (New Delhi, 1964), p. 176

p. 135 'a city designed . . .', Arvind Krishna Mehrotra, 'Partial Recall', *Civil Lines*, no. 1 (Delhi, 1994), p. 8.

p. 141 'all the lungiwallas . . .', cited in Jayant Lele, 'Saffronization of the Shiv Sena: The Political Economy of City, State and Nation', in Sujata Patel and Alice Thorner (eds), *Bombay: Metaphor For Modern India* (Bombay, 1995), p. 190

p. 143 'In Bombay . . .', Salman Rushdie, *The Moor's Last Sigh* (London, 1995), p. 350

CHAPTER FOUR: WHO IS AN INDIAN?

Epigraphs

p. 150 Jawaharlal Nehru, *The Discovery of India* (Calcutta, 1946), p. 497
p. 150 Rabindranath Tagore, 'The Message of Indian History'(1902), *Visva-Bharati Quarterly*, vol. 22, no. 2 (1956), p. 110

p. 154 'there is not . . .', John Strachey, *India* (London, 1885), p. 5
p. 158 'a man . . . may obtain', James Mill, *The History of British India* (1817), 10 vols, edited by H. H. Wilson, (5th edn, London, 1858), vol. 1, p. xxiii
p. 159 'We must have . . .', Bankimchandra Chattopadhyay, cited in Ranajit Guha, *An Indian Historiography of India: A Nineteenth-Century Agenda and Its Implications* (Calcutta, 1988), p. 57
p. 160 'Hindutva is not . . .', V. D. Savarkar, *Hindutva: Who is a Hindu?* (1923), (6th edn, New Delhi, 1989), p. 3

p. 162 'We know that . . .', Muhammad Ali Jinnah, Presidential Address
to the All-India Muslim League, Lahore, in *Speeches and Writings
of Mr. Jinnah*, edited by Jamil-ud-din Ahmed (Lahore, 1942),
p. 161

p. 164 'I look upon Gibbon . . .' M. K. Gandhi, 'My Jail Experiences XI',
Young India, 11 September 1924, in *Collected Works of Mahatma
Gandhi*, vol. xxv (Ahmedabad, 1967), p. 128

p. 164 'I believe that . . .', ibid.

p. 165 Both India and Pakistan . . .', M. K. Gandhi, *Collected Works of
Mahatma Gandhi*, vol. lxxxviii (Ahmedabad, 1983), p. 265

p. 169 'The history of India . . .', Rabindranath Tagore, 'The Message of
Indian History' (1902), *Visva-Bharati Quarterly*, vol. 22, no. 2
(1956), p. 105

p. 169 'an ancient palimpsest . . .', Jawaharlal Nehru, *The Discovery of
India* (Calcutta, 1946), pp. 38–9

p. 170 'If my mind was full . . .', ibid., p. 46

p. 170 'Indian culture was . . .', Jawaharlal Nehru, *An Autobiography*
(London, 1936), p. 430

p. 170 'lonely and homeless . . .', ibid., p. 374

p. 171 'he never showed . . .', Isaiah Berlin, 'Rabindranath Tagore and
the Consciousness of Nationality', *The Sense of Reality* (London
and New York, 1996), p. 260

p. 180 'the dream of a minority . . .', T. N. Madan, 'Secularism in its
Place', *Journal of Asian Studies*, vol. 46, no. 4 (1987), p. 748

p. 180 'in an open society . . .', ibid.

p. 187 'with the ubiquity . . .', Tapan Basu *et al.*, *Khaki Shorts and Saffron
Flags: A Critique of the Hindu Right* (New Delhi, 1993), p. 100

p. 187 'As far as . . .', Sadhvi Rithambhra, cited in Sudhir Kakar, *The
Colours of Violence: Cultural Identities, Religion and Conflict*
(Chicago, 1996), p. 157

p. 188 'It is out of the past . . .' Swami Vivekananda, cited in Bharatiya
Janata Party, *Party Manifesto: Our Vision, Our Faith, Our Commitment* (New Delhi, 1996), p. 5

p. 194 'All the "best" . . .', Henri Michaux, *A Barbarian in Asia*, trans.
Sylvia Beach (New York, 1949), p. 26

EPILOGUE: THE GARB OF MODERNITY

Epigraph

p. 196 A. K. Ramanujan, 'Annayya's Anthropology', trans. Narayan Hegde, in Ramachandra Sharma (ed.), *From Cauvery to Godavari: Modern Kannada Short Stories* (New Delhi, 1992), p. 44

p. 196 'When he lived . . .', ibid., p. 47

p. 198 'A country is not . . .', Rabindranath Tagore, *Rabindra-Rachanabali*, vol. 1, p. 1, cited in Ashis Nandy, *The Illegitimacy of Nationalism: Rabindranath Tagore and the Politics of the Self* (Delhi, 1994), p. ix

p. 199 'A couple of years . . .', Saadat Hasan Manto, 'Toba Tek Singh', *Kingdom's End and Other Stories*, trans. Khalid Hassan (London, 1987), p. 11

p. 200 'Shut up . . .', W. H. Auden, 'Partition', *Collected Poems* (London, 1976), pp. 803–4

p. 201 'I thought you . . .', Cyril Radcliffe to Mark Radcliffe, cited in Edmund Heward, *The Great and the Good: A Life of Lord Radcliffe* (Chichester, 1994), p. 42

p. 204 'When asked why . . .' Aung San Suu Kyi, 'In Quest of Democracy', in *Freedom From Fear and Other Writings* (London, 1995), p. 173

BIBLIOGRAPHICAL ESSAY

This is intended as a guide to further reading. It is not a comprehensive bibliography for the book, far less for the entire period; the selections are personal, from a literature that is bewildering in its scale. A glossary of abbreviations can be found at the end.

A great deal of initial information about India can be gleaned rapidly and at a glance from three useful atlases: Joseph E. Schwartzberg, *A Historical Atlas of South Asia* (Chicago, 1978); *A Social and Economic Atlas of India* (Delhi, 1987); and Gordon Johnson, *A Cultural Atlas of India* (New York, 1996). A fascinating historical survey of Indian cartography is Susan Gole, *Indian Maps and Plans: From Earliest Times to the Advent of European Surveys* (New Delhi, 1989). There are a number of specialist bibliographies, but the single most comprehensive one for the Indian subcontinent is Maureen Patterson, *South Asian Civilizations: A Bibliographic Synthesis* (Chicago, 1981). An accessible general reference work is Francis Robinson (ed.), *The Cambridge Encyclopedia of India* (Cambridge, 1989). Many have tried their hand at 'introductions' to India's culture and society. The most engaging and reliable of these are Nirmal Kumar Bose, *The Structure of Hindu Society* (New Delhi, 1975), and more elaborately, A. L. Basham, *The Wonder That Was India* (London, 1954) and Richard Lannoy, *The Speaking Tree: A Study of Indian Culture and Society* (Oxford, 1971); specifically on art and religion, Heinrich Zimmer, *Myths and Symbols in Indian Art and Civilization* (New York, 1962) is valuable. The *New Cambridge History of India*, still in progress, is the most important attempt to provide a systematic general history of India, and several volumes in the series have already established themselves as historiographical benchmarks. In particular, the volume on the eighteenth century and the coming of colonialism, C. A. Bayly, *Indian Society and the Making of the British Empire* (Cambridge, 1988) is an essential starting point for understanding modern India. Unfortunately, no comparable work exists on the nineteenth or twentieth centuries: there are virtually no works of any ambition or achievement that offer synoptic interpretative accounts of the last 150 years. The nearest approximations are: Judith Brown, *Modern India: The Origins of an Asian Democracy* (Oxford, 1985), which is a serviceable if rather pedestrian narrative; from a leftist 'social history' perspective, Sumit Sarkar, *Modern India 1885–1947* (New Delhi, 1983); and for a left nationalist view, Bipan Chandra *et al.*, *India's Struggle for Independence* (New Delhi, 1988). Ayesha Jalal, *Democracy and Authoritarianism in South Asia: A Comparative and Historical Perspective* (Cambridge, 1995) begins with a good and important comparative question – why have the experiences of India, Pakistan and Bangladesh been so different since their independence? Its treatment and conclusions, however, are eccentric. Two brief and incisive attempts at a historical sociology are: Arun Bose, *India's Social Crisis* (Delhi, 1989); and Satish Saberwal, *The Roots of Crisis: Interpreting Contemporary Indian Society* (New Delhi, 1996). For a thought-provoking historiographical essay, see Dipesh Chakrabarty, 'Postcoloniality and the Artifice of History: Who Speaks for "Indian" Pasts?', *Representations*, no. 37 (Winter 1992).

Most writing on India's post-1947 politics is unhistorical, and easily prone to the methodological fashions that swept through the post-war social sciences, especially functionalism, behaviourism, Marxism, and most recently, post-modernism. The best general introductions to Indian politics are: W. H. Morris Jones, *Government and Politics of India* (London, 1964); Rajni Kothari, *Politics in India* (New Delhi, 1970); Paul Brass, *The Politics of India Since Independence* (2nd edn, Cambridge, 1994); Ramesh Thakur, *The Government and Politics of India* (Basingstoke, 1995); and from a Marxist perspective, Achin Vanaik, *The Painful Transition: Bourgeois Democracy in India* (London, 1990). Kothari's volume remains intellectually the most impressive. But any adequate understanding of the politics of modern India must begin with the rich vein of historical writing.

For long-range perspectives on forms of political authority and on the social bases of power, see Romila Thapar, *From Lineage to State: Social Formations in the Mid-First Millennium B. C. in the Ganga Valley* (Oxford, 1990): of wider import than its title might suggest and with an interesting if oblique argument about the emergence of 'states' and a 'state-system' in ancient India. A very useful collection of important contributions to debates about political forms and their relation to social power is Hermann

Kulke (ed.), *The State in India 1000–1700* (Delhi, 1995). Also necessary reading on this subject is chapter two of Lloyd Rudolph and Susanne H. Rudolph, *In Pursuit of Lakshmi: The Political Economy of the Indian State* (Chicago, 1987). The past three decades have produced significant new historical research that bears on struggles between central and regional power, on the social bases of political authority, and on conceptions of territoriality and sovereignty. It is impossible to list this work, but of particular note are: Burton Stein, *Peasant, State and Society in Medieval South India* (Delhi, 1980); Nicholas Dirks, *The Hollow Crown: Ethnohistory in an Indian Kingdom* (Cambridge, 1987); Sanjay Subrahmanyam, *The Political Economy of Commerce: Southern India 1500–1650* (Cambridge, 1989); Andre Wink, *Land and Sovereignty in India: Agrarian Society and Politics under the Eighteenth-Century Maratha Swarajya* (Cambridge, 1986); Muzaffar Alam, *The Crisis of Mughal Empire in North India* (Delhi, 1986); and chapters three and four in C. A. Bayly, *Indian Society and The Making of the British Empire* (Cambridge, 1988).

The impact of colonial rule upon India continues to attract full-throated controversy. Since the 1970s the historiographical trend has stressed continuities as opposed to breaks, and has highlighted the ineffectuality of colonialism in reshaping Indian society. The argument was advanced with eloquence by Eric Stokes, 'The First Century of British Colonial Rule: Social Revolution or Social Stagnation?', *Past and Present*, no. 58 (1973). A range of revisionist studies followed, all designed to demonstrate how the British Raj had to adapt to existing Indian patterns and regimes. For retrospects on some of this work, see Frank Perlin, 'State Formation Reconsidered', *MAS*, vol. 19, no. 3 (1985); and David Washbrook, 'Progress and Problems: South Asian Economic and Social History c. 1720–1860', *MAS*, vol. 22, no. 1 (1988). The continuity thesis is the central motif of C. A. Bayly's work, developed further in *Empire and Information: Intelligence Gathering and Social Communication in India, 1780–1870* (Cambridge, 1996), which demonstrates the extent to which 'Orientalist' knowledge actually relied on local informants. Elements of this historiography find parallels in the arguments of Indian Marxists, who have advanced their own notions of 'abortive modernization', 'failed capitalism', and 'historic failure' on the part of both colonialism and the nationalist bourgeoisie. In some cases they have inducted the Gramscian concept of 'passive revolution' to try to explain modern India's trajectory: see, for instance, the essays in V. C. Joshi (ed.), *Rammohun Roy and the Process of*

Modernization in India (Delhi, 1975); and the argument succinctly stated by Partha Chatterjee, 'The Constitution of Nationalist Discourse', in Bhikhu Parekh and Thomas Pantham (eds), *Political Discourse: Explorations in Indian and Western Political Thought* (New Delhi, 1987). The Raj *did*, however, result in decisive discontinuities and disturbances, especially of a conceptual kind. Some of these are suggested in Sudipta Kaviraj, 'On State, Society, and Discourse in India', in James Manor (ed.), *Rethinking Third World Politics* (Harlow, 1991); and 'On the Construction of Colonial Power: Structure, Discourse, Hegemony', in Dagmar Engels and Shula Marks (eds), *Contesting Colonial Hegemony: State and Society in Africa and India* (London, 1994). Specific studies of how the Raj's techniques of administration and rule altered political possibilities for Indians include: David Washbrook, 'Law, State and Agrarian Society in Colonial India', *MAS*, vol. 15, no. 3 (1981); Richard Saumarez Smith, 'Rule-by-Records and Rule-by-Report: Complementary Aspects of the British Imperial Rule of Law', *Contributions to Indian Sociology* n.s., vol. 19, no. 1 (1985); Bernard Cohn, 'The Census, Social Structure and Objectification in South Asia', in *An Anthropologist Among the Historians and Other Essays* (Delhi, 1987); and Arjun Appadurai, 'Number in the Colonial Imagination', in Carol A. Breckenridge and Peter van der Veer (eds), *Orientalism and the Postcolonial Predicament* (Philadelphia, 1993). For an illuminating study of the modification of caste categories during the colonial period, see Rashmi Pant, 'The Cognitive Status of Caste in Colonial Historiography', *IESHR*, vol. 24, no. 2 (1987). The effects of colonialism on the religious imagination are studied in Gyanendra Pandey, *The Construction of Communalism in Colonial North India* (Delhi, 1990); and Romila Thapar, 'Imagined Religious Communities? Ancient History and the Modern Search for a Hindu Identity', *MAS*, vol. 23, no. 2 (1989). The impact of liberal forms of political representation on ideas of Muslim community is discussed in Farzana Shaikh, *Community and Consensus in Islam: Muslim Representation in Colonial India 1886–1947* (Cambridge, 1989). On the ideological theories that shaped nineteenth-century colonial rule and practice, essential primary sources are: James Mill, *History of British India* (10 vols, London, 1817), (abridged in 2 vols, Chicago, 1972); Henry Sumner Maine, *Village Communities in the East and West* (London, 1871); and James Fitzjames Stephen, *Liberty, Equality, Fraternity* (London, 1873). Eric Stokes, *The English Utilitarians and India* (Oxford, 1959) is the classic study of the relation between these metropolitan doctrines and the Raj; worth comparing is Ranajit

Guha, *A Rule of Property for Bengal: An Essay on the Idea of Permanent Settlement* (New Delhi, 1982); recently, the theme has been revisted in Thomas R. Metcalf, *Ideologies of the Raj* (Cambridge, 1994); and more narrowly in Javeed Majeed, *Ungoverned Imaginings: James Mill's The History of British India and Orientalism* (Oxford, 1992). On British views of India, Francis Hutchins, *The Illusion of Permanence: British Attitudes to India* (Princeton, 1967) is still useful. For an attempt to connect recent developments in British historiography to themes in the study of Indian history, see C. A. Bayly, 'Returning the British to South Asian History: The Limits of Colonial Hegemony', *South Asia*, vol. xvii, no. 2 (1994).

Histories of Indian nationalism have focused on the history of the Congress Party, itself dominated by a few towering individuals. Most of this literature is firmly in the mode of nationalist epic, and the classic study is Pattabhi Sitaramayya, *The History of the Indian National Congress* (2 vols, Bombay, 1946–7). Nationalist orthodoxies came under question from the 1960s by historians, some in Cambridge, who began to rethink the historical function of empire, and its strategies of indirect rule. These strategies, they argued, drew Indian elites into 'collaboration' and helped to stimulate political competition between them, leading ultimately to the emergence of nationalism. This antidote to nationalist epics shifted attention from a story of an idealistic elite towards the arduous and often ungainly processes whereby support at the national level was built upon provincial and local power-brokering: see Anil Seal, *The Emergence of Indian Nationalism* (Cambridge, 1968); John Gallagher, Gordon Johnson and Anil Seal (eds), *Locality, Province and Nation: Essays on Indian Politics 1870 to 1940* (Cambridge, 1973); David Washbrook, *The Emergence of Provincial Politics: The Madras Presidency 1870–1920* (Cambridge, 1976); Judith Brown, *Gandhi's Rise to Power* (Cambridge, 1972); and C. A. Bayly, *The Local Roots of Indian Politics* (Oxford, 1975). More general accounts of the pre-independence Congress can be found in B. R. Tomlinson, *The Indian National Congress and the Raj* (London, 1976), and two useful collections of essays: David Low (ed.), *Congress and the Raj: Facets of the Indian Struggle 1917–1947* (London, 1977); and Paul Brass and Francis Robinson (eds), *The Indian National Congress and Indian Society 1885–1985* (Delhi, 1987). For an important Indian perspective, see Bipan Chandra (ed.), 'The Left in India', special issue *Studies in History*, vol. 3, nos. 1–2 (1981), especially the contributions by Joshi and Josh. On pre-1947 tensions within Congress which surfaced after independence, see Ravinder Kumar, 'The Structure of Politics in India on the Eve of Independence', *Occasional Papers on History and Society*, second series, xvi, NMML (Delhi, 1989). Gandhi and Gandhian politics are explored in Ravinder Kumar (ed.), *Essays on Gandhian Politics* (Oxford, 1971) and Sumit Sarkar, 'The Logic of Gandhian Nationalism: Civil Disobedience and the Gandhi-Irwin Pact (1930–1931)', *IHR*, vol. 3, no. 1 (1976). On popular perceptions of Gandhi, see Shahid Amin, 'Gandhi as Mahatma: Gorakhpur District, Eastern UP, 1921–2', in Ranajit Guha (ed.), *Subaltern Studies*, vol. 3 (Delhi, 1984).

The work of the historians associated with the Subaltern Studies project, initiated by Ranajit Guha, represents the most sustained critique both of nationalist histories of nationalism, and of revisions to this picture by the 'Cambridge school'. The 'Subaltern historians' focused their attentions outside the circles of elite politics, and have emphasized the insurrectionary activities and potential of the 'subaltern classes' (artisans, poor peasants, landless labourers), who they claim possessed self-conscious and coherent conceptions of resistance – that were variously directed against rich peasant, urban merchant or colonial Collector. See *Subaltern Studies*, vols. i–viii (Delhi, 1982–94), and for a selection, Ranajit Guha and Gayatri Chakravorty Spivak (eds), *Selected Subaltern Studies* (New York, 1988). Explaining why this revolutionary potential was so effectively dissipated poses awkward problems for this approach: to stress the conservative bent of the Congress leadership merely restores focus to the character of the elite. The question of how these putative radical energies were domesticated and harnessed to the purposes of a nationalist elite underlies the important but ultimately evasive book by Partha Chatterjee, *Nationalist Thought and the Colonial World: A Derivative Discourse?* (New Delhi, 1986). Chatterjee's attention to the ideological forms and content of Indian nationalism helped to stimulate significant re-interpretations of its character: see in particular Sudipta Kaviraj, 'The Imaginary Institution of India', in Partha Chatterjee and Gyanendra Pandey (eds), *Subaltern Studies*, vol. vii (Delhi, 1992), and *The Unhappy Consciousness: Bankimchandra Chattopadhyay and the Formation of Nationalist Discourse in India* (Delhi, 1995), and Chatterjee's own later book, *The Nation and its Fragments: Colonial and Postcolonial Histories* (Princeton, 1993).

Partition, and the intricate sequence of events leading up to it, remains embedded in controversy. Studies of decisive episodes from the 1930s include: on the formation of provincial governments after the 1937 elections, Ravi S. Vasudevan, 'Why the Congress Accepted Office in 1937',

Studies in History, vol. 4, nos. 1 and 2 (1988); on the alienation of Muslim support from Congress, Mukul Kesavan, 'Invoking a Majority: The Congress and the Muslims of the United Provinces, 1945–47', in P. C. Chatterji (ed.), *Self-Images, Identity and Nationality* (Simla, 1989). Ayesha Jalal's *The Sole Spokesman: Jinnah, the Muslim League and the Demand for Pakistan* (Cambridge, 1985) is the most energetic and successful critique of the 'two-nation theory', but its interpretative ingenuities beg a number of questions. Some of the implications of Jalal's work are lucidly considered in Asim Roy, 'The High Politics of India's Partition: The Revisionist Perspective', in an excellent collection edited by Mushirul Hasan, *India's Partition: Process, Strategy, Mobilization* (Delhi, 1994); and for an earlier attempt to assemble the variety of positions on Partition, see C. H. Philips and M. D. Wainwright (eds), *The Partition of India: Policies and Perspectives 1935–1947* (London, 1969). The 'Subaltern' perspective informs Gyanendra Pandey's research on Partition, and his forthcoming work will be of major importance. In the meanwhile, see his 'The Prose of Otherness', in David Arnold and David Hardiman (eds), *Subaltern Studies*, viii (Delhi, 1994); and for an initial polemical reaction to this, Ayesha Jalal, 'Secularists, Subalterns and the Stigma of "Communalism": Partition Historiography Revisted', *IESHR*, vol. xxxiii, no.1 (1996). For introductions to the vast and disputatious literature on what is variously called 'independence' or the 'transfer of power', see R. J. Moore, 'The Transfer of Power: An Historiographical Survey', *South Asia*, vol. ix, no. 1 (1986); and H. V. Brasted and Carl Bridge, 'The Transfer of Power in South Asia: An Historiographical Review', *South Asia*, vol. xvii, no.1 (1994). Ravinder Kumar, 'Introduction', in A. K. Gupta (ed.), *Myth and Reality: The Struggle for Freedom, 1945–47* (New Delhi, 1987) is an important Indian statement of the issues.

Most studies of post-independence politics are confined within the constitutional frame of the nation state. On the process of Constitution-making, the debates themselves make fascinating reading: *Constituent Assembly Debates 1946–1950*, (12 vols, Delhi, 1946–50); see also, B. Shiva Rao *et al.*, *The Framing of India's Constitution* (5 vols, New Delhi, 1965–71); and most accessibly, Granville Austin, *The Indian Constitution: Cornerstone of a Nation* (Oxford, 1966). A rare study of the sociological character of the Constituent Assembly is S. K. Chaube, *Constituent Assembly of India: Springboard of Revolution* (New Delhi, 1973). On the more general place of constitutional law since 1947, see Upendra Baxi, *The Indian Supreme*

Court and Politics (Lucknow, 1980); and R. Sudarshan, 'The Political Consequences of Constitutional Discourse', in T. V. Satyamurthy (ed.) *State and Nation in the Context of Social Change* (Delhi, 1994). India's administrative system, inherited from the Raj, is examined in B. B. Misra, *Government and Bureaucracy in India, 1947–1976* (Delhi, 1986); the best account of the social background and training of Indian bureaucrats is David Potter, *India's Political Administrators, 1918–1983* (Oxford, 1986). There is a vast literature on political parties, leaders and parliamentary politics. W. H. Morris Jones, *Parliament in India* (London, 1957) is a thorough account of India's politics during the 1950s, which saw it as a close approximation to the textbooks. The seminal essay on the operations of the political system during the period of Congress dominance is Rajni Kothari, 'The Congress "System" in India', *Asian Survey*, vol. iv, no. 2 (1964). Although Congress has exercised such a powerful presence in post-1947 India, there are no detailed studies of Congress as an organization since the important studies published in the late 1960s by Myron Weiner, *Party Building in a New Nation: The Indian National Congress* (Chicago, 1967), and Stanley Kochanek, *The Congress Party of India: The Dynamics of One-Party Democracy* (Princeton, 1968); but see the article by James Manor, 'Parties and the Party System', in Atul Kohli (ed.), *India's Democracy* (Princeton, 1990).

Biography ought to be an important source for understanding modern politics, and library shelves certainly heave with the biographies of political figures; unfortunately most of them are useless. Those that are not include: Sarvepalli Gopal, *Jawaharlal Nehru: A Biography* (3 vols, London, 1975–84), which is weighted towards a diplomatic history of the post-1947 period; Judith Brown, *Gandhi* (New Haven and London, 1989), and an insightful memoir by a close associate, Nirmal Kumar Bose, *My Days with Gandhi* (New Delhi, 1953; New Delhi, 1974); on the Congress Right, Rajmohan Gandhi, *Patel: A Life* (Ahmedabad, 1991) and his *The Rajaji Story* (2 vols, New Delhi, 1984) are both essential; Leonard Gordon, *Brothers Against the Raj: A Biography of Sarat and Subhas Chandra Bose* (New Delhi, 1990); C. P. Srivastava, *Lal Bahadur Shastri* (Delhi, 1995); Zareer Masani, *Indira Gandhi*, (London, 1975); and Pupul Jayakar, *Indira Gandhi* (New Delhi, 1992). Ramachandra Guha's forthcoming study of the British-born anthropologist, Verrier Elwin, recovers an important voice on the subject of India's tribal populations: in the meanwhile, see Guha's 'Savaging the Civilized: Verrier Elwin and the Tribal Question in Late Colonial

India', *EPW*, vol. xxxi, special nos. 35–7 (1996). For first-hand accounts by some of the decisive actors in modern Indian politics, see Mahatma Gandhi, *Moral and Political Writings*, 3 vols, edited by Raghavan Iyer (Oxford, 1986–7); Jawaharlal Nehru, *Autobiography* (London, 1936) and *The Discovery of India* (Calcutta, 1946). An insight into the mind of the Congress Right can be gathered from K. M. Munshi, *Pilgrimage to Freedom 1902–1950* (New Delhi, 1967); and Rajendra Prasad, *Autobiography* (New Delhi, 1957). The Congress Muslim position is articulated in Maulana Abul Kalam Azad, *India Wins Freedom* (Madras, 1989). The post-independence period is not very well served, but see Jayaprakash Narayan, *A Revolutionary's Quest: Selected Works*, edited by Bimal Prasad (Delhi, 1980), and Ram Manohar Lohia, *Wheel of History* (Hyderabad, 1955). An interesting memoir by an intellectual of the Nehru and Indira Gandhi periods is Raj Thapar, *All These Years: A Memoir* (New Delhi, 1991).

The study of India's national and regional electoral politics is a busy and second-rate sub-discipline, apart from some notable exceptions. Recent efforts to connect the study of elections to wider concerns is very welcome, and the research emerging out of the major National Election Study launched in 1996 and coordinated by V. B. Singh and Yogendra Yadav at the Centre for the Study of Developing Societies, Delhi, promises significantly to enrich the field. This project builds on the earlier work of Bashiruddin Ahmed, and very preliminary results are available in Yogendra Yadav *et al.*, 'The Maturing of A Democracy', *India Today*, vol. xxi, no.16 (1996). The popular bible of Indian psephology, and an indispensable factual compendium is David Butler, Ashok Lahiri and Prannoy Roy, *India Decides: Elections 1952–1995* (New Delhi, 1995), updated after each general election. On the 'critical election' of 1967, see Rajni Kothari, 'The Political Change of 1967', *EPW*, annual number 1967; and W. H. Morris Jones, 'From Monopoly to Competition', in *Politics Mainly Indian* (Bombay, 1978); on the 1980 election which returned Mrs Gandhi to power, see James Manor, 'The Electoral Process amid Awakening and Decay: Reflections on the Indian General Elections of 1980', in Peter Lyon and James Manor (eds), *Transfer and Transformation: Political Institutions in the New Commonwealth* (Leicester, 1983). Two important collections on electoral studies are R. Kothari and Myron Weiner (eds), *Indian Voting Behaviour* (Calcutta, 1965), and D. L. Sheth (ed.), *Citizens and Politics: Aspects of Competitive Politics in India* (Bombay, 1975). A very interesting study is Harry Blair, 'Caste and British Census in Bihar: Using

Old Data to Study Contemporary Political Behaviour', in Gerald Barrier (ed.), *The Census in British India* (New Delhi, 1981). A thoughtful account which touches on the wider effects of electoral politics upon agrarian society is Oliver Mendelson, 'The Transformation of Authority in Rural India', *MAS*, vol. xxvii, no. 4 (1993). On recent realignments and the emergence of a 'post-Congress' system, see Yogendra Yadav, 'Reconfiguration in Indian Politics: State Assembly Elections, 1993–1995', *EPW*, vol. 32, nos. 2–3 (1996). On the 1996 elections, see Sudipta Kaviraj, 'The General Elections in India', *Government and Opposition*, vol. 32, no. 1 (1997).

There is a large literature aimed at identifying the social bases of Indian politics and lines of cleavage and conflict: caste, class, region, language and religion all are variously highlighted in this work. The most important single collection that addresses these themes is Francine Frankel and M. S. A. Rao (eds), *Dominance and State Power in India: Decline of a Social Order* (2 vols, Delhi, 1990); see also Ramashray Roy and Richard Sisson (eds), *Diversity and Dominance* (2 vols, New Delhi, 1990), especially the essays by Chibber and Petrocik, Blair, Vanderbok, Shah and Wood. Caste, generally assumed to be the basic unit of the Indian social order, has inevitably attracted considerable attention. The classic work on caste as a doctrinal and ideological system is Louis Dumont, *Homo Hierarchicus: The Caste System and its Implications* (London, 1970), governed primarily by Dumont's own preoccupations with identifying the distinctiveness of the West. Dumont provoked a host of critical responses; the best are Arjun Appadurai, 'Is Homo Hierarchicus?', *American Anthropologist*, vol.13 (1986); Geoffrey Hawthorn, 'Caste and Politics in India since 1947', in Denis MacGilvray (ed.), *Caste Ideology and Interaction* (Cambridge, 1984); Andre Beteille, 'Homo Hierarchicus, Homo Equalis', in *The Idea of Natural Inequality & Other Essays* (Delhi, 1983); see also the essays in Dipankar Gupta (ed.), *Social Stratification* (Delhi, 1991). Nicholas Dirks, 'Castes of Mind', *Representations*, no. 37 (1992) is a sharp historical critique of the category of caste. The influential idea of 'Sanskritization', as a channel of social mobility and modernization was first advanced by M. N. Srinivas; see his *Social Change in Modern India* (California, 1966); *Caste in Modern India and Other Essays* (London, 1962); and M. N. Srinivas (ed.), *Caste: Its Twentieth Century Avatar* (New Delhi, 1996), which has some critical essays on the policy of caste 'reservations' recommended by the Mandal Commission Report. For the report itself, see B. P. Mandal (chairman),

Report of the Backward Classes Commission, (7 vols, New Delhi, 1981). Another recent and useful collection is C. J. Fuller (ed.), *Caste Today* (Delhi, 1996), especially the contributions of Fuller and Beteille. For the role of caste in politics, see R. Kothari (ed.), *Caste in Indian Politics* (New Delhi, 1970); D. L. Sheth, 'Caste and Politics: A Survey of the Literature', *Contributions to South Asian Studies*, vol. 1 (Delhi, 1979). Perhaps the best empirical study of the effects of caste upon local political mobilization and outcomes is the study of Modasa in Gujarat by Rajni Kothari and Ghanshyam Shah, 'Caste Orientation of Political Factions', in Rajni Kothari *et al.*, *Party Systems and Election Studies* (Bombay, 1967). For two high-altitude perspectives on the Brahminic order, see the Gellner-like argument of John A. Hall, 'The Land of the Brahmans', in *Powers and Liberties: The Causes and Consequences of the Rise of the West* (Oxford, 1985); and, more sociologically grounded, Satish Saberwal, *Wages of Segmentation: Comparative Historical Studies on Europe and India* (New Delhi, 1995).

On the intricate relations between caste and class, see Geoffrey Hawthorn, 'Some Political Causes of Class and Caste Hostility in India', in C. Clarke, D. Ley and C. Peach (eds), *Geography and Ethnic Pluralism* (London, 1984). There are several good studies of Indian communist and left politics: G. Overstreet and W. Windmiller, *Communism in India* (Berkeley, 1959); and Paul Brass and Marcus Franda (eds), *Radical Politics in South Asia* (Cambridge MA, 1973). Revolutionary communism and the Naxalite movements in Bengal are examined in Sumanta Banerjee, *In the Wake of Naxalbari* (London, 1985); and more reflectively in Rabindra Ray, *The Naxalites and Their Ideology* (Delhi, 1988). Parliamentary communism is the subject of T. J. Nossiter, *Marxist State Governments in India* (London, 1988), and Ross Mallick, *Indian Communism* (Delhi, 1994). The emergence of lower-caste and Dalit politics, which transformed the political arena during the 1980s and 90s, is covered in Gail Omvedt, *Dalit Visions: The Anti-Caste Movement and the Construction of an Indian Identity* (London, 1995). It is essential to hear the Dalit voice first-hand: see in particular the extraordinary essay by Kancha Ilaiah, *Why I am not a Hindu: A Sudra Critique of Hindutva Philosophy, Culture and Political Economy* (Calcutta, 1996).

There are relatively few good general accounts of the complex and increasingly important politics of the regions. Useful collections for earlier periods include Myron Weiner (ed.), *State Politics in India* (Princeton, 1968); Iqbal Narain (ed.), *State Politics in India* (Meerut, 1976); and John

R. Wood (ed.), *State Politics in Contemporary India* (Boulder CO, 1984); the forthcoming work by James Manor on Indian chief ministers will be a useful addition to this literature. There are some good studies on specific regions: in particular, the crises in Punjab, Assam and Kashmir are the subject of a growing literature. From a long list, the following are helpful: on Punjab, Paul Brass, 'The Punjab Crisis and the Unity of India', in Atul Kohli (ed.), *India's Democracy* (Princeton, 1990), and Robin Jeffrey, *What's Happening to India? Punjab, Ethnic Conflict and the Test for Federalism*, (2nd edn, London, 1994); on Assam, Sanjib Baruah, '"Ethnic" Conflict as State–Society Struggle: The Poetics and Politics of Assamese Micro-Nationalism', *MAS*, vol. 28, no. 3 (1994). There is no single guide to the vexed history of Kashmir: compare Alastair Lamb, *Kashmir: A Disputed Legacy 1846–1990* (Hertingfordbury, 1991) with Prem Shankar Jha, *Kashmir 1947: Rival Versions of History* (Delhi, 1996); see also Sumit Ganguly, *The Crisis in Kashmir* (Cambridge, 1997), and for an impassioned account of the sequence of events from the early 1980s to the most recent crisis, Tavleen Singh, *Kashmir: A Tragedy of Errors* (New Delhi, 1995). The Nehruvian perspective on the Kashmir issue is stated in Sisir K. Gupta, *Kashmir: A Study in Indian–Pakistan Relations* (London, 1967). The politics of language is dealt with in Jyotirindra Das Gupta, *Language Conflict and National Development: Group Politics and National Language Policy in India* (Berkeley, 1970); and Paul Brass, *Language, Religion and Politics in North India* (London, 1974); an admirably lucid survey of the more recent vexations surrounding these issues is D. L. Sheth, 'The Great Language Debate: Politics of Metropolitan versus Vernacular India', in Upendra Baxi and Bhikhu Parekh (eds), *Crisis and Change in Contemporary India* (New Delhi, 1995). Since the late 1970s, non-party – or what is sometimes called 'grassroots' – politics, has become a very active and important arena of political struggle: these developments are discussed by Smitu Kothari, 'Social Movements and the Redefinition of Democracy', in Philip Oldenberg (ed.), *India Briefing 1993* (Boulder CO, 1993) and in the journal *Lokayan Bulletin*, published since 1983 from Delhi. For longer studies, see Gail Omvedt, *Reinventing Revolution: New Social Movements and the Socialist Tradition in India* (New York, 1993), and on feminism and women's political movements, Omvedt's *We Will Smash This Prison: Indian Women in Struggle* (London, 1980); the monthly *Manushi*, published from New Delhi since 1979, is also an essential source on women's politics.

Remarkably, there are no authoritative studies of the Indira Gandhi period. An illuminating journalistic account is Kuldip Nayar, *Between the Lines* (New Delhi, 1969), and *In Jail* (New Delhi, 1978). The Emergency is a much evoked but little studied episode: for attempts to identify its significance for the Indian political system, see Max Zins, *Strains on Indian Democracy* (New Delhi, 1988); and more obliquely Sudipta Kaviraj, 'Indira Gandhi and Indian Politics', *EPW*, vol. xxi, nos. 38–9 (1986). Emma Tarlo's forthcoming research on popular responses to the Emergency in New Delhi, which suggests a far from victimized populace, promises to be a pioneering contribution. The rise of the Youth Congress, and of Sanjay Gandhi, has been entirely neglected (more generally, the crucial role of the young in Indian politics has not received the attention it deserves).

While particular wars and incidents have been studied, there is little worthwhile on the relationship between the Indian military and politics: nothing of any substance has been produced since Stephen Cohen's valuable *The Indian Army: Its Contribution to the Development of a Nation* (Berkeley, 1971); Raju Thomas, *India's Security Policy* (Princeton, 1987), ranges no wider than its title suggests. On the increasing uses of paramilitary forces in domestic politics, see Kuldip Mathur, 'The State and the Uses of Coercive Power in India', *Asian Survey*, vol. 32, no. 4 (1992); and Stephen Cohen, 'The Military and Indian Democracy', in Atul Kohli (ed.), *India's Democracy* (Princeton, 1990). For statistics on communal violence until the mid-1980s, see Gopal Krishna, 'Communal Violence in India: A Study of Communal Disturbance in Delhi', *EPW*, vol. 20, no. 2 (1985); and P. R. Rajgopal, *Communal Violence in India* (New Delhi, 1987). For more general reflections on the place of violence in India, see Veena Das (ed.), *Mirrors of Violence: Communities, Riots and Survivors in South Asia* (Delhi, 1990); Gyanendra Pandey, 'In Defense of the Fragment: Writing about Hindu–Muslim Riots in India Today', *Representations*, no. 37 (Winter 1992); and for a comparative perspective on South Asia, Stanley Tambiah, *Leveling Crowds: Ethnonationalist Conflicts and Collective Violence in South Asia* (Berkeley, 1996). Two powerful documentary accounts of the infringement of citizens' rights by the state are Luingam Luithui and Nandita Haksar, *Nagaland File* (New Delhi, 1984); and A. R. Desai (ed.), *Violation of Democratic Rights in India* (New Delhi, 1986). The complex issues surrounding the relation between imperatives of *raison d'etat* and the protection of individual rights in the Indian context have been rarely addressed.

Political developments after the Emergency spurred a rapidly growing literature on the 'crisis of the Indian state'. For the most important examples, see Rajni Kothari, 'The Crisis of the Moderate State and the Decline of Democracy' in Peter Lyon and James Manor (eds), *Transfer and Transformation* (Leicester, 1983) and his *State Against Democracy: In Search of Humane Governance* (Delhi, 1988); Sudipta Kaviraj, 'On the Crisis of Political Institutions in India', *Contributions to Indian Sociology* n.s., vol. 18, no. 2 (1984) and 'A Critique of the Passive Revolution', *EPW*, special vol. xxiii, nos. 45–7 (1988); D. L. Sheth, 'The Crisis of Representation', in Asha Kaushik (ed.), *Democratic Concerns: The Indian Experience* (Jaipur, 1994); Atul Kohli, *Democracy and Discontent: India's Growing Crisis of Governability* (Cambridge, 1990); Satish Saberwal, *India: The Roots of Crisis: Interpreting Contemporary Indian Society* (New Delhi, 1996); and 'Democratic Political Structures', in T. V. Satyamurthy (ed.), *State and Nation in the Context of Social Change* (Delhi, 1994).

There is little successful writing on the subject of political culture. The work of Ashis Nandy is essential: apart from his classic *The Intimate Enemy: Loss and Recovery of Self under Colonialism* (Delhi, 1983), see two collections of his essays, *At the Edge of Psychology: Essays in Politics and Culture* (Delhi, 1980), and *The Savage Freud* (Delhi, 1995); and two essays, 'The Political Culture of the Indian State', *Daedalus*, vol. 118, no. 4 (1989), and 'Culture, State and the Rediscovery of Indian Politics', *EPW*, vol. xix, no. 49 (1984). Also worth reading is Lloyd and Susanne Rudolph, *The Modernity of Tradition* (Chicago, 1967).

The most accessible historical introduction to the regional variations of India's agrarian economy are the essays in Dharma Kumar (ed.), *The Cambridge Economic History of India vol. 2 c.1757–c.1970* (Cambridge, 1983), especially those by Stokes, Kumar and Chaudhuri. The essays in K. N. Chaudhuri and C. J. Dewey (eds), *Economy and Society: Studies in Indian Economic and Social History* (New Delhi, 1978) offer further detail on the historical background; a synoptic account of the subcontinental economy before colonialism is K. N. Chaudhuri, *Asia before Europe: Economy and Civilization of the Indian Ocean Before the Rise of Islam* (Cambridge, 1990). On the twentieth-century economy, B. R. Tomlinson, *The Economy of Modern India 1860–1970* (Cambridge, 1993) brings out some of the continuities across 1947; Pramit Chaudhuri, *The Indian Economy* (London, 1978) is also lucid and helpful. Francine Frankel, *India's Political Economy,*

1947–1977 (Princeton, 1978) is a detailed study, essential for the period it covers; Lloyd and Susanne Rudolph, *In Pursuit of Lakshmi: The Political Economy of the Indian State* (Chicago, 1987) is relentlessly committed to the language and models of American political science, sometimes to illuminating effect. An authoritative study of fiscal and macroeconomic policy is Vijay Joshi and Ian Little, *Macroeconomics and Political Economy 1964–1991* (Washington DC and Delhi, 1994). For an elegant statement of a Marxian argument, see Pranab Bardhan, *The Political Economy of Development in India* (Delhi, 1984). On the post-1991 liberalization of economic controls, see Jagdish Bhagwati, *India in Transition: Freeing The Economy* (Delhi, 1993); and Vijay Joshi and Ian Little, *India's Economic Reforms 1991–2001* (Delhi, 1997). Two critical perspectives on liberalization are Amit Bhaduri and Deepak Nayyar, *The Intelligent Person's Guide to Liberalization* (New Delhi, 1996); and Jean Dreze and Amartya Sen, *India: Economic Development and Social Opportunity* (Delhi, 1995).

The role of India in the creation of British *raison d'etat* still awaits its historian; in the meanwhile, see W. J. Barber, *British Economic Thought and India 1600–1858* (Oxford, 1975); and S. Ambirajan, *Classical Political Economy and British Policy in India* (Cambridge, 1978). The consequences of such policy for India itself are, as might be expected, the subject of bitter dispute. For a statement of the negative effects of colonial rule, see Amiya Kumar Bagchi, 'De-industrialization in India and the Nineteenth Century: Some Theoretical Implications', *Journal of Development Studies*, vol. xii, no. 2 (1976); and compare Ian Little, 'Indian Industrialization Before 1945', in M. Gersovitz (ed.), *The Theory and Experience of Economic Development* (London, 1982). On some of the intellectual and institutional consequences of the Raj, see S. Ambirajan, 'India: The Aftermath of Empire', *History of Political Economy*, vol. 13, no. 3 (1981). The only major study of the contemporary response of Indian 'economic nationalists' to colonial rule is Bipan Chandra, *The Rise and Growth of Economic Nationalism in India* (New Delhi, 1966); while this is useful, there continues to be a need for an intellectual history of modern Indian economic thought and argument. On the interests produced by economic activity during the Raj, and on the politics of these interests, see Aditya Mukherjee, 'The Indian Capitalist Class and Congress on National Planning and Public Sector 1930–47', in K. N. Pannikar (ed.), *National and Left Movements in India* (Delhi, 1980); and Claude Markovits, *Indian Business and Nationalist Politics* (Cambridge, 1985). An important study of the difficulties facing the creation of a unified industrial working class in India is Rajnarayan Chandavarkar, *The Origins of Industrial Capitalism in India: Business Strategies and the Working Classes in Bombay 1900–1940* (Cambridge, 1994).

The literature on the post-1947 economy is dominated by planning. The essential work on the historical background to Indian planning remains A. H. Hanson, *The Process of Planning: A Study of India's Five-Year Plans 1950–1964* (Oxford, 1966). Also of interest are Pramit Chaudhuri, 'The Origins of Modern India's Economic Development Strategy', in Mike Shepperdson and Colin Simmons, *The Indian National Congress and the Political Economy of India 1885–1985* (Aldershot, 1988) and his 'Economic Planning in India', in T. V. Satyamurthy (ed.), *Industry and Agriculture in India since Independence* (Delhi, 1995); B. R. Tomlinson, 'Historical Roots of Economic Policy', in Subroto Roy and William E. James (eds), *Foundations of India's Economic Policy* (New Delhi, 1992); and Baldev Raj Nayar, *The Modernization Imperative and Indian Planning* (Delhi, 1972). The literature on the economic consequences of planning is enormous; for the best, see Sukhamoy Chakravarty, *Development Planning: The Indian Experience* (Delhi, 1987) and his 'Nehru and Indian Planning', *South Asia Research*, vol. 9, no. 2 (1989); Jagdish Bhagwati and Sukhamoy Chakravarty, 'Contributions to Indian Economic Analysis', *American Economic Review*, LIX, no. 4, Supplement (1969); Francine Frankel, *India's Political Economy, 1947–1977*, noted above, is also essential. On the mutual influences between Western and Indian economists, George Rosen, *Western Economists and Eastern Societies: Agents of Social Change in South Asia* (Delhi, 1985) is on the whole disappointing, but something may be gleaned from it. On Mahalanobis, a rather inadequate biography has now appeared by Ashok Rudra, *P. C. Mahalanobis* (Delhi, 1996). The mounting difficulties of Indian planning were noted in Paul Streeten and Michael Lipton (eds), *The Crisis of Indian Planning: Economic Planning in the 1960s* (London, 1968); and Jagdish Bhagwati and Padma Desai, *India: Planning for Industrialisation* (London, 1970). The actual process of policy-making during the post-1947 period is a glaringly understudied subject; some perspectives on the politics of planning can be found in T. J. Byres (ed.), *The State and Development Planning in India* (Delhi, 1994).

A comprehensive survey of the literature on agrarian reform is P. C. Joshi, *Land Reforms in India: Trends and Perspectives* (Bombay, 1975). On the failure of land reforms, Ronald Herring, *Land to the Tiller: The Political Economy of Agrarian Reform in South Asia* (New Haven, 1983) is necessary.

An early useful study of the 'Green Revolution' is Francine Frankel, *India's Green Revolution: Economic Gains and Political Costs* (Princeton, 1971). Some light on why agrarian interests have been unable to shape economic policy actively to their advantage is shed by Ashutosh Varshney, *Democracy, Development, and the Countryside: Urban–Rural Struggles in India* (Cambridge, 1995). The 'informal' agrarian economy, where many of India's very poorest have to seek employment, is the subject of Jan Breman, *Footloose Labour: Working in India's Informal Economy* (Cambridge, 1996).

The Indian experience has been a prime source for the theory and practice of development economics. Succinct introductions to the issues are Amartya Sen, 'The Concept of Development', in H. Chenery and T. N. Srinivasan (eds), *Handbook of Development Economics*, vol.1 (Oxford, 1988), and Amartya Sen, 'Indian Development: Lessons and Non-Lessons', *Daedalus*, vol. 118, no. 4 (1989). For two sophisticated theoretical works that widen the concept of development, see Amartya Sen, *Inequality Re-examined* (Oxford, 1992), and Partha Dasgupta, *An Inquiry into Poverty, Destitution and Well-Being* (Oxford, 1993). The role of foreign aid is discussed in Michael Lipton and John Toye, *Does Aid Work in India?* (London, 1990). Since the publication of Kingsley Davis's magisterial work on subcontinental demography, *The Population of India and Pakistan* (Princeton, 1951), there has been nothing that quite compares; but see Robert Cassen, *India: Population, Economy, Society* (London, 1978) and the forthcoming book by Patricia and Roger Jeffrey, *Population, Gender and Politics* (Cambridge). For a critical perspective on the orthodoxies of population policy, see the essay by Amartya Sen, 'Population: Delusion and Reality', *New York Review of Books* (22 September 1994).

In keeping with a general disregard for the historicity of the concepts it employs, the development literature has used the concept of poverty without any sense of its shifting historical meanings in the Indian context. A conceptual history of the term is urgently needed. In the meanwhile, see Pramit Chaudhuri, 'Changing Perceptions of Poverty in India: State and Poverty', *Sankhya: Indian Journal of Statistics*, special vol. 55, pt 3 (1993); and more empirically, Angus Madison, 'The Historical Origins of Indian Poverty', *Banca Nazionale Del Lavoro Quarterly Review*, vol. 23, no. 92 (1970). On the historical emergence of 'the poor' as a subject of government, the work of Nandini Gooptu on North India is of interest: see her 'The "Problem" of the Urban Poor: Policy and Discourse of Local Administration', *EPW*, vol. xxxi, no. 50 (1996). Atul Kohli, *The State and Poverty in India* (Cambridge, 1978) compares the relative success of poverty-alleviation policies in different regional states of the Union. An essential work on the practical and moral issues surrounding the subject of poverty is Jean Dreze and Amartya Sen (eds), *The Political Economy of Hunger*, 3 vols (Oxford, 1990). The vital subject of education has not really commanded the attention it deserves. On the initial inconsistencies in education policy, see Krishna Kumar, *Political Agenda of Education: A Study of Colonialist and Nationalist Ideas* (New Delhi, 1991); and on the subsequent failures, see J. P. Naik, *Policy and Performance in Indian Education 1947–1974* (New Delhi, 1975); Myron Weiner, *The Child and the State in India: Child Labour and Education Policy in Comparative Perspective* (Princeton, 1991); and the essays in Jean Dreze and Amartya Sen (eds), *Indian Development: Selected Regional Perspectives* (Delhi, 1996).

For an attempt to assess the scale of India's 'black economy', see Suraj B. Gupta, *Black Income in India* (New Delhi, 1992). The causes behind India's poor economic performance are examined in Isher Judge Aluwalia, *Industrial Growth in India: Stagnation Since the Mid-Sixties* (Delhi, 1985); Prem Shankar Jha, *India: A Political Economy of Stagnation* (Bombay, 1980); and more tendentiously in Deepak Lal, *The Hindu Equilibrium* (Oxford, 1988). An explanation of why efforts at liberalization were limited during the 1980s is essayed in Atul Kohli, 'Politics of Economic Liberalization in India', *World Development*, vol.17, no. 3 (1989). The crisis of 1991 is helpfully explained in Vijay Joshi, 'Macroeconomic Policy and Economic Reform', in K. Banerji and T. Vakil (eds), *India: Joining the World Economy* (New Delhi, 1995). The political and economic issues surrounding the economic reforms are discussed in Robert Cassen and Vijay Joshi (eds), *India: the Future of Economic Reform* (Delhi, 1995), while the more specifically political context of the reform process is illuminated by Robert S. Jenkins, 'Theorizing the Politics of Economic Adjustment: Lessons from the Indian Case', *Journal of Commonwealth and Comparative Politics*, vol. xxxiii, no. 1 (1995) and forthcoming publications based on Jenkins's D.Phil, *Democratic Adjustment: Explaining the Political Sustainability of Economic Reform in India* (University of Sussex, 1997).

While there are many empirical comparisons between India's economic performance and that of other countries (see, for instance, chapters three and four in Dreze and Sen, *India: Economic Development and Social Opportu-*

nity, Delhi, 1995), there have been virtually no comparative studies of the institutional context of policy-making; for an example of the kind of work that could be usefully developed, see the article by Robert Wade, 'How to make "Street Level" Bureaucracies Work Better: India and Korea', *IDS Bulletin*, vol. 23, no. 4 (1992).

The genre of urban history is underdeveloped in India, although particular Indian cities have been the subject of detailed study. Two attractive general books on India's cities are Norma Evenson, *The Indian Metropolis* (London and New Haven, 1989), which focuses on the four largest (Calcutta, New Delhi, Bombay and Madras); and Giles Tillotson, *The Tradition of Indian Architecture* (London and New Haven, 1989), concerned mainly with architectural and aesthetic matters. The classic statement of the contrast between the European and the 'Asiatic' city is Max Weber, *The City* (Glencoe, 1958). For Asian evidence that qualifies the Weberian view, William Rowe's remarkable study of nineteenth-century Hankow, *Hankow: Commerce and Society in a Chinese City 1796–1889* (Stanford, 1984), and *Hankow: Conflict and Community in a Chinese City 1796–1895* (Stanford, 1989), is worth consulting; there is no equivalent work on any Indian city. An important comparative critique of the Weberian thesis is Jack Goody, *The East in the West* (Cambridge, 1996). On the links between traditional and modern commercial activities in urban centres, see Thomas Trimberg, *The Marwaris: From Traders to Industrialists* (Delhi, 1978); and for a fascinating biographical study, see Dwijendra Tripathi, *Kasturbhai Lalbhai and his Entrepreneurship* (New Delhi, 1978). During the 1950s there were a number of ambitious theoretical studies of India's cities that remain of interest: see, for example: Robert Redfield and Milton Singer, 'The Cultural Role of Cities', *Man in India*, vol. 36, no. 3 (1956); Milton Singer, 'The Great Tradition in a Metropolitan Centre: Madras', in Milton Singer (ed.), *Traditional India: Structure and Change* (Philadelphia, 1959); and G. S. Ghurye, 'Cities of India', *Sociological Bulletin*, vol. ii (1953). On the standard contrast to the city, the village, see: Louis Dumont, 'The "Village Community" from Maine to Munro', *Contributions to Indian Sociology*, vol. ix (1966); Clive Dewey, 'Images of the Village Community: A study in Anglo-Indian Ideology', *MAS*, vol. 6, no. 2 (1972); M. N. Srinivas, 'The Indian Village: Myth and Reality', in *The Dominant Caste and Other Essays* (Delhi, 1987); and Rhoads Murphey, 'City and Countryside as Ideological Issues: India and China', *CSSH*, vol. xiv, no. 3 (1972).

The impact of colonialism on urban life in India is one of the themes of C. A. Bayly, *Rulers, Townsmen and Bazaars: North Indian Society in the Age of British Expansion 1770–1870*, (2nd edn, Delhi, 1992). Also useful are the essays in Richard G. Fox (ed.), *Urban India: Society, Space and Image* (Duke University, 1970); and Anthony D. King, *Colonial Urban Development* (London, 1976). On the emergence of public politics in provincial cities of India, see the study of Surat by Douglas Haynes, *Rhetoric and Ritual in Colonial India* (Berkeley, 1991), and of Benares by Sandra Freitag, *Collective Action and Community: Public Arenas and the Emergence of Communalism in North India* (Berkeley, 1989). Kenneth Gillion's *Ahmedabad* (Berkeley, 1968) is an excellent account of a 'traditional' Indian city. On the Raj's determination to reform Indian cities, see, for instance, the essay by J. B. Harrison, 'Allahabad: A Sanitary History', in K. Ballhatchet and J. Harrison (eds) *The City in South Asia: Premodern and Modern* (London, 1980). The career and ideas of Patrick Geddes offer an interestingly different view of what such reform might involve: see J. Tyrwhitt (ed.), *Patrick Geddes in India* (London, 1947); and Geddes's own attempt to detect the harmonies between culture, history and urban form in 'The Temple Cities', *Modern Review* (India), no. 25 (1919).

Two helpful accounts of social change and the emergence of nationalist politics in urban India are Ravinder Kumar, 'The Changing Structure of Urban Society in Colonial India', *IHR*, vol. 5, nos. 1–2 (1978); Ravinder Kumar, 'The Role of Urban Society in Nationalist Politics', in Indu Banga (ed.), *The City in Indian History: Urban Demography, Society and Politics* (Delhi, 1991). The role of the cities in nationalism is studied in Rajat K. Ray, *The Urban Roots of Indian Nationalism: Pressure Groups and Conflict of Interests in Calcutta Politics 1875–1939* (New Delhi, 1975). The emergence of popular forms of political action in the cities, often in tension with the ambitions of Congress leaders to control such forms, is considered by Ranajit Guha, 'Discipline and Mobilize', in Partha Chatterjee and Gyanendra Pandey (eds), *Subaltern Studies*, vii (Delhi, 1992); and Jim Masselos, 'Audiences, Actors and Congress Dramas: Crowd Events in Bombay City in 1930', in Jim Masselos (ed.), *Struggling and Ruling: The Indian National Congress, 1885–1985* (Delhi, 1987).

The literature on India's urban demography and sociology is large. The standard introduction is Ashish Bose, *India's Urbanization 1901–2001* (New Delhi, 1980); see also Roy Turner (ed.) *India's Urban Future* (Berkeley, 1962); and more technically and narrowly, Charles Becker, Jeffrey Williamson and Edwin Mill, *Indian Urbanization and Economic Growth since 1960* (Baltimore, 1992). For a comparative perspective on urbanization in the third world, see Paul Biaroch's magisterial *Cities and Economic Development* (Oxford, 1988), Part IV. The controversial idea of 'urban bias' was advanced in Michael Lipton, *Why Poor People Remain Poor: Urban Bias In World Development* (Cambridge MA, 1977). Two helpful if now dated collections on social structure and politics in the cities are Satish Saberwal (ed.), 'Process and Institution in Urban India', *Contributions to Indian Sociology* n.s., vol. XI, no. 1 (1977), especially the Introduction by Saberwal; and Donald B. Rosenthal (ed.), *The City in Indian Politics* (Faridabad, 1976). On migration and its political consequences, see Myron Weiner, *Sons of the Soil: Migration and Ethnic Conflict in India* (Princeton, 1978).

Individual Indian cities have attracted an abundant literature, often quite lavish and sometimes of high quality. On Benares, Diana L. Eck, *Banaras: City of Light* (New York, 1982), is the best general account; Nita Kumar, *The Artisans of Banaras: Popular Culture and Identity, 1880–1986* (Princeton, 1988), and Jonathan Parry, *Death in Banaras* (Cambridge, 1994) are also necessary reading. The construction of New Delhi is lovingly told in Robert Grant Irving, *Indian Summer: Lutyens, Baker, and Imperial Delhi* (Newhaven and London, 1981); the earlier history is covered in Robert Frykenberg (ed.), *Delhi Through the Ages* (Delhi, 1986): especially worthwhile are the essays by Bayly and Narayani Gupta. On Calcutta, an engrossing collection is Sukanta Chaudhuri (ed.), *Calcutta: The Living City*, 2 vols (Calcutta, 1990); the city's popular culture is also examined in Sumanta Banerjee, *The Parlour and the Street* (Calcutta, 1989). The literature on Chandigarh is extensive, and mainly focused on the architecture. Essential for understanding the form of the city itself, and the history of its construction, are Norma Evenson, *Chandigarh* (Berkeley, 1966), and Ravi Kalia, *Chandigarh: The Making of an Indian City* (Delhi, 1987). The political disputes over Chandigarh are examined in Yogendra Malik, 'Conflict over Chandigarh: A Case Study of an Inter-state Dispute in India', *Contributions to Asian Studies*, vol. 3 (1973). An account critical of the city's neglect of the poor is Madhu Sarin, *Urban Planning in the Third World: The Chandigarh Experience* (London, 1982). Two books that deal with the symbolic significance of cities like Chandigarh in the creation of a national identity are Sven Nilsson, *New Capitals of India, Pakistan, Bangladesh* (London, 1973); and Lawrence J. Vale, *Architecture, Power, and National Identity* (New Haven, 1992). An excellently illustrated historical

THE IDEA OF INDIA

account of Bombay is Sharada Dwivedi and Rahul Mehrotra, *Bombay* (Bombay, 1995); also Gillian Tindall, *City of Gold: a Biography of Bombay* (London, 1982). An essential and wide-ranging collection on social, political and cultural aspects of Bombay are the two volumes by Sujata Patel and Alice Thorner (eds) *Bombay: A Metaphor for Modern India* (Bombay, 1995), especially good are the essays by Lele and Heuze on the Shiv Sena, and Sharma on the 1993 riots; and Sujata Patel and Alice Thorner (eds), *Bombay: Mosaic of Modern Culture* (Bombay, 1995), which deals with cultural and literary aspects of the city. The essays in both volumes are motivated by a desire to explain why the cosmopolitan dream of Bombay soured in the 1980s and 90s. The Shiv Sena as an organization, and its social bases, are studied in Dipankar Gupta, *Nativism in a Metropolis: Shiv Sena in Bombay* (New Delhi, 1982). The 1992–3 riots are tackled in Jim Masselos, 'The Bombay Riots of January 1993: The Politics of Urban Conflagration', *South Asia*, vol. xvii, special issue (1994); the events themselves are reported in V. K. Ramachandran, 'Reign of Terror: Shiv Sena Pogrom in Bombay', *Frontline* (Madras), 12 February 1993; and Dileep Padgaonkar (ed.), *When Bombay Burned* (New Delhi, 1993). The literature on Bangalore is not very accessible. Two detailed, often quite technical studies, are: V. L. S. Prakasa Rao and V. K. Tewari, *The Structure of an Indian Metropolis: A Study of Bangalore* (Bombay, 1979); and Vinod Vysalu and A. K. N. Reddy (eds), *Essays on Bangalore* (Bangalore, 1986). An interesting analysis of the underbelly of the city, based on a case-study of a liquor-poisoning disaster, is James Manor, *Power, Poverty and Poison: Disaster and Response in an Indian City* (New Delhi, 1993). The new and rapidly growing provincial cities, and their distinctive politics, have received virtually no academic notice: for an engaging journalistic evocation of these places, see Pankaj Mishra, *Butter Chicken in Ludhiana: Travels in Small Town India* (New Delhi, 1995). Two stimulating conceptual pieces on poverty and slums, that both take a long historical view, are Dipesh Chakrabarty, 'Open Space/Public Space: Garbage, Modernity and India', *South Asia*, vol. xiv, no. 1 (1994); and Sudipta Kaviraj, 'Filth and the "Public Sphere"', *Osterreichische Zeitschrift fur Soziologie*, vol. 21, no. 2 (1996). For more specific studies, see Paul Wiebe, *Social Life in an Indian Slum* (Delhi, 1975); Jeremy Seabrook, *Life and Labour in a Bombay Slum* (London, 1987); and, more comparatively, *In the Cities of the South: Scenes from a Developing World* (London, 1996).

*

For obvious reasons, since the 1980s the politics of religion has become a highly charged subject in India: with the rise of political Hinduism, debates about religion have become linked to the subject of Indian identity. Good introductions to Hindu philosophies and doctrines are: K. M. Sen, *Hinduism* (London, 1961); and Heinrich von Stietencron, 'What is Hinduism? On the History of a Religious Tradition', in Hans Kung *et al.*, *Christianity and the World Religions* (London, 1987). A very interesting essay on Indian conceptions of tradition and of 'Sanatan Dharma' is Baidyanath Saraswati, *Thinking about Tradition: The Indian Vision* (Varanasi, 1987). On Islam in South Asia, see Asim Roy, *The Islamic Syncretistic Tradition in Bengal* (Princeton, 1983) and Asim Roy (ed.), *Islam in South Asia: A Regional Perspective* (New Delhi, 1996), which also has a useful bibliography. Aspects of the historical background to the emergence of a Hindu political identity are covered in Partha Chatterjee, *The Nation and its Fragments: Colonial and Postcolonial Histories* (Princeton, 1993); and Gyanendra Pandey (ed.), *Hindus and Others: The Question of Identity in India Today* (New Delhi, 1993). The pivotal figure in the emergence of a modern Hindu political identity is V. D. Savarkar, but he has only been studied by his admirers; for want of anything better, see Dhananjay Keer, *Veer Savarkar* (3rd edn, Bombay, 1988). The formation of Hindu nationalist political organizations is examined in Bruce Graham, *Hindu Nationalism and Indian Politics: The Origins and Development of the Bharatiya Jana Sangh* (Cambridge, 1990); and in greater depth by Christophe Jaffrelot's important study, *The Hindu Nationalist Movement and Indian Politics, 1925 to the 1990s* (London, 1996). The voice of Hindu nationalism needs to be heard first-hand; although there are few accessible English texts, worth consulting are the writings of Balraj Madhok, a politician and intellectual of the older generation: see his *Indianisation: What, Why and How?* (Delhi, 1970) and *Rationale of Hindu State* (Delhi, 1982). Debates about Indian secularism provoke a constantly growing literature. The following are essential: Donald E. Smith, *India as a Secular State* (Princeton, 1963); T. N. Madan, 'Secularism in its Place', *JAS*, no. 46, no. 4 (1987); and 'Whither Indian Secularism?', *MAS*, vol. 27, no. 3 (1993); also T. N. Madan (ed.), *Religion in India* (Delhi, 1991) and *Modern Myths, Locked Minds* (Delhi, 1997); Ashis Nandy, 'An Anti-Secularist Manifesto', *Seminar* (Delhi), no. 314 (1985), and 'The Politics of Secularism and the Recovery of Religious Tolerance', in Veena Das (ed.), *Mirrors of Violence* (Delhi, 1990); and the articles in *EPW*, vol. xxix, no. 28 (1994), special issue on 'Secularism, Modernity and the State', especially by Bhargava, Bilgrami and Chatterjee. An unusual and stimulating essay is Ramchandra Gandhi, *Sita's Kitchen: A Testimony of Faith* (New Delhi, 1992). On popular religion, see C. J. Fuller, *The Camphor Flame: Popular Hinduism and Society in India* (Princeton, 1992). An illuminating essay on the historical uses of the Ram myth is Sheldon Pollack, 'Ramayana and Political Imagination in India', *JAS*, vol. 52, no. 2 (1993). For a wide-ranging account of the city of Ayodhya and how violence engulfed it, see Ashis Nandy *et al.*, *Creating a Nationality: The Ramjanmabhumi Movement and Fear of the Self* (Delhi, 1995). Two important and contrasting accounts of the historical bases of religious violence are C. A. Bayly, 'The Pre-History of "Communalism"? Religious Conflict in India, 1700–1860', *MAS*, vol. 19, no. 2 (1985); and Gyanendra Pandey, *The Construction of Communalism in Colonial North India* (Delhi, 1990).

Apart from religion, challenges to an Indian identity have also come from regional and 'ethnic' groups. The literature on ethnicity is large and very uneven. Three good examples are: Jyotirindra Das Gupta, 'Ethnicity, Democracy and Development in India: Assam in a General Perspective', in Atul Kohli (ed.), *India's Democracy* (Princeton, 1990); Dipankar Gupta, 'The Indispensable Centre: Ethnicity and Politics in the Indian Nation State', *Journal of Contemporary Asia*, vol. 20, no. 4 (1990); and L. M. Khubchandani, 'Self-images and Identities of the Punjabi People: Ethnic and Linguistic Realities', in P. C. Chatterji (ed), *Self-images, Identity and Nationality* (Simla, 1989). On regional identities since the 1980s, see the essays by Paul Brass on Punjab, and Sanjib Baruah on Assam, referred to earlier. Two historical studies of the Sikh case are: Richard G. Fox, *Lions of the Punjab: Culture in the Making* (Berkeley, 1985); and, as a corrective to Fox, Harjot Oberoi, *The Construction of Religious Boundaries: Culture, Identity and Diversity in Sikh Tradition* (Delhi, 1994). The emergence of tribal political movements is the subject of Susanna B. Devalle, *Discourses of Ethnicity: Culture and Protest in Jharkhand* (New Delhi, 1992). For historical perspectives on regional and national identities, see Paul Wallace (ed.), *Region and Nation in India* (New Delhi, 1985), especially the essays by Embree, Lloyd and Susanne Rudolph; and Richard G. Fox (ed.), *Realm and Region in Traditional India* (New Delhi, 1977) – particularly instructive is the essay by Ainslie Embree, 'Frontiers into Boundaries: From the Traditional to the Modern State'. C. A. Bayly's 1996 Radhakrishnan Lectures (University of Oxford) on patriotism argue against the presumption that Indian nationalism is purely an outcome of processes of modernity, and propose an older, indigenous, genealogy. For an argument about the place of language in the formation of identities in India, which emphasizes the role of modernity in creating both regional and national identities, see Sudipta Kaviraj, 'Writing, Speaking, Being: Language and the historical formation of identities in India', in Dagmar Hellman-Rajanayagam and Deitmar Rothermund, *Nationalstaat und Sprachkonflikte in Sud und Sudostasien* (Stuttgart, 1991). There is a growing literature on the role of cinema in the formation of regional and national identities: see M. S. S. Pandian, *The Image Trap: M. G. Ramachandran in Film and Politics* (New Delhi, 1992), interesting but committed to the notion of 'false consciousness'; and Chidananda Das Gupta, *The Painted Face: Studies in India's Popular Cinema* (Delhi, 1991). The vigorous debate on Indian cinema and politics can be followed in the pages of the *Journal of Arts and Ideas* (New Delhi) and *Economic and Political Weekly* (especially since 1993).

India's relationship with other cultures, particularly the West, is an academic growth area. The classic work is Raymond Schwab, *The Oriental Renaissance: Europe's Rediscovery of India and the East 1660–1880* (1950; new edn New York, 1984); see also William Halbfass, *India and Europe* (New York, 1988). A polemical work of scholarship and verve is Ronald Inden, *Imagining India* (Oxford, 1990). Tapan Raychaudhuri, *Europe Reconsidered: Perceptions of the West in Nineteenth Century Bengal* (Delhi, 1988), tries to tell something of the story from the other side. For a view of this relationship by an intellectual of the Nehruvian generation, see K. M. Pannikar, *Asia and Western Domination* (London, 1959).

Fiction, in English and in Indian languages is probably the most seductive entry into different aspects of contemporary India. From a vast pool, the following are especially rewarding. Among Indian writers writing in English: Mulk Raj Anand, R. K. Narayan, Khushwant Singh, Nayantara Sahgal, Salman Rushdie, Vikram Seth, Amitav Ghosh, Firdaus Kanga, Upamanyu Chatterjee, Rohinton Mistry, and the best-selling Shobha De; in other languages, and available in good translations: Saadat Hasan Manto, U. R. Ananthamurthy, O. V. Vijayan, Maheswati Devi, Bhisham Sahni and Nirmal Verma.

ABBREVIATIONS

CSSH: *Comparative Studies in Society and History*
EPW: *Economic and Political Weekly*
IHR: *Indian Historical Review*
IESHR: *Indian Economic and Social History Review*
JAS: *Journal of Asian Studies*
MAS: *Modern Asian Studies*

Index

Abbas, Khwaja Ahmad (1914–87): grandson of the Urdu poet Hali, prolific journalist, novelist and scriptwriter; committed to Nehru's anti-communal and socialist ideas; wrote film scripts for a series of influential socialist-realist films which were also popular hits, 137

Advani, Lal Kishinchand (1927–): born Karachi; joined RSS 1942, Jana Sangh 1951; General Secretary, Janata Party 1977, Minister of Information and Broadcasting 1977–9; leader of the Opposition in Lok Sabha, 1990–95, President BJP, 146–7

Agra, 114

agrarian power, 66, 74–5, 78–80, 90–91

Ahmedabad, 70, 112–14, 135

Akali Dal (Sikh party), 50–51

Alberuni (973–1048), 197

Ambedkar, Bhim Rao (1891–1956): born into an 'untouchable' caste, educated himself and went on to study law in England and America; became leader of the 'untouchables' during the Raj; opposed Congress, which he saw as representative of the upper castes; pressured by Gandhi into pact with Congress in 1932; instrumental in drafting Indian Constitution; served as Law Minister in Nehru's cabinet, but finally distanced himself from the government; shortly before his death, converted to Buddhism in anger at Hindu caste practices, and urged his followers to do the same, 7, 13, 14, 34–5, 36, 57, 127–8, 185

America, see United States of America

Amritsar, 53, 83

Anand, Mulk Raj (1905–): novelist and writer, 127

Andhra Pradesh, 51

anna: one-sixteenth of a rupee, 73

army, see military

Artha: realm of human action conforming to self-regarding interest, 19